ON THE THRESHOLD
OF THE UNSEEN

ON THE THRESHOLD OF THE UNSEEN

AN EXAMINATION OF THE PHENOMENA OF SPIRITUALISM AND OF THE EVIDENCE FOR SURVIVAL AFTER DEATH

BY

SIR WILLIAM F. BARRETT, F.R.S.S

"Men are wont to guess about new subjects from those they are already acquainted with, and the hasty and vitiated fancies they have thence formed: than which there cannot be a more fallacious mode of reasoning." — Bacon *"Novum Organum,"* Bk. i, par. cix.

www.whitecrowbooks.com

TO THE DEAR MEMORY OF ONE WHOSE RADIANT FAITH GAVE HER "THE ASSURANCE OF THINGS HOPED FOR" AND NEEDED NOT THE EVIDENCE OF THINGS UNSEEN WHICH THIS BOOK MAY POSSIBLY GIVE TO SOME STRICKEN SOULS AND OTHER SEEKERS AFTER TRUTH.

On the Threshold of the Unseen

William F. Barrett

Copyright © 2012 by White Crow Books. All rights reserved.

Published and printed in the United States of America and the United Kingdom by White Crow Books; an imprint of White Crow Productions Ltd.

No part of this book may be reproduced, copied or used in any form or manner whatsoever without written permission, except in the case of brief quotations in reviews and critical articles.

For information, contact White Crow Books
at P. O. Box 1013 Guildford, GU1 9EJ United Kingdom,
or e-mail to info@whitecrowbooks.com.

Cover Designed by Butterflyeffect
Interior production by essentialworks.co.uk
Interior design by Perseus Design

Paperback ISBN 978-1-908733-70-2
eBook ISBN 978-1-908733-71-9

Non Fiction / Body, Mind & Spirit / Parapsychology

Published by White Crow Books
www.whitecrowbooks.com

Disclaimer: White Crow Productions Ltd. and its directors, employees, distributors, retailers, wholesalers and assignees disclaim any liability or responsibility for the author's statements, words, ideas, criticisms or observations. White Crow Productions Ltd. assumes no responsibility for errors, inaccuracies, or omissions.

PREFACE

"A mind unwilling to believe, or even undesirous to be instructed, our weightiest evidence must ever fail to impress. It will insist on taking the evidence in bits and rejecting item by item. The man who announces his intention of waiting until a single absolutely conclusive bit of evidence turns up, is really a man not open to conviction, and if he be a logician he knows it. For modern logic has made it plain that single facts can never be 'proved' except by their coherence in a system. But as all the facts come singly anyone who dismisses them one by one is destroying the conditions under which the conviction of new truth could ever arise in his mind."

Dr. F. C. S. Schiller,
"Proceedings of the Society
for Psychical Research,"
Vol. XVIII, p. 419.

During the greater part of the last century, and that which preceded it, the learned world as a whole treated with scorn and contempt all those obscure psychical phenomena which lie between the territory already conquered by science and the dark realms of ignorance and superstition.

Many causes have in recent years contributed to lessen this aversion, which is not only passing away but giving place to an earnest desire to know what trustworthy evidence exists on behalf of super-normal, — often, but erroneously, called super-natural, — phenomena.

Although many eminent scientific men in the past and present generation, both in England and abroad, have testified to the genuineness and importance of these phenomena official science still stands aloof. This no doubt is largely due to the essential difference between physical and psychical phenomena, a difference by no means clearly recognized and which can never be broken down.

The main object of physical science is to measure and forecast, and from its phenomena free will must be eliminated. Psychical states on the contrary can neither be measured nor forecast, and from them the disturbing influence of life and will can neither be eliminated nor foreseen.

The association of ideas and methods of investigation in physical research are therefore widely different from those in psychical research.

Accordingly minds working in the former line of thought become more or less impervious to facts belonging to the other line of thought, however well attested those facts may be. The new association of ideas is foreign and uncongenial and has apparently no harmonious relation to accepted scientific truths. Nevertheless, as I have endeavoured to point out in the introductory chapters, when these differences are realized, and the rapidly accumulating weight of evidence on behalf of phenomena, hitherto unrecognised by official science, is critically and fairly examined, the general acceptance of these phenomena by science can only be a question of time.

That this is likely to be the case is seen from the fact that all enduring additions to our knowledge of the universe rest upon a similar basis.

They are the result of prolonged and cautious enquiry, the investigation and discussion of a number of circumstances, each of which by itself may appear to be insignificant, but taken collectively point to some wide generalization. Such evidence though conclusive to a trained observer makes little appeal to the popular mind, which has no time nor inclination to master the necessary details, and asks for some one piece of conclusive evidence, — some "knockdown blow", — to compel its attention and assent. This however cannot be given, — as that acute thinker Dr. F. C. S. Schiller has pointed out in the quotation at the head of this Preface, — and there is nothing for it but a tiresome study of detailed evidence, the strength of which rests on its cumulative character.

In the following pages I have given some of this evidence with as little tedium as possible, and also ventured to touch, perhaps too daringly, upon many subjects which need fuller exposition than was possible in a small volume, the history of which is as follows.

More than twenty years ago an address on the phenomena of spiritualism, which I delivered in London, was expanded into a little book, — the nucleus of the present volume, — entitled *On the Threshold of a New World of Thought*. Although an edition of that book was printed off in 1895, its publication was delayed for more than a dozen years for the following reason. Considerable public interest was at that time being taken in a well known Italian medium, Eusapia Paladino; several eminent continental savants, and subsequently a few distinguished members of the Society for Psychical Research, after a searching investigation in 1894, had attested the genuineness of many remarkable phenomena occurring with this medium. Their report was quoted in my former book, but just before it was issued an opposite opinion was arrived at by others, equally competent, after a subsequent investigation in 1895. It seemed wiser therefore to delay the publication of the volume until more conclusive evidence, one way or the other, was forthcoming. Moreover I felt that if Eusapia were really nothing more than a clever and systematic impostor, able to deceive several eminent investigators, both English and foreign, this fact would certainly shake the value of other scientific testimony to the supernormal, and undermine the stability of many of the conclusions reached in my book.

As will be seen by referring to the history of this case, repeated critical investigation in later years showed that this notorious medium really possessed genuine supernormal power, albeit, like so many professional mediums of a low moral type, she sometimes lapsed into fraudulent practices, which however were quickly detected by trained observers.

Accordingly *On the Threshold of a New World of Thought* was issued in 1908 and the edition quickly sold out. The remarkable series of experiments, carried out by the Society for Psychical Research, on the evidence for survival after death was then in progress and I postponed the publication of a new edition until further trustworthy evidence on this vital question was attainable. This, in my opinion, has now been obtained; my early book was therefore recast, an outline of some of the evidence on survival included, and the present volume is the result.

Meanwhile the editors of the *Home University Library* had asked me to write the volume on "Psychical Research" for their series, and after this was published, various circumstances prevented the completion of this book until the present year. Now, alas, the war has rendered printing and paper a great difficulty for the publishers, to whom my readers will I trust extend their indulgence for any shortcomings in this respect.

It will thus be seen that the conclusions reached in this book are not the result of hasty and superficial examination. Upwards of forty years ago I began the investigation of alleged super-normal phenomena with a perfectly detached and open mind. The urgent need for a Society which should preserve continuity of records of investigation and a high standard of experimental work became apparent, and with the co-operation of one or two friends the Society for Psychical Research was founded early in 1882. Forty-six volumes of its *Proceedings* and *Journal* have now been published, and in addition its sister society in America, — which through the assistance of some eminent friends in Boston and Harvard I was enabled to initiate in 1884, — has also published a large library of its Proceedings and Journal, under the indefatigable editorship of Professor Hyslop. Thus a vast collection of sifted evidence is being accumulated and printed, which will be of immense value for future reference and study.

As regards the so-called "physical phenomena" of spiritualism, given in Part 2, bizarre and sometimes repellent as such manifestations are, — and meaningless except as affording illustrations of the operation of some unknown intelligence and power, — the evidence cited seems to me indisputable, though some of my readers may hesitate to accept it. A wholesome scepticism is desirable, but to attribute imbecility or hallucination to eminent and cautious scientific investigators, or fraud to men of high intelligence and probity like the Rev. Stainton Moses ("M.A. Oxon") is simply puerile. Nevertheless, in the *British Weekly*, the writer of a lengthy review of Sir Oliver Lodge's book *Raymond* expresses amazement that Sir Oliver refers "without a word of caution to the record of Stainton Moses." He justifies this stricture by quoting from the writings of the late Mr. F. Podmore, who did useful work in connection with psychical research, but was chiefly known for his ingenuity in discrediting, or attributing to telepathy, any psychical phenomena outside his limited range of view. Those who, like myself, knew both the Rev. S. Moses and Mr. Podmore would be indignant if the latter attributed wilful deception to the former, but the writer in the *British Weekly* is mistaken and has no adequate grounds for thinking this was the case. It was necessary to refer to this matter, as the evidence of phenomena associated with Mr. Stainton Moses, which I have quoted in Part 2, might otherwise be regarded with suspicion by those who do not know the facts.

In selecting some illustrations from the growing mass of trustworthy evidence on behalf of survival after death, given in Part 4, it will be noticed that I have refrained from citing any such evidence obtained through paid professional mediums, who are naturally regarded by the public with more or less distrust. Nor can the love of notoriety, or other inducement to deceive, be brought against those through whom the evidence for survival given in this book has come.

The question has naturally and often been asked, — if communication with those who have passed into the unseen be possible, why should it be necessary to have a connecting link in a so-called medium, usually a perfect stranger and of another order of mind? Surely our loved ones who have recently entered the spiritual world would try to communicate directly with those dearest to them! a father or mother would be more likely to be sensitive to the spiritual presence of their beloved child than an uncongenial stranger. This question I have discussed in Chapter 10 and would also beg my readers to refer to the Cautions and Suggestions given in Chapter 20.

Those who like St. Thomas cannot believe in survival after bodily death, without some material demonstration, will probably find in continued sittings with one or two friends, in the manner described in Appendix D, a response to their yearnings and an aid to their faith.[1] Having attained this assurance I do not advise them to pursue the matter further, but rather learn more of the spiritual world and spiritual communion from the Christian mystics of all countries; especially would I commend a book by the late Mr. J. H. Spalding, where

---

[1] Anyone wishing to make experiments on, and a study of, automatic writing, are advised to read the late Mrs. Verrall's account of her own experience and method given in the "Proceedings of the Society for Psychical Research," Vol. XX, and also Mr. Myers' paper in Vol. IV, p. 209, etc.

the teaching of that gifted seer Swedenborg is luminously and dispassionately set forth.[2]

None will find in automatic writing, or other spiritualistic phenomena, the channel for the "communion of saints," which is independent of material agency and attained only in stillness and serenity of soul. For the psychical order is not the spiritual order; it deals, as I have said elsewhere, only "with the external, though it be in an unseen world; and its chief value lies in the fulfilment of its work whereby it reveals to us the inadequacy of the external, either here or hereafter, to satisfy the life of the soul."

The paramount importance of psychical research is found in correcting the habit of Western thought, — of the average men we meet, — that the physical plane is the whole of Nature, or at any rate the only aspect of the universe which really concerns us. Under this false and deadly assumption all wider views and spiritual conceptions wither and die as soon as they are born. This vast and devastating war has, however, brought certain spiritual tendencies and aspirations into the lives of a multitude of men and led many to the conviction, which Lowell expresses, that — "We see but half the causes of our deeds, Seeking them wholly in the outer life, And heedless of the encircling spirit world, which though unseen, is felt, and sows in us All germs of pure and world-wide purposes." My warmest thanks are due to my friend the Rev. M. A. Bayfield, M.A. for kindly reading the proof sheets of this book and for many valuable suggestions.

31 Devonshire Place, London, W.
March, 1917.

---

[2] *The Kingdom of Heaven*, by J. H. Spalding (Dent & Co., 3/6 net; my little book on "Swedenborg" (J. H. Watkins, 1/net), may also interest the reader.

CONTENTS

PREFACE vii

PART 1
1. INTRODUCTION 1
2. PSYCHICAL RESEARCH AND PUBLIC OPINION 9
3. CONFLICTING OBJECTIONS OF
   SCIENCE AND RELIGION 15

PART 2
4. PHYSICAL PHENOMENA OF SPIRITUALISM............................ 21
5. PHYSICAL PHENOMENA OF SPIRITUALISM CONTINUED..... 31
6. LEVITATION AND IMPUNITY TO FIRE 43
7. ON CERTAIN MORE DISPUTABLE PHENOMENA OF
   SPIRITUALISM; ECTOPLASMS; DIRECT VOICE;
   MATERIALIZATION; SPIRIT PHOTOGRAPHY: THE AURA .. 51

PART 3
8. THE CANONS OF EVIDENCE IN PSYCHICAL RESEARCH 59
9. THEORIES 65
10. THE PROBLEM OF MEDIUMSHIP 73
11. HUMAN PERSONALITY: THE SUBLIMINAL SELF 79

PART 4

12. APPARITIONS 87
13. AUTOMATIC WRITING. THE EVIDENCE FOR IDENTITY 101
14. PROOF OF SUPERNORMAL MESSAGES; THE OUIJA BOARD 109
15. FURTHER EVIDENCE OF SURVIVAL AFTER DEATH 119
16. EVIDENCE OF IDENTITY IN THE DISCARNATE 129
17. EVIDENCE FROM ABROAD OF SURVIVAL 139

PART 5

18. CLAIRVOYANCE, PSYCHOLOGY OF TRANCE PHENOMENA 149
19. DIFFICULTIES AND OBJECTIONS CONSIDERED 155
20. CAUTIONS AND SUGGESTIONS 159

PART 6

21. THE LESSON OF PHILOSOPHY IN THE INTERPRETATION OF NATURE 167
22. THE MYSTERY OF HUMAN PERSONALITY 175
23. THE DIVINE GROUND OF THE SOUL: REINCARNATION 179
24. TELEPATHY AND ITS IMPLICATIONS 185

APPENDICES

A. SUPERSTITION AND THE SUPERNATURAL: MIRACLES 191
B. NOTE BY THE LATE PROF. BALFOUR STEWART, F.R.S 197
C. EUSAPIA PALADINO 201
D. SUGGESTIONS FOR INVESTIGATORS 207
E. 213

INTRODUCTION

I feel that it is somewhat presumptuous on my part to introduce a work by Sir William Barrett to the American public. He should be well enough known in this country to make an introduction by a much less qualified person unnecessary. But if it will help any one to read his book I shall gladly send it on the mission for which it was written. Sir William Barrett was for many years Professor of Experimental Physics in the Royal College of Science for Ireland, and also spent many years investigating psychic phenomena, having worked in the subject long before the English Society for Psychical Research was organized.

Hence this work is the ripe fruit of many years of investigation. It is the best work of the kind that has ever appeared in English and readers may study it without offense at either its data or its manner. It is thoroughly scientific in method and spirit, and practices no evasions or subterfuges in the discussion of its problems. The manner is calm and tolerant of scepticism, perhaps because the author came to the subject as a sceptic himself, and he selects all his facts with reference to the objections which sceptics and believers in other theories than the spiritualistic one would bring forward. The author faces issues boldly and makes no concessions to mere respectability, though not attacking or shunning it. In many writers there is fear of compromising one's standing by telling the truth. There is nothing of the kind in this book, and that characteristic makes it refreshingly frank and clear.

Every aspect. and difficulty of the subject is canvassed and evidence produced for the claims made in the book.

Readers cannot fail to find in it the light they desire on this complicated subject.

James H. Hyslop.
New York, December 21st, 1917.

Part 1

CHAPTER 1

INTRODUCTION

> "If anyone advances anything new which contradicts, perhaps threatens to overturn, the creed which we have for years repeated, and have handed down to others, all passions are raised against him, and every effort is made to crush him. People resist with all their might; they act as if they neither heard nor could comprehend; they speak of the new view with contempt, as if it were not worth the trouble of even so much as an investigation or a regard, and thus a new truth may wait a long time before it can make its way." [1]

There are many people, and their number is rapidly increasing, who feel, as the late Professor Henry Sidgwick has said, "it is a scandal that the dispute as to the reality of the marvellous phenomena of Spiritualism should still be going on,— phenomena of which it is quite impossible to exaggerate the scientific importance, if only a tenth part of what has been alleged by generally credible witnesses could be shown to be true." Taking an unprejudiced view of the subject, such persons are anxious to know what amount of truth underlies the alleged facts. To these this little book may be of service.

There are others who, whilst not denying that the subject may possibly be a legitimate object of scientific investigation, prefer to give the whole matter a wide berth; contending either that it is a worthless will-

---
[1] *Conversations of Goethe* (Bohn's Library, p. 47)

o'-the-wisp, luring its victims, by an imaginary prospect of knowledge, into a miserable morass, or that it is distinctly forbidden by the Scriptures and condemned by the Church, so that its practice, and some would even add its investigation, is unlawful.

On the other hand, the popular habit of thought, whether lay or scientific, regards the whole thing as too contemptible for any inquiry, that it reeks, not of the bottomless pit, but of the dunghill; superstition, fraud, and tomfoolery amply accounting for all the alleged "phenomena." Hence they regard with complacency the many shallow *quidnuncs*, ever on the lookout for something new, who find in fourth-hand stories of "spooks" abundant material for the entertainment of their friends. In a busy world, occupied with other things— where the fierce struggle for material existence, wealth, and position dominates everything — such a state of mind is very natural. But I have failed to find that a single person who ridicules Spiritualism has given to the subject any serious and patient consideration; moreover, I venture to assert that any fair-minded person who devotes to its careful and dispassionate investigation as many days, or even hours, as some of us have given years, will find it impossible to continue sitting in the seat of the scornful, whatever other position he may take up.

No doubt the popular hesitation in accepting unseen intelligences as a cause of these phenomena arises not so much from inability to explain the *modus operandi*, but from a preconceived theory that such an explanation is impossible, and perhaps also from the fear of being laughed at as unscientific or superstitious in adopting it.

There are, however, some able thinkers who decline to accept or even investigate these phenomena on the ground that with our limited faculties successful investigation is impossible, and with our present limited knowledge, whatever results are obtained would probably be misinterpreted by us, so that any conclusions drawn as to the supernormal character of the phenomena are worthless, or, at any rate, to be distrusted.

Even those who do not go so far as this, regard psychical research, whether it be telepathy or Spiritualism, as unworthy of serious attention, because the phenomena are either impossible or utterly trivial; therefore in either case a sheer waste of time.

There are some things, I admit, which it would be utter folly to waste our time upon, such as "circle squaring," or "perpetual motion," etc. These things are beyond the pale of rational investigation at the

INTRODUCTION

present day on account of the extent of our knowledge in those particular regions. But there are other things which today appear impossible only from the extent of our ignorance in those directions. Such, for example, as, say, the sea serpent, thought-transference, or Spiritualistic phenomena; a few years ago we should also have included the telephone and wireless telegraphy. The essential difference between these two classes of improbable events is^ that the first involves a contradiction of experience or of laws well established, the second involves an unforeseen extension, but no contradiction, of existing knowledge and experience.

To assert that mind can act upon mind independently of any recognised channel of sense, or that mind can exist associated with an imperceptible form of matter, is a considerable extension of our knowledge, — if true as I believe it to be — but involves no rejection or contradiction of other knowledge equally true.

On the other hand, to assert that 2 and 2 makes 5, and also make 4, would involve intellectual confusion; similarly, to believe in materialism, as now understood, and also in these phenomena, would involve a contradiction of thought and consequent intellectual confusion; hence one or the other must be rejected. So that the "impossibility" that is urged refers, not to the phenomena themselves, but only to certain popular theories or conceptions about those phenomena.

But it is urged that the utterly trivial character of the phenomena renders them too contemptible for serious inquiry. "Even if true, we don't care for the results you obtain," is a common observation. This was doubtless the feeling that prompted the illustrious Faraday to decline any further investigation; for he stated in his well-known letter to Sir Emerson Tennant[2] that he had found in the phenomena "nothing worthy of attention," or capable of supplying "any force or information of the least use or value to mankind." With all deference to one whom I knew and revered so highly, this surely was a wrong position to take up. Long ago Benjamin Franklin, most practical of men, disposed of that argument; but the whole of Faraday's great career showed he valued truth for its own sake, irrespective of any commercial consideration, and supplies the best answer to the words of his I have quoted. Nevertheless, we still find some scientific men of the highest eminence taking precisely the same ground. Thus Professor Huxley replying to

---

[2] Pall Mall Gazette, May 19th, 1868. The whole correspondence is given in Light, February and March, 1888.

Mr. A. R. Wallace, O.M. (who had described some spiritualistic phenomena he had witnessed) said "It may be all true for anything I know to the contrary, but really I cannot get up any interest in the subject." Some time ago, in 1894, the distinguished physicist and courageous investigator Sir Oliver Lodge answered such objectors in the columns of the official scientific journal *Nature*, as follows: —

> "This attitude of 'not caring' for the results of scientific investigation in unpopular regions, even if those results be true, is very familiar to some of us who are engaged in a quest which both the great leaders in the above-remembered controversy [Lord Kelvin and Professor Huxley] agree to dislike and despise. It is an attitude appropriate to a company of shareholders, it is a common and almost universal sentiment of the noble army of self-styled 'practical men', but it is an astonishing attitude for an acknowledged man of science, whose whole vocation is the discovery and reception of new truth. Certain obscure facts have been knocking at the door of human intelligence for many centuries, and they are knocking now, in the most scientific era the world has yet seen. It may be that they will have to fall back disappointed for yet another few centuries; it may be that they will succeed this time in effecting a precarious and constricted right of entry; the issue appears to depend upon the attitude of scientific men of the present and near future, and no one outside can help them."

But fifty years ago Professor A. De Morgan, with inimitable satire, had already exposed the unphilosophical and illogical position still taken up on these questions by such honoured leaders of science as Lord Kelvin and Professor Huxley. Nothing more brilliant or amusing has ever been written on the whole subject than De Morgan's preface to his wife's book, *From Matter to Spirit*, and I earnestly commend its perusal to the scientific men of today. And to those who prefer Bishop Butler to De Morgan for their guide let me quote the following words from the "Analogy"; "After all, that which is true must be admitted; though it should show us the shortness of our faculties, and that we are in no wise judges of many things, of which we are apt to think ourselves very competent ones."

Nevertheless the argument is sometimes heard that if these supernormal psychical phenomena are true they ought to be reproduced and demonstrated at pleasure. This was urged by that eminent physiologist

INTRODUCTION

Dr. Carpenter, speaking in reply to my paper at the British Association in 1876, when for the first time evidence on behalf of thought transference and other psychical phenomena was brought before a scientific society. That able publicist Mr. R. H. Hutton in his journal the *Spectator* showed the absurdity of such an argument, remarking that if it were valid we should have to reject as imaginary many of the psychological and pathological facts given by Dr. Carpenter and other writers on mental physiology.[3] And as the late Professor Henry Sidgwick said, "I have never seen any serious attempt to justify this refusal [to accept the evidence of rare and fitful phenomena] on general principles of scientific method." We do not know at present all the conditions of success, and it is to be expected they may be sometimes present and sometimes absent.

Moreover, whether the phenomena originate in the unconscious self of the medium, or the operation of some unseen intelligence, in neither case can we control the exercise of the will.

Before proceeding further it is desirable to define the exact meaning of the word Spiritualism. On the Continent this word is often replaced by the term "Spiritism" to distinguish it from the broad sense of the word as used by philosophical writers, to denote a metaphysic opposed to materialism. But the generally accepted sense in which the word is used today is defined (1) by Mrs. Henry Sidgwick, in the article "Spiritualism," in the last edition of the *Encyclopaedia Britannica*, as "a belief that the spiritual world manifests itself by producing in the physical world effects inexplicable by the known laws of nature", or (2) by Dr. A. R. Wallace, in *Chambers Encyclopaedia*, as "the name applied to a great and varied series of abnormal or preter-normal phenomena, purporting to be for the most part caused by spiritual beings," or (3) by a writer in the "Spiritual Magazine", whose definition I curtail, as "a belief based solely on facts open to the world through an extensive system of mediumship, its cardinal truth, established by experiment, being that of a world of spirits, and the continuity of the existence of the individual spirit through the momentary eclipse of death."

These definitions, it will be noticed, are somewhat progressive; the last is doubtless the usual meaning attached to the word by Spiritualists. I see nothing to dissent from in it, and, speaking for myself, I do not hesitate to affirm that a careful and dispassionate review of my own experiments, extending over a period of forty years, together with the

---

[3] See Spectator for September 30, 1876.

investigation of the evidence of competent witnesses, compels my belief in Spiritualism, as so defined.

There can be little doubt that the impatience with which orthodox science regards spiritualism and psychical research in general arises from the difficulty of finding any explanation of the phenomena which is related to existing scientific knowledge. Hence, as Goethe remarked, in one of his conversations quoted at the head of this chapter, "a new truth may wait a long time before it can make its way." My friend the late Mr. C. C. Massey has well pointed out: —

"When we see how a thing can have happened we are much more ready to give a fair hearing to evidence that it has happened, than when the material offered is quite indigestible by our intelligence. And thus an explanatory hypothesis is hardly less necessary for the reception of facts of a certain character, than are facts for the support of a hypothesis."[4]

So also more recently the late Professor William James has said: "It often happens a fact is strenuously denied until a welcome interpretation comes with it, then it is admitted readily enough."

The insistence of the demand for some explanation of these phenomena which we find within us, is only a special case of that "continuous pressure of the causal instinct" which characterises our reason; and it is because of the difficulty of finding any adequate explanation of them in known and familiar causes, that science distrusts the existence of the phenomena themselves. The reasoning faculty, in rejecting every known cause as inadequate, satisfies its unrest by rejecting the occurrences as improbable or unproved. In truth, there is, strictly speaking, no scientific explanation of the higher phenomena of Spiritualism. Secondary causes, with which science deals, are only antecedents or previous states of a phenomenon, and have more remote antecedents or previous states, which, in turn, need to be accounted for, and so on in an endless chain; thus to the scientific materialist God necessarily becomes an infinite *et cetera*.

With a real or true cause — still less with the ultimate cause of things — science cannot grapple.[5] A real cause, though of limited range, we find in ourselves, in our personality; and such a cause, perhaps of wider

---

[4] Preface to Du Prel's "Philosophy of Mysticism."

[5] See on this subject the remarkably suggestive and able work, "Personality, Human and Divine," by the late Canon Illingworth.

range, we find in the intelligence that lies behind many of the phenomena here discussed. But the operation of unseen intelligences — who, in some unknown manner, can affect us, and also affect material things around us, just as our personality can affect the grey matter of our brain, and through it things outside ourselves — this, although it may be a true cause, is as far beyond scientific explanation, as the phenomena of consciousness itself. Until science can explain how consciousness is related to the brain, — which, although a fact of daily experience, is wholly incomprehensible, — we cannot expect from it any explanation as to how discarnate intelligences can operate upon matter, or whence the energy is derived. (See Note at end of chapter.)

But a change of thought on this subject is coming over the educated world. Some of the most cultured minds and acute investigators of recent years have satisfied themselves of the genuineness of the phenomena of Spiritualism, or at least that there is a strong *prima facie* case for serious investigation, and are profoundly impressed with the issues opened up and the vast movement of thought the general acceptance of these phenomena would create. Some, it is true, desire to suspend their judgment as to the explanation of the facts, whilst a surprisingly large number unreservedly accept the facts as an "assurance of things hoped for, the proving of things not seen." "When we last met," said Holman Hunt to Ruskin, "you declared you had given up all belief in immortality."

"I remember well," replied Ruskin, "but what has mainly caused the change in my views is the unanswerable evidence of spiritualism. I know there is much vulgar fraud and stupidity connected with it, but underneath there is, I am sure, enough to convince us that there is personal life independent of the body, but with this once proved, I have no further interest in spiritualism."[6]

Many stricken men and women in this gigantic and devastating war have found similar solace in the dark hours of their bereavement. They have seen in it a ray of heavenly light falling —

> "Upon the great world's altar-stairs
> that slope through darkness up to God."

Note. — There are of course various philosophical theories to account for consciousness and its relation to brain processes; in Chapter 10 I have briefly referred to this subject. Ultimately, as Dr. W. McDougall,

---

[6] *The Pre-Raphaelite Brotherhood*, by Holman Hunt, O.M., Vol. II, p. 271.

F.R.S., has shown, we are compelled to choose between Materialism and Spiritualism, using this latter word in its true metaphysical sense, "the soul theory." This theory involves psycho-physical interaction, and the argument that such interaction is impossible because it is inconceivable, has been answered by Lotze as follows: — "It is easy to show that in the interaction between body and soul there lies no greater riddle than in any other example of causation, and that only the false conceit that we understand something of the one case, excites our astonishment that we understand nothing of the other." I quote this from Dr. McDougall's masterly and well-known work, "Body and Mind." It is a significant fact — although Prof. W. James said some time ago, "Souls have gone out of fashion" (in science and philosophy) — that today not only Dr. McDougall, but many other distinguished psychologists and metaphysicians, support the soul theory.

CHAPTER 2

PSYCHICAL RESEARCH AND PUBLIC OPINION

"Wherever there is the slightest possibility for the mind of man to know, there is a legitimate problem for science." — *Professor Karl Pearson.*

It will I think be generally admitted that public opinion has taken a new departure with regard to the large class of important and interesting phenomena which lie on the boundary of an unseen world. We are on the Threshold of a new World of Thought, and the existence of the Society for Psychical Research, with the long list of distinguished men who are members of the Society or have given it their cordial support, is of itself a proof that a profound change of thought has taken place in recent years. Among the past presidents of that Society is a former Prime Minister of this country, the Right Hon. A. J. Balfour, who in his presidential address to the Society in 1894 spoke as follows: — [1]

"I think the time has now come when it is desirable in their own interests, and in our interests, that the leaders of scientific thought in this country and elsewhere should recognise that there are well attested facts which, though they do not easily fit into the framework

---

[1] "*Proceedings Society for Psychical Research,*" Vol. X, p. 6, et seq. The lapse of time since the foundation of the Society in 1882 has left Mr. Balfour and myself the sole survivors of the original Vice-Presidents of the Society.

of sciences, or of organised experience as they conceive it, yet require investigation and explanation, and which it is the bounden duty of science, if not itself to investigate at all events to assist us in investigating . . . . All arbitrary limitations of our sphere of work are to be avoided. It is our business to record, to investigate, to classify, and if possible to explain, facts of a far more startling and impressive character than these modest cases of telepathy. Let us not neglect that business . . . .

If many are animated by a wish to get evidence, not through any process of laborious deduction, but by direct observation, of the reality of intelligences not endowed with a physical organisation like our own, I see nothing in their action to criticise, much less to condemn. If I rightly interpret the results which these many years of labour have forced upon the members of this Society, and upon others not among our number, who are associated by a similar spirit, it does seem to me that there is at least strong ground for supposing that outside the world (as we have, from the point of view of science, been in the habit of conceiving it), there does lie a region . . .not open indeed to experimental observation in the same way as the more familiar regions of the material world are open to it, but still with regard to which some experimental information may be laboriously gleaned. Even if we cannot entertain any confident hope of discovering what laws these half-seen phenomena obey, at all events it will be some gain to have shown, not as a matter of The Psychical Research Society speculation or conjecture, but as a matter of ascertained fact, that there are things in heaven and earth not hitherto dreamed of in our scientific philosophy."

These are the words of a statesman not of a dreamer or a fanatic; they express the opinion moreover of a singularly acute and philosophic mind, accustomed to sift and weigh evidence, and experienced in the errors and illusions as well as in the knowledge and thought of his fellow men.

Another famous Prime Minister, the Right Hon. W. E. Gladstone, also gave his great name to the support of the Psychical Research Society, and for many years before his death was an Honorary Member. So also was the poet Laureate, Alfred Tennyson, the great painters G. F. Watts and Lord Leighton, as well as the famous writers John Ruskin and R. L. Stevenson.

Foremost men of science both in England and abroad have shown their hearty approval by joining the Council or becoming members of the Society. Among these are to be found the recent Presidents of the Royal Society, on all of whom have been conferred the Order of Merit: Lord Rayleigh, Sir Arch. Geikie, Sir W. Crookes, and Sir J. J. Thomson. Another past president of the Royal Society, also given the O.M., Sir William Huggins, assured me of his support, when I issued invitations to the conference which led to the foundation of the Society for Psychical Research in 1882.[2]

Sir Wm. Huggins, however (like Archbishop Benson, who was also in hearty sympathy), for various reasons did not wish to become a member of the Society, though he had been convinced of the genuineness of certain super-normal phenomena he himself had witnessed.

The active work of Sir Oliver Lodge in connection with the Society, of which he has been President, is well known to everyone.

On the Continent and in America many eminent savants have given their valued adhesion to the Society, e.g. Professor Charles Richet of Paris and Professor William James of Harvard, both of whom have been Presidents of the Society, and among other foreign members are to be found the names of Professors Janet, Bernheim, Lombroso, Schiaparelli, Flammarion, and that most strenuous worker Dr. Hyslop; nor must we forget the late Professor Hertz, "the lustre of whose name," as Mr. Balfour remarked in his presidential address, gave an added dignity to our proceedings. Nor have the more enlightened clergy held aloof, such as the late Bishop of Carlisle, the Rev. R. J. Campbell, The Psychical Research Society and Bishop Boyd Carpenter, who has been a recent President of the Society, his successors being Mrs. Henry Sidgwick, D. Litt, Dr. Schiller of Oxford, and Professor Gilbert Murray, D. Litt who was in 1916 the President of the Society.

There can be little doubt that much of the success the Society has won is due to the wise guidance and indefatigable labour so long given by the first President, Professor Henry Sidgwick, — work most ably and zealously continued by his widow. It is almost needless to mention the immense service rendered to psychical research by the well-known names of those brilliant and gifted men — both Fellows of Trinity College, Cambridge. — Mr. Ed. Gurney and Mr. F. W. H. Myers, who were the first Honorary Secretaries of the Society.

Some of us know the disinterested courage, the eminent fairness, and the self-sacrificing labour which Sidgwick, Myers and Gurney, brought

---

[2] I may mention here that in the foundation of the Society my friends the late Mr. Dawson Rogers and Mr. P. W. Myers cooperated.

to bear on the study of these difficult problems, and there can be little doubt that in another generation or two the names of these eminent pioneers will be held in honour throughout the educated world.

Some think, not unnaturally, that the S.P.R., as its title is usually designated, proceeds too slowly and cautiously and has not shown a sufficiently open mind towards the physical phenomena of spiritualism. There is no doubt some truth in this latter criticism, but we must remember that the caution with which the Society for Psychical Research proceeds is characteristic of all scientific investigation, and is doubly necessary in a region where there are so many pitfalls for the unwary. But if it builds up slowly it builds securely, and next to the addition of fresh knowledge within its domain, it welcomes most heartily that investigator who can prove that any of the conclusions at which it has arrived are incorrect. It has no retaining fee on behalf of telepathy or of ghosts, no vested interest in the super-normal. Theories, however plausible, that do not cover the whole of the facts observed must be rejected; superstition reverses this process, but science should know nothing of prejudices and prepossessions. As Sir John Herschel has well said: "The perfect observer will have his eyes, as it were, opened, that they may be struck at once with any occurrence which, according to received theories, ought not to happen, for these are the facts which serve as clues to new discoveries."[3]

It was this openness of mind which led the brave pioneers in the investigation of spiritualistic phenomena, to risk their reputation and encounter ridicule and obloquy by their enquiry; and when they had obtained what appeared to them conclusive evidence of the genuineness of the phenomena, they published their opinions with what then required rare courage. Foremost amongst these was our own great exposer of fallacies and paradoxes, the eminent mathematician, Professor A. De Morgan, who wrote in 1863: "I am perfectly convinced that I have both seen and heard, in a manner which should make unbelief impossible, things called spiritual which cannot be taken by any rational being to be capable of explanation by imposture, coincidence, or mistake."[4] Similar testimony has been borne by Dr. A. R. Wallace, O.M., and others of note, whilst Sir W. Crookes' famous researches in Spiritualism are known to all.

---

[3] "Discourse on Natural Philosophy," sec. 5

[4] Preface to *From Matter to Spirit* (Longmans'). An admirable summary of the statements made by distinguished individuals who have been led to a belief in Spiritualism, is given by Dr. A. R. Wallace in his *Miracles and Modern Spiritualism*.

But not only these and other eminent men have been convinced of the facts, multitudes of men and women in all parts of the world have come to a similar belief. Long ago Dr. A. R. Wallace stated in an article in *Chambers' Encyclopaedia*, "Spiritualism has grown and spread continuously till, in spite of ridicule, misrepresentation, and persecution, it has gained converts in every grade of society and in every civilised portion of the globe." They have had in their own experience indubitable evidence of the existence of phenomena entirely new to the science of today — phenomena which receive their simplest solution upon the hypothesis of a spiritual world and of intelligent beings therein, able through certain channels at times to communicate with us. Neither the blazing light of public opinion, nor the rogues that have too often duped the credulous, have shaken a faith which stretches back to a remote past,[5] and which has grown in strength with the accumulating evidence forthcoming from time to time and place to place.

Now the philosopher Fichte has said: "Everything great and good upon which our present existence rests, and from which it has proceeded, exists only because noble and wise men have resigned the enjoyments of life for the sake of ideas."[6] What a man affirms is the idea he has made his own, and this is always interesting and generally worth listening to; and what a number of men affirm and continue unshaken to affirm through years of opposing prejudice, or may be of persecution, is certainly a matter to which every honest lover of truth should give some heed.

---

[5] Cf. Myers' *Classical Essays*, p. 83, ct seq. See also Howitt's *History of the Supernatural*, Vol. I, Chapter IX. Delitzsch, in his *Biblical Psychology*, Sect. XVII, shows that "table turning" was practised in many Jewish circles in the seventeenth century; the "table springs up even when laden with many hundredweight." In a work published in 1614 this is denounced as magic. Zebi, in 1615, defends the practice as not due to magic but to the power of God, "for we sing to the table sacred psalms and songs, and it can be no devil's work where God is remembered." But, going back 2,000 years, I am informed a prominent feature in the enlightened creed of the early Essenes was their belief in Spiritualism, tending to angel worship. In fact, the tenets of this mystic sect resembled in several other things the views held by many modern Spiritualists.

The early Church Councils, e.g. of Elvira, A.D. 305, — a little later of Ancyra, — warned Christians against augury and spiritualistic phenomena as the work of the devil and his demons, but in the Ancyra "Canon Episcopi" about 900 A.D., these phenomena were denounced as pure illusions. This was not, however, the opinion of St. Thomas Aquinas in the 13th century nor of the Roman Catholic Church then and now. See Canon McClurc's brochure on Spiritualism published by S.P.C.K.

[6] "Fichte's Works," Vol. VII, p. 41.

On the other hand, what men deny is either valueless, or evidence of the rarity or novelty of the occurrences denied, — unless indeed the denial be a mode of affirming another truth, like the denial of perpetual motion. Thus for anyone to deny the possibility of the electric telephone, as some scientific sceptics did in my hearing in 1877, is of no importance compared with competent witnesses who have seen and heard the telephone.

How comes it then that the denials of the ignorant or the prejudiced as regards spiritualistic phenomena have had more weight in scientific and popular estimation than the affirmative evidence of the many witnesses we have referred to? The consideration of this question must be deferred to the next chapter.

CHAPTER 3

CONFLICTING OBJECTIONS OF SCIENCE AND RELIGION

"Is anything of God's contriving endangered by inquiry? Was it the system of the universe or the monks that trembled at the telescope of Galileo? Did the circulation of the firmament stop in terror because Newton laid his daring finger on its pulse?" — *Lowell.*

Why, we may well ask, in an age preeminent for its fearless inquiry, and for the daring advance that has been made in regions where ignorance has for centuries reigned supreme, has there not been much more advance in a direction which would appear to be so important? Surely the supreme problem for science to solve if she can, is whether life, as we know it, can exist without protoplasm, or whether we are but the creatures of an idle day; whether the present life is the entrance to an infinite and unseen world beyond, or "the Universe but a soulless interaction of atoms, and life a paltry misery closed in the grave." And although the province of religion is the region of faith, yet, surely, as a handmaid to faith, the evidence afforded by Spiritualism ought to be welcomed by it. Yet, strangely enough, it is these two great authorities, Science and Religion, which have largely blocked the way. And when we ask the leaders of thought in each to give us the ground for their opposition, we rind their reasons are mutually destructive.

Our scientific teachers of the last generation, largely influenced by German materialism, denied, and many still deny the possibility of mind without a material brain, or of any information or knowledge being gained except through the recognised channels of sensation. But our religious teachers stoutly oppose this; they assert that a spiritual world does exist, and that the inspired writings contain a system of knowledge supersensibly given to man. Both views cannot be true, yet both are urged in antagonism to Spiritualism.

Their common ground is that all extension of our existing knowledge in their respective departments must only come through the legitimate channels they prescribe; in the one case the channel is that bounded by the known senses, and the known properties of matter, and in the other the channel is that sanctioned by Authority. Everything outside these channels is heresy, and must be discredited.

I am, of course, speaking generally, for we all know eminent men, both in science and theology, who take a broader and more rational view.

At the same time there is much to be said on behalf of orthodoxy. The inertia of Conservatism is useful, nay, even necessary, in helping to suppress rash or hasty deviation from the recognised order of things; hence mere aberrations of intellect meet with a steady resistance, but that which is true, however novel it may be, has a resiliency which grows stronger the greater the resistance it encounters, and finally wins its way among our cherished and enduring possessions.

There are some cogent reasons which both science and religion might give for their opposition to this subject. The effect of their opposition has not been by any means an unmixed evil. In the address already referred to Mr. A. J. Balfour has well-stated one of these reasons. He says: "If we took it by itself we should say that scientific men have shown in connection with it a bigoted intolerance, an indifference to strictly scientific evidence, which is, on the face of it, discreditable. I believe that although the course they pursued was not one which it is very easy rationally to justify, nevertheless there was a great deal more of practical wisdom in it than might appear at first sight."[1] He then proceeds to show that as no nation or age can do more than the special work which lies before it at the time, so natural science, during its comparatively short life, has had enough to do in building up the whole body of the natural and experimental sciences, which within

---

[1] *Proceedings of the Society for Psychical Research*, Vol. X, p. 4. Mr. Balfour is here speaking of mesmerism, but the remarks equally apply to Spiritualism.

the last century have been reconstructed from top to bottom. "If science had at first attempted to include in its survey not only physical but psychical phenomena, it might for a century have lost itself in dark and difficult regions, and the work of science today would then have been less, not more, complete."

I quite agree with this. Not only had our knowledge of nature to be first learnt, but the foundation of our scientific faith in the undeviating order of nature had also to be laid by the investigation of the laws of matter and motion and the discovery of the orderly evolution of life. What science has now established, and holds as eternally true, is that the universe is a cosmos, not a chaos, that amidst all the mutability of visible things there is no capriciousness, no disorder; that in the interpretation of nature, however entangled or obscure the phenomena may be, we shall never be put to intellectual confusion.

The magnificent procession of phenomena in the midst of which we stand; the realms and magnitudes above us, too vast for the mind to grasp; the molecules and movements around us, too minute or too rapid for the eye to see or the mind to conceive, are all marching to the music of a Divine and Eternal order. On this system of the orderly government of the world, our faith in a Supreme Being is rooted; and the progress of modern science has made this faith an integral part of our daily life, whether we regard the Supreme as an impersonal power or as a beneficent Father. Now, if instead of investigating natural phenomena (I use that term in its common meaning, all phenomena are, strictly speaking, natural, only the Deity is supernatural) science had first grappled with supernormal phenomena, I doubt whether it would have yet emerged from the abyss; certainly it would not have reached its present assured belief in a reign of law. For psychical phenomena are so elusive, the causes so obscure, that we need the steadying influence of the habit of thought engendered by science to enable us patiently and hopefully to pursue our way.

A similar argument holds good in relation to religion. The seers and prophets of the Old Testament were the statesmen and men of science of their day: they were in advance of the people, because their thinking was based upon a philosophy illuminated with the Divine idea, — the idea that through all the strife of nature and men one eternal purpose runs. And from Moses to Isaiah we find them united in warning the people against any attempts to peer into and forecast the future, or to meddle with psychical phenomena for this or any lower purpose.

Divination, enchantment, witchcraft, astrology, and sorcery were various methods of augury, or of attempts to inflict injury on an enemy, veiled in a cloud of mystery to impress the beholder; and necromancy, or the attempt to hold communication with the dead, seems to have been resorted to chiefly for the same purpose.

These practices were condemned in unmeasured terms by the Hebrew prophets, and this irrespective of any question as to whether the phenomena were genuine or merely the product of trickery and superstition. They were prohibited — as a study of the whole subject undoubtedly shows — not only, or chiefly, because they were the practice, and part of the religious rites of the pagan nations around, but mainly because they tended to obscure the Divine idea, to weaken the supreme faith in, and reverent worship of, the One Omnipotent Being, whom the nation was set apart to proclaim. And the reason was obvious. With no knowledge of the great world-order such as we know possess, the intellectual and moral sense of the people would only have been confounded by these psychical phenomena.

Still worse, a sense of spiritual confusion would have ensued. Not only might the thought, the industry, and the politics of the nation have been hampered or paralysed by giving heed to an oracle rather than to the dictates of reason, but the calm unwavering faith of the nation in an infinitely wise and righteous Ruler of all might have been shaken.

Instead of the "arm of the Lord" beyond and above them, a motley crowd of pious, lying, vain, or jibbering spirits would have peopled the unseen; and weariness, perplexity, and, finally, despair would have enervated and destroyed the nation. As a learned and suggestive theologian has said: "Augury and divination wearied a people's intellect, stunted their enterprise, distorted their conscience.

Isaiah saw this and warned the people: 'Thy spells and enchantments with which thou hast wearied thyself have led thee astray.' And in later years, Juvenal's strong conscience expressed the same sense of the weariness and waste of time of these practices."[2]

With these feelings many of us can sympathise, as we have felt much the same in the quest of these elusive phenomena. But beyond this weariness, which in the search for truth we must endure, the perils that beset the ancient world in the pursuit of psychical knowledge do not apply to scientific investigation today, which is based on the acknowledged omnipresence of order.

---

[2] Principal G. A. Smith's "Isaiah," Vol. I, p. 199.

The aversion that undoubtedly still exists among many Christian men and women to the whole scope of these enquiries is based, I believe, partly upon the warnings contained in the Scriptures, to which I have alluded, and partly upon the more general ground that our investigations are an attempt to force an illegitimate entrance into the spiritual realm, a presumptuous effort to draw aside the veil, which both Scripture and our most sacred feelings have closed over the portals of death.

What can we reply to this? I think the feeling largely arises from a misconception of the position. I have already dealt with the ground upon which those magnificent men, the Jewish prophets, so strenuously forbade all psychical inquiry — grounds most wise and rational then, but inapplicable now. In the New Testament the condition, to some extent, changes; unmistakable warnings are uttered of the spiritual dissipation and danger that the early Christians would suffer if they allowed their religion to be degraded by the spiritual thaumaturgy still prevalent among neighbouring nations.

The civilised world at that time believed in the existence of spirits in the air, and the illuminated spiritual insight of the Apostles saw (and I, for one, believe we shall all see this more clearly as our knowledge grows) that the unseen around us is tenanted by many spiritual creatures whose influence is sometimes good and sometimes evil. Hence the apostolic injunction 'to try the spirits,' i.e. use our moral judgment and not be led astray by the foolish but common notion that every communication that comes from the unseen is good and worthy of credence. In fact the messages often spring from, and are invariably influenced by, the medium's own sub-conscious life.

Moreover, the Apostle saw clearly, as every Christian sees, that the foundation of religious life, which consisted of faith in a risen Lord, is seriously imperilled when the seen is substituted for the unseen, the phantasms of the spiritualistic séance for the realities of the Kingdom of Heaven, which cometh not with observation.

The same peril exists today, and always will exist. This every thoughtful and reverent mind must admit, and it is a distinct warning against making a religion of Spiritualism.

But this is not an argument against the study of the phenomena as a branch of psychical or psychological science. Whatever be the power or intelligence behind these phenomena, the fact that it manifests itself to us — that, directly or indirectly, it impinges on our senses, and so affects our perceptive faculties, or can leave some permanent record of its presence — this fact not only places Spiritualism within the pale of legitimate experimental inquiry, but invites and demands the attention of science.

It may be that these psychical phenomena are so elusive, depend so largely on conditions beyond our control, such as the activities of the subliminal self, or the volition of discarnate agents, that we shall never arrive at the laws that underlie them. But that need not prevent our observing, recording, and classifying the phenomena, noting the physical and psychical conditions most favourable to their production, and the variations induced by a change in these conditions. Only thus can we hope to link the unknown to the known, and so to correlate these obscure phenomena with the general body of recognised knowledge. Until this is done they will remain an outstanding puzzle, and the educated world will continue to shun them.

Part 2

CHAPTER 4

THE PHYSICAL PHENOMENA OF SPIRITUALISM

"Science is bound by the everlasting law of honour to face fearlessly every problem which can fairly be presented to it." — *Lord Kelvin.*

It is now time to turn from the somewhat lengthy discussion in the preceding pages, and submit some of the evidence which has come under my own observation and has convinced me of the genuineness of the phenomena themselves. It is however hardly possible to convey to others who have not had a similar experience an adequate idea of the strength and cumulative force of the evidence that has compelled one's own belief.

Unfortunately, where there is good coin there is also false, and Spiritualism has suffered from a fraudulent imitation trading on the credulity of the ignorant or uncritical.

In a paper[1] I contributed to the proceedings of the Society for Psychical Research in 1886 I stated that "reviewing the numerous séances I

---
[1] "Proceedings, Society for Psychical Research," Vol. IV, p. 28. See Appendix B, where I have reprinted a note on this paper which was written by that distinguished and far-seeing scientific man the late Professor Balfour Stewart.

have attended with different private and professional mediums during the last 15 years I find that by far the larger part of the results obtained had absolutely no evidential value in favour of Spiritualism; either the condition of total darkness forbade any trustworthy conclusions, or the results were nothing more than could be explained by a low order of juggling. A few cases, however, stand out as exceptions." These I proceeded to cite, and will here give the substance of two of them, as they offer, in my opinion, unexceptionable evidence of what has been called the "physical phenomena" of Spiritualism, — that is to say, the movement of objects, raps and other sounds displaying an unseen intelligence, for which no normal explanation can be found.

For these manifestations Mr. Myers has suggested the term *telekinetic*, as spiritualistic is a question-begging expression, for they afford in themselves no evidence of the survival of human personality after death. As a rule they are grotesque and meaningless, is only when the content of some of the messages that are conveyed by telekinesis are examined, that any slight and dubious evidence is found of another personality than that of the medium. The main question is the genuineness of telekinesis itself.

It is therefore important to note that not only did the phenomena I am about to describe take place either in broad daylight or in sufficient artificial light to enable me to detect any fraud, had such been attempted, but there were no paid or professional mediums present, and the sittings were held in any place I selected and even in my own house; notes were taken at the time of the sittings, or shortly after.

The first case I will cite occurred when I was writing an article giving reasons for the opinion expressed in a paper I read before the British Association in 1876, that where fraud did not explain these physical phenomena, and the observers were men of unimpeachable integrity and competence, such as Sir W. Crookes and Professor De Morgan, the witnesses thought they saw what they describe, owing to mal-observation or some hallucination of the senses such as occurs in incipient hypnosis. In fact I began the whole investigation of these phenomena convinced that this was their true explanation, and it was not until after stretching this hypothesis to illegitimate lengths that I found the actual facts completely shattered my theory.

An English solicitor of high standing, Mr. C, had taken for the summer season the suburban residence of a friend of mine, not far from my own house in Kingstown, Co.

Dublin. Upon making Mr. C.'s acquaintance I was surprised to find that he had in his own family what appeared to be spiritualistic phenomena then and there going on. They were not spiritualists and were puzzled and somewhat annoyed by the raps and other inexplicable noises that frequently occurred when their daughter Florrie was present — a frank, intelligent child at that time about ten years old. They naturally thought their young daughter was playing some childish tricks, but they soon convinced themselves this was impossible. The governess complained of rapping's in different parts of the schoolroom whenever Florrie was idle, and the music mistress asserted that often loud raps would come inside the piano, when Florrie was listlessly playing her scales.

Mr. and Mrs. C. gladly acceded to my request for a personal investigation, and I came the next day after breakfast. It was 10 o'clock and a bright summer morning — Mr. and Mrs. C. with Florrie and myself, no one else present, sat at a large dining table, with no cloth on, and the French windows opening on to the lawn, let in a flood of sunlight, so that the sitter's hands and feet could be perfectly well seen. A scraping sound was soon heard, then raps, sometimes on the table, sometimes on the backs of our chairs. Florrie's hand and feet were closely watched; they were absolutely motionless when the sounds, which rapidly grew in loudness, were heard. The noise was exactly such as would be made by hammering small nails into the floor, and my first thought was that some carpenters were in the room above or below, but on examination no one was there. We found the raps grew in intensity when a merry song was struck up, or music was played; the raps in a most amusing way keeping time with the music, occasionally changing to a loud rhythmic scraping, as if the bow of a 'cello were drawn on a piece of wood. Again and again I placed my ear on the very spot whence this rough fiddling appeared to proceed and felt distinctly the rhythmic vibration going on in the table, but no tangible cause was visible either above or below the table.

Doubts have been suggested as to the possibility of localising sounds; with some kinds of sounds this is difficult, but direct experiments which I made for this purpose showed that when blindfolded most people can pretty accurately locate the position of sounds such as I heard on this occasion.

Sometimes the raps travelled away and were heard in different parts of the room out of reach of anyone present. On one occasion I asked for the raps to come on a small table near me, which Florrie was not touching, they did so; I then placed one of my hands on the upper and the other on the under surface of the table, and in this position I felt the slight jarring made by the raps on the part of the table enclosed between my hands.

It made no difference whether Florrie and I were alone in the room, as was often the case, or other observers were called in. This latter was done occasionally when the raps were going on, to test my hallucination theory, but everyone heard the sounds.

The alphabet was slowly repeated and questions were answered by the unseen intelligence giving a rap when the right letter was arrived at. In this way we were told the communicator was a lad named 'Walter Hussey,' and Mrs. C. later on told me that frequently when she went to her child's bedroom to say good-night to her daughter, she heard raps going on and Florrie having an animated conversation with her invisible companion, the alphabet being rapidly spelt over and raps occurring at the right letters. I took down some of the answers obtained by means of the alphabet, they were just such as the child herself would have given, merry and meaningless, the unseen intelligence corresponded to that of the child and to my surprise the spelling was also that of the child! For upon asking Florrie to write down some words that occurred in the messages, the same childish misspelling occurred.

Of course the sceptic will say the whole thing was due to a clever child, who enjoyed bamboozling a professor. The sceptic is quite welcome to hold this opinion if it pleases him. All I can say is that after some weeks searching investigation every theory propounded by myself and by sceptical friends — some of whom were allowed to join in the enquiry — caused me and my friends likewise, to abandon all preconceived theories of fraud and illusion and mal-observation. The phenomena were inexplicable except on the supposition of an unseen intelligence like or actually that of the child. But the force that was sometimes exerted far exceeded that which the child could exert. Movements of furniture occasionally took place. On one occasion in full sunlight when seated with Mr. and Mrs. C. and Florrie at the large mahogany dining table, big enough to seat twelve at dinner, all our fingers visibly resting on the top of the table, suddenly three legs of the table deliberately rose off the floor to a height sufficient to enable me to put my foot beneath the castors. Let anyone try to imitate this by using all the muscular force he possesses, and he will find, as I did, that even allowing the hands to grasp the table, which those present did not attempt to do, the feat can only be done with difficulty and practice by a strong man.

To test a favourite anatomical theory that the raps were due to a trick which the medium might have acquired of slipping the toe or knee joints partially in and out with a click, I asked Florrie to put her hands Oat against the wall and to see whether, when I did the same, she could stretch out her feet away from the wall as far as I could, pretending it was a new game between us. When we were both in this strained position, and any muscular movement of the limbs impossible, I asked 'Walter' if he was amused at our game; instantly a brisk pattering of raps came in the room, the child's hands and feet being absolutely motionless, while no one but Florrie and myself were present in the room. Trickery by the servants was out of the question, in fact Mr. C. told me that when he was out of doors with his daughter he had obtained raps on the handle of his umbrella.

After the family had returned to England Mrs. C. informed me that the phenomena died away and they were very glad as they feared the health of their daughter might have suffered, but so far no injury whatever had occurred. "Of the genuineness of the phenomena (Mrs. C. wrote) I never had the slightest doubt, then or now." The manifestations, they informed me, were often more violent than any I had witnessed and always of a meaningless or frivolous nature.

Let me now narrate a second case where the medium was an adult, a lady who lived with the family of her cousin, a leading photographer in Dublin. I will call her Miss L.; needless to say she was neither a paid nor a professional medium, and I was greatly indebted to Mr. and Miss L. for giving me every opportunity to investigate the phenomena, often at considerable inconvenience to themselves. None of the sittings were in darkness; when held in the evening there was sufficient gas light to enable me to read small print, and of course to see any movement on the part of those present. On one occasion, only Mr. L., Miss L. and myself being present, loud raps which quite startled me, were given on the table at which we sat, and when I asked the unseen visitor to rap the number of fingers I held open, my hand being held out of sight and the opened fingers unseen by anyone, the correct number was rapped out; this was done twice. Knocks came in answer to my request, when we all removed our hands and withdrew a short distance from the table.

Whilst the hands and feet of all were clearly visible and no one touching the table it sidled about in an uneasy manner. It was a four-legged table, some 4 feet square and heavy.

In obedience to my request, first the two legs nearest me and then the two hinder legs rose 8 or 10 inches completely off the ground and thus remained a few moments; not a person touched the table the whole time. I withdrew my chair further, and the table then moved towards me, — Mr. and Miss L. not touching the table at all, — finally the table came up to the armchair in which I sat and imprisoned me in my seat. When thus under my very nose the table rose repeatedly, and enabled me to be perfectly sure, by the evidence of touch, that it was quite off the ground and that no human being had any part in this or the other movements. To suppose that the table was moved by invisible and non-existent threads, worked by an imaginary accomplice, who must have floated in the air unseen, is a conjecture which sceptics are at liberty to make if they choose.

Subsequently at my request Mr. and Miss L. came to my house at Kingstown, which they had never visited before, and we three had a sitting in the afternoon, with plenty of daylight enabling me to see everything in the room. After a short time raps, varying from faint ticks to loud percussive sounds, were heard, not muffled sounds as would be made by the feet in the carpeted room, but clear and distinct, and not the slightest movement of the hands or feet of any of the three present could be seen. Suddenly, the tips of our fingers only being on the table, the heavy loo table at which we sat began a series of prancing movements; so violently did the claws of the table strike the floor that I had to stop the performance fearing for the safety of the chandelier in the room below. I tried to imitate this movement afterwards and found it could only be done by a person using both hands and all his strength.

As in the previous case the messages that were spelt out were just such as the medium, who was a Methodist, would have given, serious and pious platitudes.

The foregoing were among my earliest experiences of the physical phenomena of Spiritualism, and taken along with my later experience and the evidence of others to which I will refer presently, left no shadow of doubt on my mind of the super-normal character of the manifestations. I will now briefly narrate my latest experience which occurred only a few months ago, Christmas 1915.

In the following case I was indebted for my introduction to the sitting to Dr. Crawford —lecturer on Mechanical Engineering at the Queen's

University and at the Technical College, Belfast, a trained scientific man holding the D.Sc. degree. Dr. Crawford had for some months been investigating the remarkable physical phenomena that occurred in a small family circle of highly respectable and intelligent working people in Belfast. The medium was the eldest daughter of the family, a girl, Kathleen, of some 17 years. The family had become interested in Spiritualism and had sat regularly one or two evenings a week for a year or more, to see if they could obtain any evidence of survival after bodily death. They made a sort of religious ceremony of their sittings, always opening with prayer and hymns, and when at last phenomena came, their unseen visitors were greeted with delight and respect. Obviously they were uncritical, simple, honest, kind hearted people; Dr. Crawford having assured himself they had no pecuniary or other motive such as notoriety to gain, was allowed and indeed welcomed to make a searching and critical investigation. This he did, devising elaborate and ingenious apparatus to test the phenomena, which he is describing in a work he is about to publish. *Inter alia* he found that the weight of the medium increased as the amount of the weight of the table or other object which was levitated had decreased.

I was permitted to have an evening sitting with the family, Dr. Crawford accompanying me. We sat outside the small family circle; the room was illuminated with a bright gas flame burning in a lantern, with a large red glass window, on the mantelpiece. The room was small and as our eyes got accustomed to the light we could see all the sitters clearly.

They sat round a small table with hands joined together, but no one touching the table.

Very soon knocks came and messages were spelt out as one of us repeated the alphabet aloud. Suddenly the knocks increased in violence, and being encouraged, a tremendous bang came which shook the room and resembled the blow of a sledge hammer on an anvil. A tin trumpet which had been placed below the table now poked out its smaller end close under the top of the table near where I was sitting. I was allowed to try and catch it, but it dodged all my attempts in the most amusing way, the medium on the opposite side sat perfectly still, while at my request all held up their joined hands so that I could see no one was touching the trumpet, as it played peep-bo with me. Sounds like the sawing of wood, the bouncing of a ball and other noises occurred, which were inexplicable.

Then the table began to rise from the floor some 18 inches and remained so suspended and quite level. I was allowed to go up to the table and saw clearly no one was touching it, a clear space separating the sitters from the table. I tried to press the table down, and though I exerted all my strength could not do so; then I climbed up on the table and sat on it, my feet off the floor, when I was swayed to and fro and finally tipped off. The table of its own accord now turned upside down, no one touching it, and I tried to lift it off the ground, but it could not be stirred, it appeared screwed down to the floor. At my request all the sitters' clasped hands had been kept raised above their heads, and I could see that no one was touching the table; — when I desisted from trying to lift the inverted table from the floor, it righted itself again of its own accord, no one helping it.

Numerous sounds displaying an amused intelligence then came, and after each individual present had been greeted with some farewell raps the sitting ended.

It is difficult to imagine how the cleverest conjurer with elaborate apparatus could have performed what I have described; here were a simple family group of earnest seekers, on whose privacy i had Intruded and who had suffered Dr. Crawford for 6 months or more to put them to the greatest inconvenience without any remuneration whatever.

But it is the cumulative force of the evidence coming from different places and different witnesses, some of which will be given in the next chapter that carries conviction. The objection as to the foolish and meaningless character of the phenomena will be met later, here I will only ask my readers to imagine how a dumb and invisible visitor coming to a house at night would try to attract the attention of the inmates; his efforts to communicate would be not unlike the knockings and sounds made by these unseen visitants.

That there is an unseen intelligence behind these manifestations is all we can say, but that is a tremendous assertion, and if admitted destroys the whole basis of materialism.

I am not so foolish as to suppose anything I can say will make an appreciable difference in public opinion, or that my testimony is superior to, or ought to have more weight attached to it, than that of several other observers. But it will, I hope, lead other witnesses to come forward and relate any unexceptionable evidence they possess, until "we drive the objector into being forced to admit the phenomena as inexplicable, at least by him, or to accuse the investigators either of lying, cheating, or of a blindness or forgetfulness incompatible with any intellectual condition except absolute idiocy."

It is true that much of what passes as evidence among certain Spiritualists has no claim to this distinction, and is only evidence of the difficulty of preserving a sound judgment and uninterrupted attention when dealing with these obscure phenomena. Nor is this to be wondered at. When any of us have obtained what we deem conclusive proof of some amazing occurrence, and are thereby convinced, we are all apt to relax the stringency of our inquiry, and accept as corroborative evidence what to an unconvinced outsider may seem capable of quite a different and more familiar explanation. At the outset we all start from very much the same level; some, of course, are worse observers than others; some jump to conclusions too readily, their judgment is less valuable; but the uniformity of the laws of nature is the common experience of mankind, and the man who tells us his gooseberry bush is bearing cucumbers does not expect to be believed until he can verify so outrageous a statement.

CHAPTER 5

PHYSICAL PHENOMENA CONTINUED

"In saying that a marvel is contrary to experience we can mean no more than that it is unlike previous experience; or rather that it is unlike that portion of experience which has been collected, handed down, and systematised by competent persons. But this only means that it is entirely novel and strange: and the greater the marvel the better must be the testimony [on its behalf]." — *Henry Sidgwick.*

Let us now turn to some of the undeniable evidence of similar super-normal phenomena that has been obtained by other witnesses.

In the most searching examination of this subject which has ever been undertaken, Mrs. Henry Sidgwick, Litt.D., in a paper published in the Proceedings of the Psychical Research Society for 1886,[1] states her own conviction that "notwithstanding the absence of what may be called crucial evidence for the existence of these physical phenomena beyond the recognised laws of nature, there is still some evidence which ought not to be set aside, and affords a prima facie case for further investigation." Mrs. Sidgwick then cites in illustration the Count de Gasparin's careful experiments with his own family and friends on the movement of tables without contact, published by him in Paris in 1854; also the evidence for similar phenomena obtained by a committee

---
[1] "Proceedings S. P. R.," Vol. IV, p. 72, e t seq.

for the Dialectical Society in 1870; Sir W. Crookes experiments with D. D. Home, published in the Quarterly Journal of Science, London, 1874, and the Rev. Stainton Moses' account of phenomena occurring through his own mediumship about the same period.

Mrs. Sidgwick has been unfortunate in her own protracted experience with professional mediums, but nevertheless states "it is not because I disbelieve in the psychical phenomena of spiritualism, but because I think it more probable than not that such things occasionally occur, that I am interested in estimating the evidence for them." There is not a single sceptic in the world who has devoted as many hours to this enquiry as Mrs. Sidgwick has given years, and I doubt if there exists a more competent critical and cautious investigator than this distinguished lady. Had she been fortunate enough to witness what I have described in the previous chapter, or to have had any sittings with D. D. Home, her opinion, I venture to think, would have been not very different from my own.

The London Dialectical Society consisted of some well-known professional men, and in 1870 they published the report of a special committee appointed to investigate these so-called physical phenomena. They state no paid mediums were employed, the psychics tested being persons of good social position and integrity who had no pecuniary interest to serve. The Committee report the frequent occurrence of raps showing unseen intelligence, and the movement of solid objects without any visible or known cause. On one occasion the committee knelt on chairs placed around, and about a foot away from, a large mahogany dining table, the hands of each person held behind their backs; under these conditions in full light distinct movements of the table occurred several times and swayed about in one direction or another without contact or the possibility of contact with any person present. Raps also occurred on the floor and on the table in answer to request.[2]

This report mentions many other remarkable super-normal phenomena, but it is needless to go into further detail, for these results, and those that I have witnessed, came far short of what Sir W. Crookes obtained in his own laboratory, under the most stringent conditions that his unrivalled experimental skill could devise.

Sir Wm. Crookes asserts that his experiments demonstrate the occurrence of the following phenomena inexplicable by any known agency: —

---

[2] "Report of the Dialectical Society" (Burns & Co., London), p. 391.

PHYSICAL PHENOMENA CONTINUED

(1) Raps and percussive sounds varying in loudness from a mere tick to loud thuds, which appeared to be caused by an unseen intelligent operator.

(2) The movement both of small and light, as well as large and heavy, bodies without visible cause or the contact of any human being.

(3) The alteration in the weight of bodies.

(4) The levitation of heavy objects without contact with any person; on three occasions he saw the medium, D. D. Home, raised completely off the ground in good light no one touching him.

(5) Musical instruments played without human intervention, and under conditions rendering them impossible to be played by normal means.

(6) Luminous appearances; more than once he affirms that under strict test conditions he has seen a luminous cloud appear, which condensed into the shape of a perfectly formed hand, that presently faded away.

(7) Intelligent messages written by unseen hands, —"direct writing" as it is termed.

(8) Handling red-hot coals and placing the hand in a blazing fire without any injury.

(9) Most astonishing of all, phantom forms and faces have appeared, and, under elaborate test conditions a materialized and beautiful female figure several times appeared, clothed in a white robe, so real that not only was its pulse taken but it was repeatedly photographed, sometimes by the aid of the electric arc light, and on one occasion simultaneously with and beside the entranced medium, who was plainer, darker, and considerably smaller than the preternatural visitant, the latter coming into and vanishing from a previously searched, closed, locked room in Mr. Crookes' own house.

'Since these almost incredible phenomena occurred (many of them witnessed not only by Mr. — now Sir Wm. — Crookes' own family, but also by other persons) I have been assured by Sir William that no subsequent criticism has failed to shake his opinion of their supernormal character, the elaborate precautions he took preventing the possibility of any fraud. Moreover, Sir Wm. Crookes in his Presidential address to the British Association in 1898 had the courage to state in reference to these investigations he had nothing to retract and that he adhered to the statements he had published.

What can be said of these miracles? They are so foreign to ordinary experience that one naturally thinks the observer was a victim of hallucination or of some clever trick. In a paper I published jointly with Mr. F. W. H. Myers in 1889 we said that on general principles the testimony of no single savant, however eminent, could compel general belief in phenomena so incredible, if they remained unattested by other trustworthy investigators.

Now as regards nearly all the phenomena described by Sir W. Crookes this additional testimony has been forthcoming.

For example, an able investigator, Professor Alexander of Rio de Janeiro, published in the *Proceedings of the Society for Psychical Research* for July, 1891, the details of some carefully conducted experiments he had made which authenticate some of the things attested by Sir. Wm. Crookes. In Professor Alexander's case the medium was one or other of two little girls, daughters of a friend of his, and here, not only did the movement of heavy objects by unseen intelligences occur, but "direct writing," under test conditions, took place in full lamplight; an unseen hand wrote messages on a slate, touched by the child's fingers only, the writing being far superior in execution to the childish calligraphy of the medium. Then luminous appearances presented themselves, at first a flitting, playful light, then growing in definiteness till a form was said to be seen by the little mediums, though not by others present. The clairvoyance was apparently shared by a dog, who gazed upward and barked at the figure, and at another time shared by a baby, who, gazing with astonishment, and pointing to an unseen figure, called, "Man, man," and at last said, "All gone!" Unseen hands were felt by all the sitters, caressing those present, and eventually the imprint of a tiny baby foot, far smaller than that belonging to any of the sitters present, was obtained on a school slate, over which a coating of flour had been spread.

This brief narrative gives an imperfect description of the phenomena obtained and the precautions taken, by Professor Alexander, but it is enough to show that independent and able investigators in different parts of the world, with different psychics, have obtained similar extraordinary results.[3]

By far the most remarkable psychic or 'medium,' whose powers have ever been investigated was Mr. D. D. Home, with whom many of Sir W. Crookes' experiments were made. Both Mr. F. W. H. Myers and myself devoted considerable time to examining the evidence on behalf of his super-normal gifts, and also the charges of fraud brought against him; we found plenty of rumours of trickery but no conviction of fraud. Robert Browning's poem "Sludge the Medium," which was supposed to express his opinion about Home, may possibly have been written to discount Mrs. Barrett Browning's enthusiastic conversion to Spiritualism. Mr. Myers knew Browning personally, and he asked the poet what foundation there was for his bad opinion of Home; Browning replied that he once heard a lady (since dead) tell him that another lady, also deceased, told her, that Home was once found in the act of experimenting with phosphorus in order to produce 'spirit lights.' Of this third hand story we could find no written or any other confirmation whatever, it was an old story when Browning heard it, and probably originated, — like other gossip we have traced to its source, — in someone saying "Home must have produced these spirit lights with phosphorized oil rubbed on his hands," a pure assumption for which we could not find a particle of evidence.4[3] In fact,

---

[3] The question whether the whole of the phenomena may not be explained away by ascribing to every witness gross and persistent exaggeration may be dismissed, as it cannot be seriously maintained; neither is it possible to sustain an explanation founded on a system of laborious and disinterested deception, though isolated cases of this kind are known. Professor Sidgwick has dealt with this point ("Journal of the Society of Psychical Research," July, 1894), and, moreover, such actors not only shrink from scientific scrutiny, but sooner or later get tired of their motiveless deception, or their fraud comes to light.

[4] Another charge against Home's character was that he had by fraudulent means persuaded a Mrs. Lyon to leave him her property, a case which led to litigation that went against Home.

This case we submitted to a high legal expert, who wrote that whether it was to Home's discredit or not rests on one's belief in the reality of the communications purporting to come from Mrs. Lyon's deceased husband, who urged the gift. Mr. Y. M. Wilkinson, an eminent and upright lawyer, and other witnesses in the case declared that Mrs. Lynn made the gift to Home of her own free will, and independent

Home courted the fullest enquiry, and made no objection to the stringent tests often imposed. I quite agree with what Sir William Crookes has said, though I never had the opportunity of meeting Home: —

> "I think it is a cruel thing that a man like D. D. Home, gifted with such extraordinary powers, and always willing, nay, anxious, to place himself at the disposal of men of science for investigation, should have lived so many years in London, and with one or two exceptions no one of weight in the scientific world should have thought it worthwhile to look into the truth or falsity of things which were being talked about in society on all sides. To those who knew him Home was one of the most lovable of men, and his perfect genuineness and uprightness were beyond suspicion."

In the report which Mr. Myers and the present writer published in the "Journal of the Society for Psychical Research" for July 1889, we gave several first-hand accounts of the marvellous phenomena witnessed by our informants in the presence of Home.

I will first quote the evidence given to me by my friends the late General and Mrs. Boldero, neither of whom were Spiritualists. Notes of what took place had been written down by my friends and the evidence was given to me verbally and independently each observer. Home had been staying with the late Lord Dunraven, — who published for private circulation a small book giving an account of the marvellous phenomena he had witnessed in Home's presence, — and had never before visited the house where General, then Colonel, Boldero was staying in Scotland, where he held a high military appointment.

Here is the account given to me by General Boldero: —

> "It was at the end of February, 1870, that Home came to visit me by invitation, at my house in Cupar, Fife. He arrived immediately before dinner, and after dinner we, Mrs. Boldero, Home, and myself, sat in the drawing room for any manifestations that might occur.
>
> The room was quite light, the gas being lighted, and a bright fire burning. Home sat with his back to the fire, at a small table, with a cloth on

---

of any unfair influence from Home. But in any case this litigation has no bearing on the reality of Home's psychic powers.

it. I was opposite to him, and Mrs. Boldero was on his right hand. A piano and Mrs. Boldero's harp were at the end of the drawing room some 10 feet or 12 feet away.

"Almost immediately some remarkable manifestations occurred; in a little while the table moved towards the piano. I saw a hand come out on my side from under the table, pushing out the tablecloth and striking notes on the piano. Afterwards I saw a whole hand as far as the wrist appear without the tablecloth and strike the notes, playing some chords on the piano. At this time Home was some distance off, and it was physically impossible for him have struck the piano. It was equally impossible for him to have used his foot for the purpose. I was perfectly confident at the time and am now that trickery on the part of Home was out of the question. After that some chords were faintly struck on the harp standing immediately behind me. We asked for them to play louder, and a reply came by raps, 'We have not power.' Then voices were heard speaking together in the room, two different persons, judging from the intonation. We could not make out the words spoken as Home persisted in speaking to us all the time.

We remonstrated with him for speaking, and he replied, 'I spoke purposely that you might be convinced the voices were not due to any ventriloquism on my part, as this is impossible when anyone is speaking in his natural voice.' Home's voice was quite unlike that of the voices heard in the air."

The differences and similarities in the account given by husband and wife are instructive. On my reading to him the following account given me by Mrs. Boldero, the General said that where there was a difference his wife's account was probably the more correct. Mrs. Boldero said: —

"On February 28th, 1870, Home arrived at our house shortly before dinner. After dinner we agreed to sit in the drawing room at a square card-table near the fire. In a few minutes, a cold draught of air was felt on our hands and knockings occurred. Several messages of no consequence came, questions being asked and answered. I was exhorted to pray more. A rustling of dresses was heard, as of a stiff silk dress in the room. [General Boldero recollects this also.] My gold bracelet was unclasped whilst my hands were on the table, and fell upon the floor. [General Boldero agrees to this.] My dress was pulled several times. I think I asked if the piano could be played; it stood at least 12 feet or 14 feet away from us. Almost at once the softest music sounded. I went up to the piano and opened it. I then saw the keys depressed, but no one playing.

I stood by its side and watched it, hearing the loveliest chords; the keys seemed to be struck by some invisible hands; all this time Home was far distant from the piano. Then a faint sound was heard upon my harp, as of the wind blowing over its strings. I asked if it could be played louder; an answer came, there was insufficient power.

"Later on in the evening, we distinctly heard two voices talking together in the room; the voices appeared to come from opposite corners, near the ceiling, and apparently proceeded from a man and child, but we could not distinguish the words. They sounded far off. Home was talking the whole time the voices were heard, and gave as his reason that he might not be accused of ventriloquism. During the whole of this séance, the whole room seemed to be alive with something, and I remember thinking that no manifestation would surprise me, feeling that the power present could produce anything. Home himself remarked that he had rarely had so satisfactory a séance. Throughout, Home seemed to be intensely, and very genuinely, interested in the whole séance. I am perfectly sure that Home could not possibly have played the piano himself; his touching it was wholly out of the question. General Boldero saw a hand playing on the piano, but I did not see this."

General Boldero also informed me that at another séance with Home he saw a large round table, on the top of which the sitters' hands were placed, rise completely off the ground to a height as great as the upstretched arms of the sitters would allow and then the table gently descended. At another time the table, on which were glasses and a lamp, tilted to such an angle that ordinarily everything would have fallen off, but they remained undisturbed. A similar incident has been witnessed at other places by other persons; thus the Rector of Edmonthorpe, Rutland, the late Rev. H. Douglas, a man of acute and scholarly mind and keen intelligence, writes that at a sitting with Home in Lady Poulett's house in London: "We all saw the supper table on which there was a quantity of glass and china full of good things, rise to an angle of 45 degrees, I should say, without anything slipping in the least, and then it relapsed to its normal position." My friends the late Lord and Lady Mount Temple were present on this occasion and they confirmed not only the story, but gave me an account of many other weird phenomena they had witnessed with Home.

The late Major-General Drayson, R.E., gave me in writing some of his experiences with Home: he said he had had more than 50 sittings with Home, and though at first absolutely incredulous, was soon convinced of the genuineness of the amazing phenomena he had witnessed, as Home gave him every opportunity for close investigation. General Drayson says: "I have seen tables, chairs, boxes, etc., suddenly rise in the air, or move from distant parts of the room to positions close beside me; I have heard a locked piano in my own house play a piece of music. I have seen in Home's presence, at the late Sir W. Gomm's house, an accordion carried round the room, playing a tune when no visible hand held it." General Drayson relates many other things he has witnessed and adds, "it is of course impossible to give in detail all circumstances which convinced me that imposition or delusion was impossible, — the séances being mostly in my own house, — and finally led me to abandon my former belief in materialism."

It would be wearisome to quote further from the abundant first-hand evidence of Home's powers attested by men of probity and intelligence. There are however two or three extraordinary phenomena which Home occasionally exhibited that are worthy of more than a passing notice; these will be discussed in the next chapter.

This little book would extend beyond its limits if I were to quote even selections from the mass of first-hand evidence given by numerous critical observers of these physical phenomena, and obtained through trustworthy mediums both in England and abroad.

I would refer specially to the able work of Mr. Maxwell on metapsychical phenomena for further evidence. Before closing this chapter it is desirable to refer to another and less satisfactory aspect of this subject as illustrated by the psychic Eusapia Paladino, a paid professional medium of a very different and much lower type than D. D. Home.

In 1894 Sir Oliver Lodge read a paper before the Society for Psychical Research in which he described the phenomena that took place in his presence, and that of Professor Charles Richet of Paris, when Eusapia was secluded in a small island in the Mediterranean (Ile Roubaud) on which Professor Richet had a summer residence. After a searching and prolonged investigation, both of these savants were convinced of the genuineness of the phenomena that occurred, and Sir Oliver published the following summary of the results witnessed: —

> "The things for which I wish specially to vouch, as being the most easily and securely observed, and as being amply sufficient in themselves to establish a scientifically unrecognised truth, are (always under conditions such as to prevent normal action on the part of the medium): —
>
> (1) The movements of a distant chair, visible in the moonlight, under circumstances such as to satisfy me that there was no direct mechanical connection.
>
> (2) The distinct and persistent bulging and visible movement of a window-curtain in absence of wind or other ostensible cause.
>
> (3) The winding-up and locomotion of the untouched chalet. [A musical cigar-box, shaped like a chalet.]
>
> (4) The sounding of the notes of the untouched accordion and piano.
>
> (5) The turning of the key on the inside of the sitting-room door, its removal on to the table, and subsequent replacement in door.
>
> (6) The audible movements and gradual inversion of an untouched heavy table, situated behind the medium and out of the circle; and the finding it inverted afterwards.
>
> (7) The visible raising of a heavy table under conditions in which it would be ordinarily impossible to raise it.
>
> (8) The appearance of blue marks on a surface previously blank, without ostensible means of writing.

(9) The grasping, patting, and clutching of my head and arms, and back, while the head, and hands, and feet of the medium were under complete control and nowhere near the places touched."[5]

It is needless to add that the observers satisfied themselves that no other person had any part in these occurrences.

Subsequently, a series of experiments were made with Eusapia at Cambridge in 1895, in which Dr. Hodgson, Professor Henry. Sidgwick, Mr. Myers (all alas now deceased), and others took part, the result being that the investigators found what seemed to them clear evidence of trickery on the part of the medium. Still further experiments a little later on by Professor Richet and Mr. Myers, after taking special precautions against fraud, led to their conviction that Eusapia had unquestionably super-normal powers. She was further critically and independently tested by several notable scientific men in Italy, — including the eminent criminologist Professor Lombroso, and the neurologist Professor Morselli of Genoa; these and other competent investigators were convinced of the genuineness of the extraordinary phenomena they witnessed. Finally, three members of the Society for Psychical Research specially qualified to detect imposture, were commissioned by the Society to investigate this notorious medium, and they unanimously reported in favour of the genuineness of the supernormal phenomena they obtained.

Nevertheless, although Eusapia appears to have these super-normal powers, she is a medium of a low moral type, who has been convicted of imposture both in England and America and with whom therefore I should not care to have any sittings. My reason for referring to her at all is the notoriety she has gained, and the instructive psychological and moral considerations her career affords.

I will only add that in fairness to Eusapia, and also in corroboration of Sir Oliver Lodge's original report, I have given in Appendix C a more detailed account of the favourable results obtained through her mediumship by the Italian investigators and others, together with some remarks on this case which is, I fear, too often typical of paid professional mediums who sit for physical phenomena.

---

[5] "Journal of the S. P. R.," Vol. VI, November, 1894, p. 310.

CHAPTER 6

LEVITATION AND IMPUNITY FROM FIRE

"There is nothing that need hinder Science from dealing successfully with a world in which personal forces are the starting point of new facts. . . . The systematic denial on Science's part of personality as a condition of events . . . may conceivably prove to be the very defect that our descendants will be most surprised at in our own boasted Science." — *Professor W. James.*

Among the many amazing phenomena which numerous credible, and indeed eminent, witnesses assert that they have seen in connection with the medium D. D. Home, is that of his levitation or floating in the air, like the miracle recorded of St. Teresa and others in still more remote times. As late as 1760, Lord Elcho states that he heard, when in Rome, witnesses swear to the levitation of a holy man about to be canonized. The same fact is recorded, Mr. A. Lang tells us, in Buddhist and Neo-platonic writings and later among the Red Indians, and in Tonquin, where in 1730 a Jesuit priest asserted he saw this phenomenon, which he describes.

In 1871 the Master of Lindsay (the late Lord Crawford and Balcarres, F.R.S.) gave the following evidence, which was corroborated by the two other spectators, the late Earl of Dunraven (then Lord Adare) and Captain Wynne: —

"I was sitting on December 16th, 1868, in Lord Adare's rooms in Ashley Place, London, S.W., with Mr. Home and Lord Adare and a cousin of his. During the sitting, Mr. Home went into a trance, and in that state was carried out of the window in the room next to where we were, and was brought in at our window. The distance between the windows was about seven feet six inches, and there was not the slightest foothold between them, nor was there more than a twelve-inch projection to each window, which served as a ledge to put flowers on. We heard the window in the next room lifted up, and almost immediately after we saw Home floating in the air outside our window.

The moon was shining full into the room; my back was to the light, and I saw the shadow on the wall of the window sill, and Home's feet about six inches above it. He remained in this position for a few seconds, then raised the window and glided into the room feet foremost and sat down.

"Lord Adare then went into the next room to look at the window from which he had been carried. It was raised about eighteen inches; and he expressed his wonder how Mr. Home had been taken through so narrow an aperture. Home said, still entranced, 'I will show you,' and then with his back to the window he leaned back and was shot out of the aperture, head first, with the body rigid, and then returned quite quietly. The window is about seventy feet from the ground. The hypothesis of a mechanical arrangement of ropes or supports outside has been suggested, but does not cover the facts as described."

In an article in the *Contemporary Review* for January, 1876, Dr. Carpenter, the eminent physiologist, commenting on the foregoing says it illustrates how differently a believer and a sceptic view the same incident: "A whole party of believers will say they saw Mr. Home float out of one window and in at another, while a single honest sceptic declares Mr. Home was sitting in his chair all the time." As the only person present whose testimony was not published was Captain Wynne he was written to, and when asked if he had contradicted Lord Crawford's statement, he replied: "The fact of Mr. Home having gone out of one window and in at another I can swear to: anyone who knows me would not for a moment say I was a victim to hallucination or any other humbug of the kind." Like many other controversialists Dr. Carpenter drew on his imagination for his facts in order to support his case.

LEVITATION AND IMPUNITY FROM FIRE

One naturally supposes, however, that the witnesses must have been mistaken, or suffering from some excitement or hallucination of the senses. But it is not easy to suppose that three educated men, to whom nothing was said beforehand of what they might expect to see, could all have been hallucinated exactly in the same way: for the accounts given by each are alike. Nor is it easy to believe that the numerous witnesses of the levitation of saints and others in past times and in different countries, knowing nothing of each other, were likewise all hallucinated; nor, as Mr. A. Lang says, is it "very easy to hold that a belief — to which the collective evidence is so large and universal, as the belief in levitation, — was caused by a series of saints, sorcerers and others, thrusting their head and shoulders out of a window where the observers could not see them as one sceptic has suggested."

Another singular phenomenon reported in connection with Home, as bizarre as it is unaccountable, is the enormous elongation of his body, which sometimes occurred when he was in a trance. The numerous witnesses to this took every precaution to prevent themselves being deceived and they are unanimous in their statement that this amazing phenomenon actually occurred. My friend the late General Boldero, when Home was staying with him in Scotland, saw this occur several times, took exact measurements and assured me that neither deception nor hallucination were possible. The Neo-Platonists report that a similar thing occurred in their day to certain 'possessed' men.

Bewildering and inconceivable as were some of the phenomena associated with Home's mediumship they were not all unparalleled. For the Rev. Stainton Moses to whom I have already referred, experienced levitation no less than ten times. Of Mr.

Moses' high character, of his sanity and probity, Mr. W. H. Myers says, "neither I myself, nor so far as I know any person acquainted with Mr. Moses, has ever entertained a doubt." I knew Mr. Moses personally for many years, and like other of his friends, I believe he was wholly incapable of deceit. Mr. Sergeant Cox, not himself a Spiritualist, relates that on one occasion when Mr. Moses was in his house, in broad daylight a large, very heavy mahogany dining table, — which required the effort of two strong men to move, — suddenly and violently rocked to and fro, then it rose, or tilted up, several inches from the floor, first on one side and then on the other.

Frequent loud rapping also came upon the table, on which there was no cloth, and the light fell under it so that they could see no one was concealed beneath the table. In fact Sergeant Cox and Mr. Moses were the only persons present in the room, they were both standing some two feet distant from the table, one on each side of it, their hands not touching the table but held some 8 inches over it. The whole incident was published by Sergeant Cox, and described by him to Mr. Fred. Myers, whose detailed report of the marvels that occurred through Mr. S. Moses' mediumship is worth careful perusal.[1]

On another occasion, when Mr. Moses was in a friend's house, a child's organ on the table was lifted up, and floated round the room, playing all the time by some invisible agency. The chair on which Mr. Moses sat was suddenly drawn across the room, turned round so as to face the wall, no one touching the chair; then, Mr. Moses himself, by the same invisible agency, was steadily lifted up from the chair and raised till his head was near the ceiling; as he was close to the wall he made a pencil mark on it, level with his chest; he was then lowered into his chair again; the height of the mark when measured was found to be over six feet from the floor. All the facts were noted at the time, and even more striking cases of his levitation are described; Mr. Moses discouraged these manifestations which however continued for some time.

To return to Home, like the youths in the Babylonian fiery furnace, Home in his trance was uninjured by fire. Here I will quote Mr. A. Lang, who has given much attention to the subject of the fire-walk: —

> "Many persons in many ages, are said to have handled or walked through fire, not only without suffering pain, but without lesion of the skin. Iamblichus mentions this as among the peculiarities of his 'possessed' men; and in ***Modern Mythology*** (1897) I have collected first-hand evidence for the feat in classical times, and in India, Fiji, Bulgaria, Trinidad, the Straits Settlements, and many other places. The evidence is that of travellers, officials, missionaries, and others, and is backed (for what photographic testimony is worth) by photographs of the performance. To hold glowing coals in his hand, and to communicate the power of doing so to others, was in Home's repertoire. Lord Crawford saw it done on eight occasions, and himself received from Home's hand the glowing coal unharmed.
>
> A friend of my own, however, still bears the blister of the hurt received in the process. Sir W. Crooke's evidence follows: — "At Mr. Home's

---

[1] "Proceedings, S. P. R.," Vol. IX, pp. 245-35S.

request, whilst he was entranced I went with him to the fireplace in the back drawing-room. He [the influence controlling Home] said: 'We want you to notice particularly what Dan [i.e. Home] is doing.' Accordingly I stood close to the fire, and stooped down to it when he put his hands in. . . .

Mr. Home then waved the handkerchief about in the air two or three times, held it above his head, and then folded it up and laid it on his hand like a cushion. Putting his other hand into the fire, he took out a large lump of cinder, red-hot at the lower part, and placed the red part on the handkerchief. Under ordinary circumstances it would have been in a blaze. In about half a minute he took it off the handkerchief with his hand, saying, 'As the power is not strong, if we leave the coal longer it will burn.' He then put it on his hand, and brought it to the table in the front room, where all but myself had remained seated."

Not only have we Sir W. Crookes' evidence, but a former President of the Royal Society, the late Sir W. Huggins, O.M., witnessed the same feat with Home and gave me a detailed account of it. So also did Mr. S. C. Hall, who was present on another occasion, when a white-hot coal was put on his head and his white hair gathered over it, but he told me he felt no heat and his hair was wholly uninjured.

Various other eye witnesses have informed me that they have seen Mr. Home handle with impunity red-hot coals; among others a shrewd and able solicitor, the late Mr. W.

M. Wilkinson, writing to me from Lincoln's Inn Fields, London, states that in the winter of 1869: —

"I saw Mr. Home take out of our drawing-room fire a red-hot coal, a little less in size than a cricket ball, and carry it up and down the room. He said to Lord Adare, — now Earl Dunravcn, — who was present, 'Will you take it from me? It will not hurt you.' Lord Adare took it from him and held it in his hand Impunity to Fire for about half a minute, and before he threw it back in the fire I put my hand close to it and felt the heat like that of a live coal."

It is impossible to explain this by some fire resisting substance, surreptitiously put over the skin by Home, for Sir W. Crookes, than whom no higher authority on chemistry can be cited, tells us he knows of no chemical preparation that will accomplish this; moreover, he says he examined Home's hands carefully, after he had carried a live coal about and he could see no burning nor any preparation over the skin, "which (he remarks) was soft and delicate like a woman's."

Now these phenomena are too gross and palpable to be explained by an inaccurate description or lack of attention on the part of the observers.

They must have thought they had seen what took place, — a collective hallucination, — or else some miraculous manifestation actually occurred. For all attempts to explain the occurrences as due to clever conjuring on Home's part have signally failed. Experts in conjuring whose opinions have been taken, however little they believe in Home's pretensions, prefer to reject the testimony wholesale rather than attempt to explain these remarkable records.

Can we reject the testimony, — not because the witnesses told conscious falsehoods, that is impossible to believe, but because they were hallucinating? Now at Nancy and other medical schools, where hypnotic suggestion is used therapeutically, it is invariably found that even the best subjects exhibit marked differences in suggestibility, one subject sees the suggested object more clearly and not quite the same as another. But in these marvels recorded with Home, the witnesses were not hypnotic subjects and all perceived the same thing, and only occasionally did they receive from Home any suggestion as to what was about to occur. The manifestations are recorded by those present as having been sudden, startling and usually unannounced.

If suggestion on Home's part were the explanation, it must have been purely mental; and difficult as it is to suppose all present are equally susceptible to verbal suggestion, the difficulty is vastly intensified when we assume unspoken mental suggestion, acting equally upon all the spectators.[2] Nor must we forget that the witnesses in some cases were entire strangers to Home, and fully aware of Poltergeists, and were on their guard against any possible hallucination.[3]

---

[2] In the "Proceedings, S. P. R.," Vol. XII, p. 21, an interesting paper by Mr. Harrows shows that mental suggestion, without hypnosis, can operate at a distance upon different individuals; but only a single person is affected, and in Home's case we must assume a collective hallucination created by an unspoken suggestion, of which we have no experimental proof, though I admit this is the most plausible hypothesis of the phenomena described in this chapter.

[3] The reader who wishes for more information on Home's marvellous record should read the two volumes "Incidents in my Life," by D. D. Home, or the excellent narrative by Madame Dunglas Home called "The Gift of D. D. Home" (Kegan Paul, Trench & Co.).

Nor is it likely that the sporadic cases of levitation recorded in history can all be explained away. Teresa was not the only saint of whom levitation is recorded. In the *Acta Sanctorum* similar phenomena are attributed to more than 40 saints or other persons, and said to be attested by crowds of their contemporaries. The Bishop of Valencia was believed to have been miraculously suspended for some hours and was thus seen by his clergy and a multitude of others. In fact unless we deny the whole of the past and present records of these phenomena, attempted explanations are as difficult to accept as the miracles themselves.

Then again both in ancient and recent times we have first-hand evidence of the spontaneous occurrence of many of the physical phenomena such as were described in the last chapter. Without warning, pieces of furniture and crockery are thrown about a room, bells are constantly rung, disturbances of all kinds are produced, without any visible cause, and all attempts to catch the supposed practical joker have signally failed. In fact numerous witnesses, whom I have personally cross-examined, have assured me they have seen these things take place in broad daylight or in abundant artificial light, and no person had touched or even come near the things that were moved or thrown about the room.

I have published a lengthy paper on the evidence for these Poltergeist phenomena, as they are called; and no doubt whatever rests on my own mind as to the reality and supernormal character of these utterly meaningless phenomena.[4]

All we can do at present is to collect additional evidence and refrain from speculating on the object of these preposterous and futile occurrences, which appear not to have the smallest ethical or religious value. Scientific and philosophical value they have undoubtedly, as must be obvious to any thoughtful reader.

---

[4] 1 See "Proceedings, S. P. R. (" Vol. XXV, p. 377, and Psychical Research (Home Univ. Series), chapter 13.

CHAPTER 7

ON CERTAIN MORE DISPUTABLE PHENOMENA OF SPIRITUALISM

ECTOPLASMS "DIRECT" VOICE AND WRITING;
MATERIALIZATION; ALLEGED SPIRIT PHOTOGRAPHY;
THE AURA

"By cherishing as a vital principle an unbounded spirit of enquiry and ardency of expectation reason unfetters the mind from prejudices of every kind… guarding only against enthusiasm and self deception by a habit of strict investigation…The character of the true philosopher is to hope all things not impossible and to believe all things not unreasonable."[1]

There are certain other aspects of spiritualistic phenomena to which I have not referred in the preceding pages because the evidence on their behalf is less conclusive. The opinion of some psychical researchers is indeed adverse to their genuineness, or at least their super-normal character. I refer to the alleged "Direct Voice" and "Direct Writing"; that is the speaking and writing of the *soi-disant* spirit without controlling the medium's muscles, or using them in any way. To this may be added the transport of material objects without human agency, "apports" as they are termed. Further, there are alleged cases of "spirit

---
[1] Sir John Herschel, *Discourse on Natural Philosophy*.

photography," where impressions of persons both deceased and living, and of luminous patches, are said to occur on a photographic plate without any corresponding objective or known cause. All these phenomena, — like that of the alleged materialisation of part of the whole of the spirit form, (to which reference was made in Chapter 5) — are comparatively rare and hence less accessible to critical investigation.

So far as my own experience goes I have repeatedly witnessed all these rare phenomena, but they were nearly always with paid professional mediums, and the usual conditions were such as to prevent conclusive evidence being obtained. Nevertheless I have a perfectly open mind on these disputed phenomena; and will go even further, for in some cases, which I investigated, their genuine super-normal character was very difficult to deny.

As regards the "direct voice" and "direct writing," many years ago I had some sittings at the house of my friend the late Mr. Dawson Rogers, with a lady medium, a friend of his, where both these phenomena were produced.

The results were remarkable, and obtained under conditions which would have been perfectly satisfactory had there been enough light (which there was not) to form a conclusive opinion.

Reference has been made to the direct writing obtained by Professor Alexander, who was well known to Mr. Myers.

In this case the sitting was in full light, and the medium was the young daughter of a personal friend of the Professor, who says "it was impossible that anyone could have written without being immediately detected"; nevertheless writing by an unseen hand came several times on a slate on which a small piece of slate pencil had been placed. ("Proc. S.P.R.," Vol. VII, p. 181.) It is very difficult to explain away other cases of direct writing, such as those quoted by Dr. Walter Leaf "Proc. S.P.R.," XIX, p. 400, and the numerous cases in which it occurred with the Rev. Stainton Moses, cited in Mr. Myers' record of the experiences of this gifted medium, which were published in the "Proceedings of the S.P.R.," Vols. IX and XL.

Sir W. Crookes records a remarkable attempt at "direct writing" by an unseen hand, which took place through the mediumship of Mr. D. D. Home. The sitting was in light at his own house, and only a few private friends present. Sir W. Crookes, having asked for a written message, says: —

"A pencil and some pieces of paper were lying on the centre of the table; presently the pencil rose on its point, and after advancing by hesitating jerks to the paper, fell down. It then rose and again fell. A third time it tried, but with no better result. After this a small wooden lath, which was lying upon the table, slid towards the pencil, and rose a few inches from the table; the pencil rose again, and propping itself against the lath, the two together made an effort to mark the paper. It fell and then a joint effort was again made. After a third trial, the lath gave it up and moved back to its place, the pencil lay as it fell across the paper, and an alphabetic message told us, 'We have tried to do as you asked, but our power is exhausted.'"[2]

As this took place in the light, under the close inspection of Sir W. Crookes and in his own room, neither fraud nor hallucination can reasonably explain the occurrence.

With the well-known professional medium, Slade I had many sittings 40 years ago, and obtained what was alleged to be direct spirit writing on my own marked slate, in full daylight, and under conditions which certainly rendered any explanation by fraud or malobservation difficult to conceive. I believe Slade had genuine super-normal powers; this can hardly be doubted after reading the reports given by "M.A." (Oxon), in his book *Psychography*, or by Zollner in his *Transcendental Physics*. Nevertheless, like so many other professional mediums, it is equally true he resorted to trickery, and was convicted of cheating in a notorious case tried in London.

Whilst the evidence against Slade in this case was biased and weak, yet it is obvious we must regard with the gravest doubt all phenomena obtained through any medium who has not a perfectly clean record. Moreover, as Dr. Hodgson and Mr. S. J. Davey have shown conclusively in the "Proceedings of the S.P.R.," Vol. IV, it is very easy for an expert conjurer to simulate what many have considered to be genuine super-normal phenomena, such as occurred with Slade, Eglinton, and other professional mediums. The same volume of the Proceedings also contains a critical paper by Mrs. H. Sidgwick on her spiritistic experiences which, with the discussion thereon, should be read by all enquirers.

As regards the "direct voice," this was the usual form in which communications came from a well-known American medium, with whom I had several sittings. Here however there was complete darkness,

---

[2] *Researches in Spiritualism*, by Sir W. Crookes, p. 93.

although she did not always resort to this. Some remarkable evidence professedly came through the communicating voice, identifying the speaker with deceased friends utterly unknown to the medium, and in some cases in languages unknown to the medium. But here also the medium was not free from suspicion, hence to a critical outsider the evidence cannot have the value which many sitters have attached to it.

More remarkable are the luminous appearances accompanying the mediumship of D. D. Home, the Rev. Stainton Moses and others, which have been observed under such stringent conditions that they cannot be set aside as fraudulent. Points of light darting about the room and floating luminous patches, I have frequently witnessed, and once also, in the late Mr. W. De Morgan's studio, a "materialized" bust, under what appeared to be excellent conditions, but the inevitable darkness of the room compelled me to regard the evidence as inconclusive. Here however is a record by Sir W. Crookes, who, needless to say, took every precaution to prevent being imposed upon by phosphorized oil or other means; moreover, with all his chemical knowledge and skill he failed to imitate the appearance artificially. "Under the strictest test conditions" Sir W. Crookes says: —

> "I have seen a solid self-luminous body, the size and nearly the shape of a turkey's egg, float noiselessly about the room, at one time higher than anyone present could reach standing on tiptoe, and then gently descend to the floor. It was visible for more than ten minutes, and before it faded away it struck the table three times with a sound like that of a hard solid body. During this time the medium was lying back, apparently insensible, in an easy chair."

The still more astonishing results recorded by Sir W. Crookes of the "materialization" of spirit hands or the whole body, remain to this day absolutely inexplicable.

All these phenomena have been termed ectoplasms by Mr. Myers adapting a word suggested by Professor Ochorowicz of Warsaw, whose valuable and confirmatory researches in spiritism I have not space to describe.[3] By *Ectoplasy* is meant the power of forming outside the body of the medium a concentration of vital energy, or vitalised matter,

---

[3] Those who wish for fuller information on these phenomena may consult *Human Personality*, Vol. II, p. 544 et seq. or Mr. Henry Holt's "Cosmic Relations," Vol. I, p. 149 et seq.

which operates temporarily in the same way as the body from which it is drawn; so that visible, audible or tangible human-like phenomena are produced. This is very much like the psychic force hypothesis under a new name.

As regards "apports," those I have witnessed with professional mediums were not convincing, and one well-known medium, now dead, I caught in flagrant trickery. But a friend of mine, sitting with a few friends in the country, and no professional medium, gave me the detailed account of an "apport" brought from his own house in London which was so convincing to him and so inexplicable, that I gave a detailed account of it in Light. This formed one of a series of articles I wrote for that Journal in 1881, entitled "Pieces Justificatives," for the formation of a Society for Psychical Research.

I will now turn to the debateable subject of alleged, "spirit photography." Mrs. Henry Sidgwick, who made a careful examination of this question, came to the conclusion that the alleged cases of the appearance of a deceased person on a photographic plate were either wilfully fraudulent or capable of a normal explanation.[4]

Since Mrs. Sidgwick's investigation other cases have occurred which prima facie seem inexplicable in either of these ways. For example, Dr. Hyslop has published a lengthy paper on this subject in the "Proceedings of the American Society for Psychical Research," giving the reproduction of numerous photographs which appear to afford evidence of a super-normal origin, though I think he will agree with me the evidence is far from conclusive.

While professing, for my own part, to leave the question of spirit-photography an open one, I may here relate a very curious and interesting case of a supposed spirit photograph which some years ago I submitted to searching examination and experiment. Lady C, the relative of a friend of mine, had taken for the summer the late Lord Combermere's country house, Combermere Abbey, in Cheshire. The library in the house was a fine panelled room, and Miss C. (as she then was) was anxious to secure a photograph of it. Accordingly, placing her half-plate camera on its stand in a favourable position, — fronting the unoccupied carved oak arm chair on which Lord Combermere always used to sit, she opened a new box of photographic plates in the dark room, put a plate in the dark slide, and after focussing the camera,

---

[4] See "Proceedings, S. P. R.," Vol. VII, also "Journal S. P. R.," Vol. V, for a discussion on die subject.

inserted and exposed the plate. On developing the plate by herself, she was amazed to find the figure of a leg-less old man seated in the carved oak armchair.

Shortly after this they found Lord Combermere had died from an accident he met with in London, and was being buried in the family vault, a few miles from his country house, at the very time the photograph was taken.

This curious coincidence came out after the photograph had been developed and led to a surmise whether the ghostly figure resembled the late nobleman.

At this point the facts were communicated to me, and I received a print of the photograph. I wrote to the members of Lord Combermere's family and sent them the photograph. The figure was somewhat indistinct and opinions differed as to the likeness; on the whole it was considered to be like him, especially in the peculiar attitude which was habitual to him when seated in his chair.

In reply to my enquiries Miss C. informed me the exposure of the plate was lengthy some 15 minutes, and that she had for a short time left the empty room during the exposure of the plate. I thought it possible one of the men servants had come in and seated himself in the chair until he heard Miss C. returning. Accordingly I made a photographic test of this surmise. Exposing a half-plate in the panelled library of the house of my friend the late Mr. Titus Salt, where I happened to be staying, I asked his eldest son, then a youth, to walk into the room, sit down in the oak arm chair, cross and uncross his legs, move his head slightly, and then walk out of the room.

This was done and we developed the photograph together, when lo! there came out almost a duplicate of the Combermere photograph, a shadowy rather aged man with no legs seated in the chair, and no signs of anyone coming into or leaving the room. I wrote a paper on the whole matter and published it, with a reproduction of the two photographs, in the *Journal of the Society for Psychical Research* for December 1895.

There I thought the matter ended, with a young footman as the *soi-disant* Lord Combermere; but I found that Miss C. and some others of the family strongly dissented from my view. They had closely examined their servants and had reason to believe that the denial, by the footman and others, — of any visit to the room at the time when the exposure took place, — was perfectly correct and straightforward.

Some time later an article of mine, which appeared in the Westminster Gazette, and contained a reference to this photograph, brought me the following letter from one of Lord Combermere's married relatives, which disclosed a fact of which I was previously unaware.

> "Dear Sir, — Having read your interesting article on the supernormal in the Westminster Gazette of the 9th inst., I cannot resist adding one detail to the account of Lord Combermere's supposed spirit photograph.
>
> "You say he had not lost his legs, but he died from an accident in which they were so much injured, he could never have used them again. He was run over by a wagon in Knightsbridge, crossing the street, and only lived a few weeks.
>
> "Lord Combermere was my father-in-law and I lived some years at the Abbey with him, and was much interested in Miss C 's written account of the photograph, which she gave me. The face was always too indistinct to be quite convincing to me, though some of his children had no doubt at all of the identity. I may add, none of the men servants in the house in the least resembled the figure and were all young men; whilst the outside men were all attending the funeral, which was taking place at the Church four miles off, at the very time the photograph was being done. I give you the *pour et contre* quite disinterestedly, as I am not myself persuaded one way or the other.
> — Yours very truly, "Jane S. C."

There I leave the matter sharing Mrs. C.'s opinion.

Both the late Mr. A. R. Wallace, O.M., and Mr. W. T. Stead, with some other investigators in England and abroad, have been convinced of the genuineness and veridical character of spirit photography; but it is so easy to fake a photograph by double exposure and otherwise, and there are so many accidental causes that give a resemblance to ghostly impressions, that we need much more conclusive evidence on this subject than has yet been obtained.

In conclusion I may allude in passing to Baron Reichenbach's "odic lights" and "aura" round the human body. There is nothing inconceivable in such phenomena, in fact some experiments I made in this direction years ago led me to think Reichenbach was not mistaken. But I was more interested in the alleged luminosity which Reichenbach declared his sensitives saw round the poles of a magnet and which in 1883 I set myself to examine.

For this purpose it was necessary to construct an absolutely dark room, to try a large number of people, each of whom had to remain at least half an hour in this darkened chamber to render their eyes sufficiently sensitive to any faint luminosity. When this was done two or three sensitives were found who distinctly saw the luminosity and were able to discover the position of an artificial magnet which, unknown to them, I had secreted in the dark room. Then a powerful electro-magnet was tried and careful precautions were taken to avoid any unconscious suggestion of telepathic influence, or detection of the faint sound that accompanies magnetisation, the sound being by proper means suppressed.

The sensitives immediately drew what they had seen on their return to daylight, their drawings, made independently, agreed, and I published the results both in the official scientific journal, the *Philosophical Magazine* for April 1883, and in the *Proceedings of the Society for Psychical Research* for the same year. Nevertheless, though I myself am perfectly satisfied of the existence of this luminosity, the evidence needs further corroboration before it can be accepted by the scientific world.[5] No trace of any photographic impression of this alleged luminosity was obtained even after long exposure with extremely sensitive plates, nor after following the suggestions made to me by the late Sir Wm. Huggins, O.M., who took much interest in the matter.

In all these curious and debateable psychical developments the difficulty consists in finding the sensitive whose organization has the peculiar and necessary idiosyncrasy which enables them to become in some cases (like the dowser or water-finder) clairvoyant, in others a medium for physical phenomena or automatic writing. This leads us back to the interesting psychological problem of mediumship, which is discussed in another chapter, and which will form a fruitful field for experimental psychology in the next generation.

---

[5] The late Earl Crawford, then Lord Lindsay, tried similar experiments, at first with doubtful success; but with the medium Home, in 1871, Lord Lindsay states he obtained clear proof of the existence of this luminosity emanating from the poles of a large permanent magnet he had secreted in a dark room.

Part 3

CHAPTER 8

THE CANONS OF EVIDENCE IN PSYCHICAL RESEARCH

"Nothing can destroy the evidence of testimony in any case but a proof or probability that persons are not competent judges of the facts to which they give testimony, or that they are actually under some indirect influence in giving it in such particular case. Until this is made out the testimony must be admitted." — *Bishop Butler.*[1]

It is unlikely that those who have never witnessed any of the phenomena we have been discussing will be able to believe in them fully or at all. A natural and proper reservation of mind always accompanies the reception of evidence which is opposed to the general experience of mankind. Even Sir W. Crookes writes that, in recalling the details of what he witnessed, he finds an antagonism in his mind between his reason on the one hand, and on the other the evidence of his senses, corroborated as it was by that of other witnesses who were present. Yet, as Reid states in his essay on "Mind," and as jurists know, no counsel would venture to offer as an argument that we ought not

---

[1] *Analogy*, part II, chap. 7.

to put faith in the sworn testimony of trustworthy eyewitnesses because what they assert is incredible; few judges would listen to such pleading.

But, in spite of all logic, we are conscious that

> "Events may be so extraordinary that they hardly can be established by testimony. We should not give credit to a man who should affirm that he saw an hundred dice thrown in the air and they all fell on the same faces. If we had ourselves been spectators of such an event, we should not believe our own eyes till we had scrupulously examined all the circumstances, and assured ourselves that there was no trick or deception. After such an examination we should not hesitate to admit it, not withstanding its great improbability, and no one would have recourse to an inversion of the laws of vision in order to account for it. This shows that the probability of the continuance of the [recognised] law of nature is superior, in our estimation, to every other evidence. One may judge, therefore, of the weight of testimony necessary to prove a suspension of those laws, and how fallacious it is in such cases to apply the common rules of evidence." [2]

Hence Bertrand, in his *Traite du Somnambulisme*, says, with regard to kindred amazing phenomena, that though by listening to weighty evidence we may conclude there are sufficient reasons for believing them, "yet one really *does* believe them only after having *seen* them." We may entertain a limited belief, one tempered with scepticism, but unreserved assent to miracles, ancient or modern, requires actual experience of similar marvels, or absolute faith not only in the wisdom, but also in the strict accuracy and moral worth of the person who attests them; in fact, the inner witness of our spiritual nature to what would otherwise be incredible.

Albeit the position taken up by St. Thomas in the Gospels does not justify the scornful attitude of many sceptics. It is utterly unphilosophical to ridicule or deny well-attested phenomena because they are inexplicable. J Laplace, Abercrombie, Herschel, and many others might be quoted to this effect, but it is needless to verify so obvious a proposition. Only "in proportion to the difficulty there seems of

---

[2] Laplace, *Essai Philosophique sur les probabilités* p. 76.

admitting the facts should be the scrupulous attention we bestow on their examination."

This brings me to the perfectly legitimate position which many take up, and which is justified by the caution that characterises all sound advances in knowledge. It is that the antecedent improbability of these phenomena is so great, they are so far removed from the common experience of mankind, and, moreover, they involve ideas so unrelated to our existing scientific knowledge, that, before we can accept them, we must have, not only evidence, but incontestable evidence, on their behalf.[3]

This is common sense and obviously necessary. Such undeniable evidence I have endeavoured to place before my readers, though it may not be adequate to carry conviction of some of the amazing phenomena related, such as the "materialization" of a spirit form, — on this indeed I reserve my own opinion. On the real objective existence of most of these super-normal physical phenomena the evidence appears to me to be overwhelming.

Surely it is the business of science to extend its domain in these fruitful fields of research, and it is only because the trained scientific investigator has, until quite recently, turned his back on these phenomena, that the humble spiritualists have had to try and do the neglected work of science in this very difficult region of enquiry; and now having done it to the best of their ability, they are scorned and pelted by the educated world and told they are guilty of "intellectual whoredom," whilst their painstaking effort to enlarge the sum of human knowledge is stigmatised as the "recrudescence of superstition"; and this by the leaders and organs of scientific thought, where

---

[3] In a paper, "On the Value of Testimony in Matters Extraordinary," Mr. C. C. Massey, following Dr. A. R. Wallace, has urged that the antecedent improbability of an event is simply equivalent to the improbability that affirmative evidence, reaching a certain standard of intrinsic value, will be forthcoming, and therefore vanishes with the occurrence of such evidence; so that adverse presumption ought never to prejudice the reception and estimation of evidence on behalf of some fact outside our experience. Hence (according to this view) we must dissent from the proposition commonly adopted that "improbability" legitimates the demand for an extraordinary amount of evidence, and have regard rather to the positive presumption which experience affords, that the best human testimony, after taking account of all elements of fallacy in the particular case, is only to be found co-existing with the actual fact testified to.

In his presidential address to the S.P.R. in 1889, Professor H. Sidgwick fully discussed, and said the last word on, " The Canons of Evidence in Psychical Research."

one would have expected a welcome even to the humblest seeker after truth.[4]

I heartily agree with our great logician, De Morgan (if I may be excused quoting him again), who says: —

> "The Spiritualists, beyond a doubt, are in the track that has led to all advancement in physical science; their opponents are the representatives of those who have striven against progress. ... I say the deluded spirit-rappers are on the right track; they have the spirit and method of the grand old times when those paths were cut through the uncleared forests in which it is now the daily routine to walk.
>
> What was that spirit? It was the spirit of universal examination wholly unchecked by fear of being detected in the investigation of nonsense. When the Royal Society was founded the Fellows set to work to prove all things, that they might hold fast that which was good. They bent themselves to the question whether sprats were young herrings. They made a circle of the powder of a unicorn's horn and set a spider in the middle of it; 'but it immediately ran out'; they tried several times and the spider 'once made some stay in the powder.' Then they tried Kenelm Digby's sympathetic powder, and those members who had any of the powder of sympathy were desired to bring some of it at the next meeting."

But these childish researches, as we now see them, showed that the enquirers had really been enquiring. Then De Morgan proceeds to show that "Spiritualists have taken the method of the old time," that they have started a theory and seen how it works, for without a theory facts are a mob, not an army.

This was the method of Newton; he started one of the most outrageous ideas that ever was conceived and tried how its consequences worked. For Newton's theory was, "that there is not a particle of salt in the salt-cellars of the most remote star in the Milky Way that is not always pull, pull, pulling every particle of salt in the salt-cellars of our earth — aye, the pepper in the pepper-boxes, too — our pepper and salt, of course, using retaliatory measures."[5] So the great law of

---

[4] This was written many years ago; happily such ferocious hostility is now rarely found except amongst those steeped in German ways of thought.

[5] Preface of *Matter to Spirit*, p. xix, et seq.

gravitation came to be our heritage; rigorous investigation and overwhelming evidence on behalf of this most improbable idea has established it as a universal truth.

Again, it has now become a scientific heresy to disbelieve in an imperceptible, imponderable, infinitely rare and yet infinitely elastic all-pervading kind of matter, the so-called *luminiferous ether*, which is both interstellar and interatomic, a material medium of a wholly different order of matter from anything known to our senses, and the very existence of which is only known inferentially.

For it is to be noted that this staggering but fruitful idea is based not upon direct but indirect evidence, and this notwithstanding its "antecedent improbability." Moreover, modern science has taught us that there are myriads of waves in the ether which are too short or too long to affect our unaided senses.

They might forever have been falling on us, bringing a constant stream of energy from the sun to the earth, and still we could never have become aware of their existence, or of the medium which carried them, had we trusted solely to the direct evidence of our senses.

A recognised authority has said in a standard textbook, "in earlier times the suggestion of such a medium by anyone would probably be looked upon as strong evidence of insanity.

Even with the evidence which we now have in favour of space-filling ether, there are many who would rather doubt such evidence than believe in a thing which they cannot taste or smell [or of which we have no direct sense perception]. However, considering the medium as only hypothetical, the fact that it might certainly exist and fill important functions in the life of the universe and still never be detected or suspected by us, is a strong reason why the postulation of such a medium for the explanation of natural phenomena should not be branded as irrational or unphilosophic."[6] This leads us to ask is there any theory "not irrational or unphilosophic" that can be suggested to account for the startling and bizarre phenomena described in these chapters. To that let us now turn our attention.

---

[6] *Preston's "Theory of Heat,"* p. 56.

CHAPTER 9

THEORIES

"Hypotheses have often an eminent use; and a facility in framing them, if attended with an equal facility in laying them aside when they have served their turn, is one of the most valuable qualities a philosopher can possess." — *Sir John Herschel.*[1]

Let us now consider what hypothesis can be framed to account for the amazing phenomena we have been considering.

The popular view that all mediums are impostors and all the manifestations associated with them are due to fraud, is a convenient explanation for those who will not take the trouble to enquire. But I have never yet met with anyone who has seriously studied the evidence, or engaged in prolonged investigation of this subject, who holds that view, however strongly he may have held it beforehand.[2] Apart from the investigations of the Psychical Research Society, — the most notable

---

[1] "Discourse on Natural Philosophy," p. 304.

[2] A reviewer of Sir O. Lodge's book "Raymond" recently said, "There never yet, we believe, was a medium, unless perhaps it was D. D. Home, who was not sooner or later convicted of gross and deliberate fraud." Such a sweeping statement is simply ludicrous, when the word medium includes men of such probity as the Rev. Stainton Moses and many others, as well as distinguished ladies such as the late Mrs. Verrall and others to be named in later chapters. Moreover, we must remember that what appears to be fraud may not always be so (see p. 12 3), and further, that it is to Spiritualists themselves we mainly owe the exposure of dishonest mediums.

instance of a body of able enquirers, — with no bias in favour of spiritualism, — who proved 40 years ago that the phenomena could not be explained by imposture, is the Committee of the Dialectical Society already referred to.

No doubt fraudulent paid mediums exist, just as bad coins do, and their existence is due to the fact that there are genuine ones to imitate. Sir W. Crookes, O.M., whose high position in the scientific world shows him to be one of the most exact and accomplished of experimental investigators, — has said that he began his enquiry into the phenomena of Spiritualism, believing the whole affair was superstition and trickery, but he ended by "staking his scientific reputation" that his preconceived ideas were wrong and that a class of phenomena wholly new to science did really exist.

Putting aside the imposture theory, what reasonable hypothesis can we entertain? *Hallucination* naturally suggests itself, and I have already referred to this in an earlier chapter. I was at one time disposed to think it was an adequate explanation. In fact, in a paper read before the British Association in 1876 on "Abnormal conditions of mind," which is printed in the "Proceedings of the Psychical Research Society" (vol. 1, p. 238), I detailed some experiments I had made, showing that by suggestion it was easy to lead a subject, when in a light hypnotic trance, to hold the most extravagant beliefs, e.g., that he had floated round the room, and this for some days after complete waking. But hallucination cannot account for the permanent records Sir William Crookes obtained, even if it extended to all the numerous witnesses who were sometimes present with him on these occasions. Hence, though admitting that it is of great importance to be on one's guard against hallucination and mal-observation, as well as fraud, I am fully satisfied that these causes are quite inadequate to explain all the phenomena before us.

Let us therefore consider what other hypotheses can be framed to account for the phenomena under discussion. A provisional theory which physiologists might be disposed to accept, when they admit the genuineness of the simpler physical phenomena of spiritualism, is that of an *Exoneural action of the brain*. But this must be a sub-conscious action, an effect of the subliminal self to which we shall refer later on. Moreover, this must be supplemented by a store of available energy in the unseen, which can not only be controlled and liberated by the subliminal self, but also, in some unknown way, can be made to act directly upon lifeless matter.

So far as I am aware, the first person to suggest an exoneural action of the mind was Dr. Mayo, F.R.S., in his admirable little book on the "Truths contained in Popular Superstitions," published in 1851. He says in explanation of mesmeric clairvoyance or lucidity, "I hold that the mind of a living person in its most normal state is always, to a certain extent, acting exoneurally or beyond the limits of the bodily person, and in the lucid state this exoneural apprehension seems to extend to every object and person around." The high position held by Dr. Mayo as Professor of Physiology in King's College and the Royal College of Surgeons, London, entitled his suggestions to greater consideration than they received.

A theory of this kind was indeed proposed by Count de Gasparin, in 1854, to explain the physical phenomena of Spiritualism, as the result of his prolonged experiments, and a little later by Professor Tinny, of Geneva, and again later by Sergeant Cox. This may be called the theory of "ectenic" or *psychic force* and it attributes the phenomena to some extension in space of the nervous force of the medium, just as the power of a magnet, or of an electric current, extends beyond itself and can influence and move certain distant bodies which lie within the field of the magnetic or electric force.

It is, however, worth noting that the "psychic force," theory, often adopted at the outset by enquirers, is usually abandoned by them later on as it is inadequate to explain the phenomena we shall discuss subsequently, where an intelligence apart from those present is manifested; hence advanced enquirers usually fall back upon the spirit theory as the simplest explanation of all the manifestations.

Thus Professor Lombroso, in an article published in the "Annals of Psychical Science" for 1908, states he advocated the psychic force theory until he found it impossible to explain by that hypothesis many of the phenomena which he proceeds to detail.

Nevertheless some such theory, as an exoneural action of our organism, which covers the simpler physical phenomena of Spiritualism, may be enunciated in the future by physiologists who wish to escape from the implications involved in the theory of a discarnate intelligence.

There is another hypothesis, somewhat allied to that of psychic force, which is worth consideration. It may be that the intelligence operating at a séance is a Thought-projection of ourselves — that each one of us has his simulacrum in the unseen. That with the growth of our life and character here, a ghostly image of oneself is growing up in the invisible world; nor is this inconceivable. As thought, will, and emotion can affect, and to some extent mould, the gross matter of which our bodies are composed, —

> "For of the soule the bodie forme doth take,
> For soule is forme and doth the bodie make."[3] —

a more perfect impression is quite conceivable upon the finer matter of the unseen universe.

The phenomena of telepathy show either that thought can powerfully affect an unseen material medium, or else project particles of thought-stuff through space, or that telepathy is the direct operation of our transcendental or intuitive self, as Mr. Constable has said in his suggestive work on Personality and Telepathy. Physics teaches us that light, heat, electricity, and magnetism affect the matter of an invisible world, the all-pervading ether, more perfectly than they do the matter of the visible world. Suns and stars, as well as much of the world in which we live, would Spenser have no existence for us but for the influence they impress upon the unseen ether.

May not thought be able to act in like manner? In fact it has been suggested by two profound and distinguished scientific men, Professors Balfour Stewart and P. G. Tait, "that thought conceived to affect the matter of another universe simultaneously with this may explain a future state."[4] The ancient Buddhist doctrine of Karma also teaches that our future state is the result of our thoughts and actions, the sum of our merit or demerit, —

> "All that total of a soul
> Which is the things it did, the thoughts it had."

Karma is thus the relentless operation and spiritual embodiment of the law of cause and effect, from which none of us can escape. In

---

[3] Spenser "Hymne in honour of Beautie," line 13.

[4] The whole passage runs as follows: "If we now turn to thought, we find that inasmuch as it affects the substance of the present visible universe, it produces a material organ of memory. But the motions which accompany thought must also affect the invisible order of things, while the forces which cause these motions are likewise derived from the same region, and thus it follows that thought conceived to affect the matter of another universe simultaneously with this may explain a future state." —*The Unseen Universe*, p. 199. (Fourth Edition.)

modern Theosophy we find the same idea, developed in connection with the doctrine of reincarnation. The thoughts of each individual life generate a thought-body in the unseen, which becomes the next dwelling place of our soul on its return to earth.

Hence the innate dispositions of a child are the result of its own unconscious past, the character it has moulded for itself during a previous existence on earth.

If, in a more concrete manner than Longfellow meant,

> "No action whether foul or fair is ever done but it leaves somewhere a record written by fingers ghostly."

If our thoughts and characters are faithfully and indelibly being written on the unseen, we are, in fact, involuntarily and inexorably creating not only in our own soul, but possibly in the invisible world, an image of ourselves, a thought-projection, that embraces both our outer and our innermost life. And it may be that during a séance a quasi-vitality is given to these conceivable thought-bodies which disappears when the sitting is over: there is, as we all know, some drain on the medium's vitality during a successful séance. But whatever explanation we adopt, there appears to be some sympathetic response, something analogous to resonance in the unseen, occurring in these psychical phenomena. Possibly it is this which so often causes the manifesting intelligence to appear but a reflection of the mind of the medium, and leads to the danger, of which investigators are well aware, deceptive communications.

Or we may reverse this hypothesis and hold, with Plato, that the world of sensible things is only an image of the world of ideas existing in a super-sensible world, that objects of sense have only a borrowed existence received from the eternal realities, or ideas in the unseen. This was very much Swedenborg's view, that the objects in the natural world are merely ephemeral counterparts and effects of things and causes in the more real spiritual world into which we pass after this life. We are thus incarnate ghosts of our true selves, fleeting material phantasms of our true and enduring personality.

To return from this digression, — What other theory can be proposed to account for the physical manifestations of what appear to be active and unseen intelligences? The usual theory of Spiritualists is that the phenomena are due to the action of discarnate human beings, who thus seek to make their continued existence known to us. But although these manifestations show intelligence, they afford no proof whatever of the continued existence of human beings after death. Evidence of this, derived from other psychical phenomena, we shall consider later on, and, if the spiritualistic theory be accepted, it may then seem to be the simplest solution of all the phenomena, albeit some of the marvels connected with the medium Home will remain an outstanding puzzle.

Meanwhile it is not a very incredible thing to suppose that in the luminiferous ether (or in some other unseen material medium) life of some kind exists; and that the law of evolution — the Divine law of progress — has been at work, maybe for aeons prior to the formation of a habitable earth. If the grosser matter we are familiar with is able to be the vehicle of life, and respond to the Divine spirit, the finer and more plastic matter of the ether might more perfectly manifest and more easily respond to the inscrutable Power that lies behind phenomena. There is nothing extravagant, nothing opposed to our present scientific knowledge, in this assumption.

It is, therefore, in harmony with all we know to entertain a belief in an unseen world, in which myriads of living creatures exist, some with faculties like our own, and others with faculties beneath or transcending our own; and it is possible that the evolutionary development of such a world has run on parallel lines to our own. The rivalry of life, the existence of instinct, intellect, conscience, will, right and wrong are as probable there as here. And, in course of time, consciousness of our human existence may have come to our unseen neighbours, and some means of mental, or even material, communication with us may have been found.

For my own part,[5] it seems not improbable that many of the physical manifestations witnessed in a Spiritualistic séance are the product of human-like, but not really human, intelligences — good or bad daimonia they may be, elementals some have called them, which aggregate round the medium; drawn from that particular plane of mental and moral development in the unseen which corresponds to the

---

[5] Isaac Taylor, in his well-known and suggestive book, *Physical Theory of Another Life*, chap. 17, which I have read since the above was written, has a similar conjecture, and maintains that the Scriptures support the existence of an entire order of both good and evil beings around us; he holds that "one well attested instance of the presence and intelligent agency of an invisible being would be enough to carry the question of an invisible ecconomy pervading the visible universe" (p. 264).

mental and moral plane of the medium. The possible danger of such influences I will refer to in a subsequent chapter.

But if such unseen intelligences have for ages past existed in our midst, may they not have had some share in the history of life on this earth? We know how largely man can modify both organic and inorganic nature by the exercise of his intelligence and will; if we can even alter the varieties of plants and animals by artificial selection, is it unreasonable to suppose that the psychical operation of unseen intelligences may have influenced the course of evolution through the ages? Is it possible that some of the unsolved problems in the doctrine of evolution may have to be shifted from the world of sense and gross matter to the unseen world around us, just as in physics we are gradually shifting our penultimate explanation of perceptible things to the imperceptible ether? The great First Cause must ever lie beyond our ken, but science, which deals with secondary causes, is finding that to many obscure questions the visible world appears to offer no intelligible solution.

The existence of a fourth dimension in space is not an explanation of the origin of the phenomena of Spiritualism, but a mathematical conception that shows the possibility for some of those phenomena to fourth dimensional beings, provided they could, under certain circumstances, produce effects visible to us three-dimensional beings. Some of these effects, we can theoretically predict, e.g. the passage of matter through matter, or the knotting of a single endless cord, or loop, or ring of leather. An intelligent being, having the power to produce on this cord fourth-dimensional bending, would be able to tie one or more knots on it without loosening the scaled ends of the cord or cutting the ring of leather. Though this feat is to us, of course, impossible, it is asserted that it was successfully performed in a few minutes, in full light, in December, 1877, through the instrumentality of a well-known medium, and in the presence of some distinguished and critical German men of science, Professors Zollner, Weber, Fechner, and Scheibner. The full account, with the precautions taken to avoid deception, is given in Mr. Massey's translation of Zollner's "Transcendental Physics." Nor was this a unique experience; for a similar experiment, a knot tied in an unseamed ring of leather, is reported to have been successfully made in Russia, and vouched for by the Hon. A. Aksakof. On the other hand, I am not aware of any corroboration of these experiments in recent years, and whilst it seems impossible to explain them away by deception, or gross exaggeration or malobservation, it is wiser to suspend our judgment on these, and some other of the rarer spiritualistic phenomena and regard them as "not proven" until more abundant and conclusive evidence is forthcoming.

This long discussion of various theories has I fear wearied my readers, but psychical researchers are cutting a path through uncleared forests, and all conjectures regarding the right way are useful. To change the simile we are laying the foundations of a new and spacious annex to the temple of knowledge, and we must be prepared to see a forest of scaffolding — in the shape of theories and working hypotheses — arise. Only thus can the solid stones of fact be laid and the temple upbuilt, then in course of time, "the facts will tell their own story and supply their own explanation; at present we have to labour and to wait."

CHAPTER 10

THE PROBLEM OF MEDIUMSHIP

"Whose exterior semblance doth belie
The Soul's immensity." —*Wordsworth*

It may be asked, and many have asked scornfully, why should a medium be necessary in these Spiritualistic manifestations? As we are all aware, the production of the phenomena appears to be inseparably connected with some special living organisations that are called "mediumistic." And it may well be, granting the existence of a spiritual world, that a medium is as necessary there as here; in fact, there seems evidence in all the communications purporting to come from deceased persons that they find an intermediary between themselves and the medium on earth is necessary to them as to us. Looked at from a purely scientific standpoint, there is nothing remarkable in this. Certain persons, happily not all of us, are subject to abnormal states of body and mind, and the alienist or pathologist does not refuse to investigate insanity or epilepsy because restricted to a limited number of human beings.

Furthermore, physical science affords abundant analogies of the necessity for a medium, or intermediary, between the unseen and the seen. We know nothing of any of the physical energies, such as electricity, magnetism, light, gravitation, etc., except through their effects on material bodies. They are unseen and unknowable until manifested by their action on matter. We do not see electricity in a lightning flash, only atmospheric particles made white-hot through the resistance they offer to the electric discharge. In like manner the waves of the luminiferous ether require a material medium to absorb them before they can be perceived by our senses; the intermediary may be the photographic plate, the rods and cones of the retina, a blackened surface, or the electric resonators of wireless telegraphy, according to the respective length of those waves; but some medium, formed of ponderable matter, is absolutely necessary to render the chemical, luminous, thermal, or electrical effects of these waves perceptible to us. And the more or less perfect rendering of these effects depends on the more or less perfect synchronism between those ethereal waves and their mundane receiver.

Thus we find certain definite physical media are necessary to enable operations to become perceptible which would otherwise remain imperceptible. Through these media, energy from the unseen physical world without us enters the seen, and passing through the seen affects thereby the unseen mental world within us. The extreme ends of the operation are unknown to us, and it is only during the transition stage that the flux of energy appeals to our senses, and therefore it is only with this stage of appearances, that is to say with phenomena, that science can deal.

This is also true of life itself; for life of any kind, however lowly it may be, is unseen by and unknowable to us *per se*; we only know life through its varied manifestations in organic matter that is in living phenomena.

This is, of course, equally true of our mind, which reveals itself through the brain, and in like manner a discarnate mind requires a medium for its manifestation. And we may take it as unquestionable, whatever shrinking our religious instincts may at first feel, that anything and everything that enters the world of phenomena becomes thereby a legitimate and promising subject of scientific investigation. As Sir Oliver Lodge has well said: "The least justifiable attitude is that which holds that there are certain departments of truth in the universe which it is not lawful to investigate."

The nexus between the seen and the unseen may be, as we have shown, physical, physiological, or psychical, but whichever it may be, it is a specialised substance, or organ, or organism; in many cases it is a body in a state of unstable equilibrium, and in that case, therefore, of a delicate nature, a body to be handled carefully, and its behaviour or idiosyncrasies needing to be studied and known beforehand.

It is doubtless a peculiar psychical state that confers mediumistic power, but we know nothing of its nature, and we often ruin our experiments and lose our results by our ignorance. Certainly it is very probable that the psychical state of those present at a séance will be found to react on the medium.

We should get no results if our photographic plates were exposed to the light of the room simultaneously with the luminous image formed by the lens. In every physical process we have to guard against disturbing causes.

If, for example, the late Prof. S. P, Langley, of Washington, in the delicate experiments he conducted for so many years — exploring the ultra red radiation of the sun had allowed the thermal radiation of himself or his assistants to fall on his sensitive thermoscope, his results would have been confused and unintelligible. We know that similar confused results are obtained in psychical research, especially by those who fancy the sole function of a scientific investigator is to play the part of an amateur detective; and accordingly what they detect is merely their own incompetency to deal with problems the very elements of which they do not understand and seem incapable of learning. Investigators, who taking an exalted view of their own sagacity, enter upon this enquiry with their minds made up as to the possible or impossible, are sure to fail. Such people should be shunned, as their habit of thought and mode of action are inappropriate, and therefore essentially vulgar, for the essence of vulgarity is inappropriateness.

Inasmuch as we know nothing of the peculiar psychical state that constitutes mediumship, we ought to collect and record all conditions which attend a successful séance.

Mediumship seems in some points analogous to "rapport" in mesmeric trance, and it would be interesting to know whether a mesmeric sensitive is more open to mediumship that the rest of mankind. Again, are those who are good percipients in telepathic experiments also percipients in spontaneous telepathy, such as apparitions at the moment of death, and are these again hypnotic sensitives? Similar questions also arise as to somnambulists; in a word, is there anything in common between the obscure psychical states of these different classes of sensitives? Very probably there is, for all psychical phenomena, as we shall see directly, involve to a greater or less extent the operation of an unconscious part of our personality, a hidden self which in a medium emerges from its obscurity, as the normal consciousness and self-control subsides. This fact does, indeed, afford some clue to the peculiar psychological condition of mediumship.

Here we may remark that our conscious life expresses itself in voluntary muscular movements, such as speech or gesture; whereas our sub-conscious life expresses itself in involuntary muscular action, such as automatic writing or speaking or the motion of a planchette or the "dowsing rod," etc. Such instrumental appliances for revealing our hidden, sub-conscious self, I have called autoscopes. If the will or reason concerns itself with any of these automatic actions, the motion becomes voluntary and passes from the control of the sub-conscious to that of the conscious self. Hence under such circumstances those psychical phenomena which spring from the subconscious self, will either yield a confusing result or fail entirely.

All I wish to point out here is that mediumship depends on the emergence of the subconscious life and therefore the ordinary waking consciousness must be more or less passive. It is the lack of the normal conscious control of his thoughts and actions that renders the medium so liable to the influence of any inimical suggestion from the sitters. For a medium is eminently a suggestible subject, and may sometimes unconsciously be the victim, and not the conscious originator, of the fraud which dominates the opinion of those sceptical investigators who believe all mediums are impostors. In fact, as Dr. Hyslop and many European psychiatrists have shown, an entranced medium is not in a normal condition but shows evidence of hysteria.

It must be borne in mind that the medium understands the phenomena as little as the investigator, or even less if possible, for he has less experience of what goes on, being very often in a trance; hence the medium's opinions or explanation of the manifestations, in his normal state, is quite valueless. The medium should, in fact, be treated as has been already said, and as Sir Oliver Lodge has also said, "as a delicate piece of apparatus wherewith we are making an investigation. The medium is an instrument whose ways and idiosyncrasies must be learnt, and to a certain extent humoured, just as one studies and humours the ways of some much less delicate piece of physical apparatus turned out by a skilled instrument maker." This is quite consistent with taking all needful precautions against deception. The stricter methods which, I think wisely, the Society for Psychical Research have adopted, have no doubt eliminated much that passed as evidence amongst Spiritualists, and also cleared off a number of those detestable professional rogues who prey on the grief and credulity of mankind.

The word "medium" is certainly an objectionable one. In the public mind it is usually associated with various degrees of rascality, and so long as paid mediums and dark séances are encouraged, and rogues and fools abound, the evil odour, which surrounds the name "medium", is likely to remain.

But there is another objection to the word. A "medium" is too often taken to imply an intermediary between the spirit-world and our own; whereas, many so-called Spiritualistic communications are nothing but the unconscious revelation of the medium's own thoughts, or latent memory, or "subliminal self." I agree, therefore, with my friend the late Frederick Myers, who calls the word medium "a barbarous and question begging term," and suggests the use of the word 'automatist"; others have suggested, and some have used, the word "psychic." Either of these words is preferable, if usage were not against them, until a wider interest in, and knowledge of, the whole subject leads to a new terminology.

I have thought it better to keep to the common phraseology, disclaiming, however, the common implication, namely, that the word medium always implies an agent between us and a spiritual world, or a personality, external to the medium. It may be, and very often is, only the unconscious world or unrecognised personality within the medium. For the whole of our personality, as is well known, is not included in the normal self with which we are familiar in our waking life.

There is in each of us an outer as well as an inner court to our personality. The outer being our conscious ego and the inner our subconscious ego. To this latter, this self below the threshold (*limen*) of consciousness, a new significance and importance has been given by Mr. Myers, and the wider term he suggested, the subliminal self, is now familiar.

It may here be useful for those of my readers who have not studied psychology to consider the subject of Human personality and Consciousness more closely, as it throws some light on the nature of mediumship and the phenomena we are discussing.

Note. — It has been pointed out that the medium belongs to that class of persons whom Prof. P. Janet in his masterly work "L'Automatisme Psychologique" terms *les individus suggestibles*; persons controlled by an idea or suggestion either self-originated (auto-suggestion) or coming from without, it may be from the unseen. Something typical of this suggestibility of certain individuals, and not of others in their order, is seen even in lower forms of life, in the way their coloration is affected by the colour of their surroundings, etc.

CHAPTER 11

HUMAN PERSONALITY: THE SUBLIMINAL SELF

"What a piece of work is a man! how noble in reason! how infinite in faculty! ... in apprehension how like a god!" — *Hamlet II., 2.*

Our consciousness is the fundamental fact, the most real thing, of which we are aware, and although it consists of a succession of states of mind, no two of which are exactly alike, it is nevertheless combined into a continuous personal identity which we call "ourself." Even when there are interruptions of our self-consciousness, as in sleep, we recognise the self that wakes up in the morning as the same self that went to sleep overnight. So also throughout our life we are conscious of the same identity, the same self, albeit the whole material of body, brain and sensory organs has been repeatedly swept away and renewed.

Hence our personality is not a mere bundle of loose sensations: no succession of states of mind, no series of thoughts or feelings can fuse themselves into a single resultant consciousness, with a knowledge and memory of all the other states.

Everyone is now familiar with the rapid succession of instantaneous photographs seen in the cinematograph, where, for example, a series of pictures of a man running swiftly gives us the appearance of a single moving figure. But the photographs remain distinct; the combination is effected by something external to the pictures, our own perception.

And so there must be something lying in the background of our consciousness which combines the series of impressions made upon us, or the states of feeling within us; this unifying power we may call our Ego or soul.

Even if the stream of consciousness be, as some believe, an epiphenomenon, a series of shadows cast by the motion of brain processes, or if consciousness be an attribute of the molecules of organic matter, matter preceding mind, there must be some transcendental and permanent nexus, a soul which unites successive sensations and perceptions into a coherent self-conscious personality; something which gives a meaning to and holds together the stream of manifold ideas.

It is a remarkable fact that a multitude of impressions are constantly being made upon us, to which this Ego appears to pay no heed. Either because they are not strong enough to pierce our consciousness — for a certain intensity must be reached before an impression can stir our Ego, — a relatively feeble stimulus, such as the light of the stars in daytime, cannot cross the threshold of our consciousness and gain an entrance to our mind — or because among the crowd of strong impressions which do enter, the Ego exercises a selective power. We direct our attention upon a few, chiefly because they interest us; these we are conscious of and can afterwards recall by an effort of memory. The will, moved in the first instance by desire — that is, by what interests us, our ruling love — determines the attention we give to particular impressions; thus we become conscious of, or alive to, thoughts or sensations excited by certain impressions, and let the rest go by unheeded. Our choice thus determines our experience, what we include in our material and mental possessions, our conscious "me"; the "me" being the known, the "I" the knowing, self: all else we regard as the "not me."

Furthermore, this process of selection, if we do it regularly, soon becomes habitual or automatic; the effort of attention is no longer required, and the will is set free for some other purpose; for instance, we walk, or we combine the letters in reading instinctively without being conscious of the steps in the process.[1] And so with the world within ourselves, we do not perceive the regular and continuous beating of

---

[1] Education is, in great part, the training to do automatically and unconsciously what would otherwise have to be done with conscious effort. Genius is a still more striking example of the power of unconscious acts. And what is done by the unconscious self is more easily and better done than by the conscious self; hence it would seem as if the summit of attainment would lead to the absence of any conscious effort at all. This, indeed, is the logical outcome of all Naturalistic hypotheses of human lite. In a striking passage in the second chapter of *Foundations of Belief*, the Right lion. A. J. Balfour has dealt with this very question.

the heart, hence the processes of respiration, circulation, and nutrition go on unconsciously in a healthy body. And to some extent this is also true of the nutrition of the mind, for the character is built up, in part, by the stream of unconscious impressions made upon us.

Again, consciousness is not aroused by a continuous succession of uniform impressions.

We should be utterly unconscious of warmth, however hot things might be, if everything were at one uniform temperature, and we should be equally unconscious of light if the universe and all material objects were illuminated with a continuous and uniform brightness. It is differences of state that we perceive, or the ratio of the strength of one sensation to another. The actual span of our consciousness is, therefore, very narrow. As the late Professor W. James, of Harvard, remarks in his valuable textbook on Psychology: —

> One of the most extraordinary facts of our life is that, although we are besieged at every moment by impressions from our whole sensory surface, we notice so very small a part of them. The sum total of our impressions never enters into our *experience*, consciously so called, which runs through this sum total like a tiny rill through a broad flowery mead. Yet the physical impressions which do not count are there as much as those which do. Why they fail to pierce the mind is a mystery, and not explained when we invoke *die Enge des Bewusstseins*, "the narrowness of consciousness," as its ground.

All these impressions, whether we are conscious of them or not, leave some mark behind; they weave a visible, or invisible thread into the fabric of our life; like every trivial act we perform, they make a perceptible or an imperceptible indent on our personality. We know that this is the case, that impressions not perceived when they were made have, nevertheless, effected a lodgement within us, for although we cannot recall them at pleasure, they often emerge from their latent state in a fragmentary and disconnected manner. This is the case when the attention is withdrawn from things around us in reverie or "crystal gazing," or often in illness or dream, and still more in somnambulism or in hypnotic trance, and in many cases of automatic writing, or other so-called Spiritualistic phenomena.

Our Ego or soul is therefore not merely co-extensive with those things of which we are or have been conscious; the range of our personality must be extended to include something more than our normal self-consciousness.

Not only are there, as it were, horizontal strata in our personality, from the material or lowest "me" up to the spiritual or highest "me," but there is also a vertical division which runs through all. On one side of this vertical plane of cleavage lie all those impressions which have penetrated our consciousness, all those states of thought and feeling which in our waking life memory can restore; on the other side lie the vastly greater number of impressions made upon us of which we were unconscious at the time, or, being conscious, have completely forgotten. One part of our Ego is, therefore, illuminated by consciousness, and another part lies in the dark shadow of unconsciousness.

Thus the outer or conscious self, as said, is not our entire self, any more than the visible or earth-turned face of the moon is the whole moon. Mr. Frederick Myers has well compared our normal self-consciousness to the visible spectrum of sunlight; beyond it on either side is a wide tract, imperceptible to the eye, yet crowded with radiation. Each pencil of sunlight embraces these invisible, as well as the visible, rays, and so each human personality embraces the unconscious as well as the conscious self. And just as experimental physics has within the present century revealed the existence of ultra-violet and infra-red portions of the spectrum, and shown us how we may, in part, render these obscure rays visible, so with the growth of experimental psychology we are beginning to discover the complex nature of our personality, and how that part of our Ego which is below the threshold of consciousness may be led to emerge from its obscurity. As the bright light of day quenches the feebler light of the stars, so the vivid stream of consciousness in our waking life must usually be withdrawn or enfeebled before the dim record of unheeded past impressions, or the telepathic impact of an extraneous mind, becomes apparent.

Hence, as we have already pointed out, a state of passivity is favourable to the emergence of the subliminal consciousness, and this is one of the characteristics of mediumship.

It is true that in many cases of automatic writing by planchette or otherwise, long coherent messages are given whilst the thoughts of the medium are engaged on other matters, but the effort of attention is relaxed, and if it be directed to the writing, or any conscious effort made to assist it, the spell is broken, and the inner self sinks again into obscurity.[2] Furthermore, and singularly enough, this secondary

---

[2] A similar sensitiveness to conscious attention is seen in experiments in thought-transference, and even in the pseudo thought reading of the "willing game"; and

or subliminal self never identifies itself with the ordinary waking self. Another person seems to have taken control of the hand or voice of the medium, a distinct intelligence that has its own past history, but with little, if any, knowledge of the past of the other self. The foreign nature of the "control" naturally suggests the agency of an external intelligence, a spirit or demon, "possessing" the medium, or of another personality that alternates with the normal soul.

The well-known facts of "double consciousness" illustrate the latter;[3] a remarkable case of this kind I was personally acquainted with and investigated some years ago. The subject, since dead, was the son of a London clergyman, and the duration of the abnormal state became so extended that it was difficult to call it by that name, but however many days had elapsed since the transition from one state to the other, — a brief period of insensibility separating the two, — on the return to the previous state, the old conversation was resumed precisely at the point where it was interrupted; in the abnormal state considerable musical knowledge was possessed, of which the subject appeared to be quite ignorant in the other state; the life, the interests, the conversation were quite distinct; even the parentage and family were regarded as different in the two states.[4] These cases of alternating personality resemble some of the delusions of the insane, and from time immemorial have led to the belief that the rightful owner of the body has been temporarily or permanently displaced, and another soul has taken "possession," like a cuckoo, of a nest that is not its own.

The whole subject of the dissociation of personality has in recent years received careful study by eminent psychologists, and the reader will find an admirable discussion of this question in Chapter 2 of Mr. F. W. H. Myers' great work, on "Human Personality."

Multiple, as well as secondary, personalities, sometimes are exhibited by the same subject.

---

ignorance of this fact is what usually leads to failure. The intrusion of the will, of conscious effort, is therefore prejudicial in all such experiments. The well meaning endeavours of those who tell the percipient "to try earnestly" to guess the thing thought of, defeat the object in view. If the percipient does try, his will comes in and prevents the emergence of the hidden and responsive part of his personality. In fact, "psychical research" in general deals with the varied manifestations and operations of the unconscious part of our personality.

[3] A possible, though only partial, explanation of dual consciousness is the separate action of the two lobes of the brain caused by an alternating inhibition of the functions of each lobe.

[4] This case is given in full in "Proceedings S. P. R.," Vol. IV, pp. 230-232.

Such for example are the well known cases of Leonie, investigated by Professor P. Janet; Louis Vive; Sally Beauchamp, investigated by Dr. Morton Prince, of Boston, U.S.A.; and other instances known to psychologists.

More recently a remarkable case of multiple personality in an American girl named Doris Fischer has received minute and continuous study by Dr. Walter Prince. His report fills two bulky volumes of the Proceedings of the American S.P.R., to which Dr. Hyslop has contributed a lengthy and valuable addition.

The classical case of Miss Beauchamp, fully described in Dr. Morton Prince's work *The Dissociation of a Personality*[5] is briefly as follows:—

> A mental shock which Miss Beauchamp received at College in 1893 produced the first disintegration of consciousness, she became modified into what Dr. Prince terms B 1. This personality alternated with another B 2, at first induced by hypnotic treatment. In course of time a new and wholly different personality appeared B 3, which called itself "Sally."
>
> Whilst B 1 was cultivated, quiet and deeply religious, B 3 was the reverse and full of mischief. Later on another personality appeared B 4, proud, selfish and dignified. B 1 and B 4 knew nothing of the others, B 2 knew only B I, but B 3 (Sally) knew all the others, was always awake and alert to annoy Miss Beauchamp, B I.
>
> Dr. Morton Prince calls B 1 the Saint, B 4 the Woman, and B 3 the Devil. For Sally made B 1 tell lies, sent her things she detested, and constantly mortified and distressed the truthful and good B I. No wonder Miss Beauchamp wrote, "Oh, Dr. Prince save me from myself, from whatever it is that is absolutely merciless; I can bear anything but not this mocking devil." Eventually by hypnotic suggestion, and with the help of Sally, all except B 3, became merged into what was the original Miss Beauchamp. Sally, B 3, now tended to sink out of sight, going back, as she said, "to where I came from." Where was that? According

---

[5] Also in "Proceedings S.P.R.," Vol. XV, and "Human Personality," Vol. I, p. 360 ft seq. Mr. Norman Pearson in his recent able and suggestive work, "The Soul and its Sum," (to which I am glad to draw attention), also gives an abstract of this case. But the most important discussion of the whole subject is by Dr. W. McDougall, F.R.S., in "Proceedings S.P.K.," Vol. XIX.

to Dr. Prince it was the subliminal self of Miss Beauchamp for a time developed into an independent personality, her other personalities being cleavages from the primary conscious self.

But I agree with Dr. McDougall that Dr. Prince's explanation of Sally is unsatisfactory. It is using a hypothesis, the subliminal self, not even accepted by all psychologists, as a mere cloak for our ignorance. Dr. McDougall inclines to the view that Sally was a distinct psychic being controlling the body of Miss Beauchamp. The case of Doris Fischer, which in many respects resembles the foregoing, lends support to this view, that occasionally a human body may be the seat of a real invasion from the spirit world, a case of obsession. If we admit the spirit hypothesis there is nothing improbable in this view. In Doris, the invading spirit, if such it were, assisted, like Sally, in the cure and ultimate restoration of the subject to a normal condition, after many years of suffering and periodical alternations of personality.

One of the most extraordinary cases of changed personality is the following: —

> Lurancy Vennum was an American girl who, at the age of 14, became controlled apparently by the spirit of Mary Roff, a neighbour's daughter, who had died at the age of 19, when Lurancy was only 15 months old. The two families lived far apart, except for a short time, and had only the slightest acquaintance with each other. Nevertheless Lurancy, in her new personality, called the Roffs her parents, knew intimate details of their family life, recognised and called by name the relatives and friends of the Roffs, knew trivial incidents in the life of Mary Roff, and for four months really seemed to be a reincarnation of Mary Roff.

This brief summary gives an inadequate idea of the whole story,[6] which rests upon excellent testimony. Dr. Hodgson, who personally investigated this case, was of opinion that Lurancy was really controlled by the spirit of the deceased Mary Roff.

Probably few psychologists today would accept this conclusion, but the vital importance of an unbiased discussion of cases of multiple personality, such as Sally Beauchamp, has been pointed out by Dr. W. McDougall, F.R.S. We cannot of course lightly set aside the weight

---

[6] Given in Dr. Stevens' brochure *The Watscka Wonder*, published at Rochester, U.S.A., and also in "Human Personality," Vol. I, p. 360 et seq.

of evidence which shows the apparent dependence of memory and therefore of personality, on the persistence of the brain and the physical changes produced in it by our experience. Nevertheless, as Dr. W. McDougall remarks: —

> "If we accept Dr. Prince's description of Sally Beauchamp we can only account for her by adopting the view that the normal personality consists of body and soul in interaction, the soul being not dependent upon the brain, or other physical basis, for its memory, but having the faculty of retaining and remembering among its other faculties…. This conclusion would give very strong support of the spiritistic explanation of such cases as Mrs. Piper, and would go far to justify the belief in the survival of human personality after the death of the body."[7]

This conclusion will receive additional illustration and support in the succeeding chapters.

---

[7] "Proc. S. P. R.," Vol. XIX, p. 430.

Part 4

CHAPTER 12

APPARITIONS

> "Dare I say
> No spirit ever brake the band
> That stays him from the native land,
> Where first he walk'd when claspt in clay?"
> — *In Memoriam*, xciii.

We must now pass on from the bizarre and perplexing phenomena we have so far discussed, to the more important question of the evidence spiritualism affords of the continuance of human life after it has, to all appearance, ceased in the material body. Before entering upon the experimental part of this enquiry it is desirable to consider the evidence on behalf of survival derived from apparitions of the dying and the dead. This aspect of our subject meets with wider acceptance, and less objection from religious minds, than the evidence derived from sittings with some medium, which many regard as illegitimate.

One of the most cautious and philosophical among our distinguished men of science of the last generation, the late Dr. R. Angus Smith, F.R.S., wrote to me, forty years ago, that he was not aware of any law of nature, except the most obvious, that was sustained by so much and such respectable evidence as the fact of apparitions about the time of death.[1] In a subsequent interview I learnt from him that this opinion

---
[1] As the whole letter may be of future interest, I give it here in full:—

was arrived at only after long and careful investigation of the evidence attainable at that time. Since then the Society for Psychical Research has obtained a mass of additional and confirmatory evidence, which is incorporated in the two bulky volumes on *Phantasms of the Living and Dead* published by the Society.

In that monumental work, chiefly due to the labour and learning of Mr. Edward Gurney, the interval between death and the apparition of the dying or deceased person was limited to 12 hours. First-hand records were however received where this interval was greatly exceeded, whilst the fact of death was still unknown to the percipient at the time of his experience. After rigorous scrutiny 134 first-hand narratives are given where the coincidence between death and the recognised "appearance" (whether by a visual or auditory experience) of the deceased to a distant person, who was not aware of the death, is exact, or within an hour; in 39 cases the apparition was seen more than an hour, but within 12 hours of death, and in 38 cases the apparition was seen shortly before death, or when death did not follow, though the person was seriously ill.[2] In 104 cases it was not known whether the percipients' experience shortly preceded or followed the death; owing to this uncertainty these cases were not taken into account.

Mr. Gurney and Mr. Myers contributed a valuable paper to Vol. V of the *Proceedings of the S.P.R.*, where additional first-hand evidence

---

"Manchester,
"October l8th, 1876.

"My Dear Professor Barrett, — I see you are deep in that fascinating study, the action of mind freed from the organism.

It surprises me much that any man is found to think it of little importance, and that any man is found who thinks his own opinion so important that he cares for no evidence. I have not been able to find a book which contains all the laws of nature needed to sustain the world, but some men are easily satisfied.

"It is difficult to obtain such proofs as men demand for free mind. Visions are innumerable, and under circumstances that seem to render the sight of the absent, especially about the time of death, a reality. I am not aware of any law of nature (except the most obvious, such as are seen by common observers) which is sustained by so many assertions so well attested, as far as respectability of evidence goes. The indications we have point out to some mighty truth more decidedly than even the aberrations of Uranus to the newest of the great planets. If we could prove the action of mind at a distance by constant experiment it would be a discovery that would make all other discoveries seem trifles.

— Yours sincerely, R. Angus Smith."

[2] "Proceedings S. P. R.," Vol. V, p. 408.

was given of "apparitions occurring soon after death." This was supplemented by a paper Mr. Myers contributed to Vol. VI on "apparitions occurring more than a year after death," where 14 veridical and recognised apparitions are recorded on first-hand evidence.

The result of a critical examination of the evidence left no doubt in the mind of any student that these apparitions were veridical or truth telling, and that their occurrence was not due to any illusion of the percipient or chance coincidence. As regards this latter, to arrive at a statistical proof Mr. Gurney obtained a numerical comparison of the veridical apparitions with those which were purely accidental, i.e. did not coincide with death. For this purpose he obtained nearly 6,000 replies to the question he addressed to adults, whether they had had any such apparition or hallucination during the preceding ten years. This was followed by a still more elaborate census of a similar kind, taken by Professor Henry and Mrs. Sidgwick, wherein 17,000 replies were received. When the relative frequency of veridical to accidental hallucinations was critically examined the possibility of chance coincidence as an explanation could be proved or disproved.

The result showed, in the Sidgwick census alone, that the proportion of veridical and recognized apparitions (i.e. coincidental 144 cases) to the meaningless (i.e. non-coincidental cases) was 440 times greater than pure chance would give. The elaborate examination of this census by experts fills Vol. X. of the Proceedings of the S.P.R., and the definite but cautiously expressed conclusion is reached that—

> "Between deaths and apparitions of the dying person a connection exists which is not due to chance alone. This we hold to be a proved fact. The discussion of its full implications cannot be attempted in this paper, nor, perhaps, exhausted in this age."

Such a result refutes the common idea that it was a mere chance the apparition happened to coincide with the death of that particular person, and that the hits are remembered and the misses forgotten.

It was found in the course of these lengthy enquiries that the number of recognised apparitions decreases rapidly in the few days after death, then more slowly, and after a year or more they become far less frequent and more sporadic. This indeed might have been expected; for on any theory as to the nature of these apparitions it is likely that the power of communication between the dead and those living on earth would lessen as the time of transition from this life becomes more and more remote.

We need not conclude from this that the soul of the departed is gradually extinguished, for we cannot track the course of the soul nor know its affinities in the larger life beyond. There are, moreover, cases, to which we will refer in a later chapter, where evidence of survival has been given more than a generation after the communicator has passed from earth-life.

Those who have witnessed the apparition of a distant deceased friend, of whose death they were wholly unaware, or have heard the statement at first hand, are far more impressed by this single occurrence than by any amount of evidence derived from reading reports of apparitions. This was the case with myself when a young friend of mine narrated to me the following account of the apparition she experienced; nor did the searching cross-examination she was submitted to, at the meeting of the Psychical Research Society where I read the account, shake her testimony in the least. The full report will be found in the "Journal of the S.P.R." for May 1908. An important feature of this incident is that the percipient was at the time at school in a convent in Belgium, where she had absolutely no access to newspapers, or any other sources of information which might have suggested the apparition. Briefly the case is as follows:

> A gentleman, of some note, shot himself in London in the spring of 1907. There can be little doubt that his mind was unhinged at the time by the receipt that morning of a letter from a lady that blighted all his hopes; before taking his life he scribbled a memorandum leaving an annuity to my young friend, who was his godchild and to whom he was greatly attached. Three days afterwards (on the day of his funeral) he appeared to his godchild, who, as stated, was being educated in a convent school on the Continent, informing her of the fact of his sudden death, of its manner, and of the cause which had led him to take his life, and asking her to pray for him.

> The mother, anxious to conceal from her daughter the distressing circumstances of her godfather's death, waited to write until a few days after the funeral, and then only stated that her uncle (as he was called) had died suddenly. Subsequently, upon meeting her daughter on her return from the Continent, the mother was amazed to hear not only of the apparition, but that it had communicated to her daughter all the circumstances which she had never intended her daughter to know. Careful enquiry shows that it was impossible for the information to have reached her daughter through normal means.

A member of the S.P.R., Miss Charlton, who kindly went to the convent to make enquiries into this case, states that the girls in the convent never see any newspapers, all letters are supervised, and no one in the convent seems to have known of the deceased gentleman; hence "that any knowledge of her godfather's suicide, or of the reason for it, could have reached the percipient by ordinary channels, cannot be entertained for a moment."

The mother of the percipient, who is a personal friend of mine, assured me that neither she nor any of her relatives (had they known of the suicide, which they did not) wrote to the convent on the matter, except as narrated above.

Sometimes, as in the foregoing case, the phantasm is not only seen but apparently heard to speak; sometimes it may announce its presence by audible signals. We may regard such cases as auditory as well as visual hallucinations. Rapping was heard as well as the apparition seen, in the following case, which was investigated by Professor Sidgwick in 1892, and the house also visited by Mrs. Sidgwick. The percipient was the Rev. Matthew Frost of Bowers Gifford, Essex, who made the following statement: —

"The first Thursday in April 1881, while sitting at tea with my back to the window and talking with my wife in the usual way, I plainly heard a rap at the window, and looking round at the window I said to my wife, 'Why, there's my grandmother,' and went to the door, but could not see anyone; still feeling sure it was my grandmother, and knowing, though she was eighty-three years of age, that she was very active and fond of a joke, I went round the house, but could not see anyone. My wife did not hear it. On the following Saturday, I had news my grandmother died in Yorkshire about half-an-hour before the time I heard the rapping. The last time I saw her alive I promised, if well, I would attend her funeral; that was some two years before. I was in good health and had no trouble, and was age twenty-six years. I did not know that my grandmother was ill." Mrs. Prost writes: — "I beg to certify that I perfectly remember all the circumstances my husband has named, but I heard and saw nothing myself." Professor Sidgwick learned from Mr. Frost that the last occasion on which he had seen his grandmother, three years before the apparition, she promised if possible to appear to him at her death. He had no cause for anxiety on her account; news of the death came to him by letter, and both Mr. and Mrs. Frost were then struck by the coincidence. It was full daylight when Mr. Frost saw the figure and thought that his grandmother had unexpectedly arrived in the flesh and meant to surprise him. Had there been a real person Mrs. Frost would both have seen and heard; nor could a living person have got away in the time, as Mrs. Sidgwick found the house stood in a garden a good way back from the road, and Mr. Frost immediately went out to see if his grandmother was really there.

The following case was carefully investigated, and corroborative evidence obtained, by Mr. Ed. Gurney, soon after the experience occurred to the narrator, Mr. Husbands:[3]

— "September 15th, 1886.

"The facts are simply these. I was sleeping in a hotel in Madeira early in 1885. It was a bright moonlight night. The windows were open and the blinds up. I felt some one was in my room. On opening my eyes, I saw a young fellow about twenty five, dressed in flannel, standing at the side of my bed and pointing with the first finger of his right hand to the place I was lying in. I lay for some seconds to convince myself of some one being really there. I then sat up and looked at him. I saw his features so plainly that I recognised them in a photograph which was shown me some days after. I asked him what he wanted; he did not speak, but his eyes and hand seemed to tell me I was in his place. As he did not answer, I struck out at him with my fist as I sat up, but did not reach him, and as I was going to spring out of bed he slowly vanished through the door, which was shut, keeping his eyes upon me all the time.

"Upon enquiry I found that the young fellow who appeared to me died in the room I was occupying.

"John E. Husbands."

The following letter is from Miss Falkner, of Church Terrace, Wisbech, who was resident at the hotel when the above incident happened:
—

---

[3] "Proceedings S. P. R.," Vol. V, 1889.

"October 8th, 1886.

"The figure that Mr. Husbands saw while in Madeira was that of a young fellow who died unexpectedly some months previously, in the room which Mr. Husbands was occupying. Curiously enough, Mr. H. had never heard of him or his death. He told me the story the morning after he had seen the figure, and I recognised the young fellow from the description. It impressed me very much, but I did not mention it to him or any one. I loitered about until I heard Mr. Husbands tell the same tale to my brother; we left Mr. H. and said simultaneously, 'He has seen Mr. D.' "No more was said on the subject for days; then I abruptly showed the photograph. Mr. Husbands said at once, 'This is the young fellow who appeared to me the other night, but he was dressed differently' — describing a dress he often wore — 'cricket suit (or tennis) fastened at the neck with a sailor knot.' I must say that Mr. Husbands is a most practical man, and the very last one would expect a 'spirit' to visit.

"K. Falkner."

On further enquiry it was found that the young man who appeared to Mr. Husbands had died just a year previously, that the room in which he died had subsequently been occupied by other visitors, who apparently had not seen any apparition, and that it must have been February 2nd or 3rd that Mr. Husbands took the room and saw the figure. Miss Falkner's sister-in-law, who was also at the hotel at the time, corroborates the above facts, and remembers Mr. Husbands telling her the incident; she also gave Miss Falkner the photograph of the deceased which Mr. Husbands recognized.

Even if Mr. Husbands had heard of the death of Mr. D. and forgotten the circumstance, this would not enable him to recognize the likeness when he was shown the photograph. Mr. Gurney, as I have said, carefully investigated this case, and saw both Mr. Husbands and Miss Falkner, receiving full *viva voce* accounts from each. Mr. Gurney remarks: —

"They are both thoroughly practical and as far removed as possible from a superstitious love of marvels; nor had they any previous interest in this or any other class of super-normal experiences. So far as I could judge Mr. Husbands' view of himself is entirely correct — that he is the last person to give a spurious importance to anything that might befall him, or to allow facts to be distorted by imagination. As will be seen, his account of his vision preceded any knowledge on his part of the death which had occurred in the room."

It would extend this book unduly were I to give any further selections from the numerous, remarkable and well authenticated cases of apparitions which are recorded in the "Proceedings of the S.P.R."[4] They are in fact so common and so generally accepted that the chief scepticism regarding them has been as to "the ghosts of the clothes" they wore, as in the last case. This would be puzzling if they were regarded as objective realities, external to the percipient. But if we regard apparitions of the dying and dead as phantasms projected from the mind of the percipient, the difficulties of clothes, and the ghosts of animal pets which sometimes are seen, disappear.

There is nothing improbable in this subjective theory of apparitions, for all the things we see are phantasms projected from our mind into the external world. It is true that a minute and real inverted picture of the objects around us is thrown on the retina by the optical arrangements in the eye, but we do not look at that picture as the photographer does in his camera; it creates an impression on certain brain cells, and then we mentally project outside ourselves a large erect phantasm of the retinal image. It is true this phantasm has its origin in the real image on the retina, but it is no more a real thing than is the virtual image of ourselves we see in a looking glass. If now, instead of the impression being made on certain cells in the brain through the fibres of the optic nerve, an impression be made directly on those same brain cells by some telepathic impact, it may reasonably be supposed that a visual reaction follows, and a corresponding image would be projected by our mind into external space.

Nor is this pure hypothesis. Actual experiments in telepathy have been repeatedly made where the percipient has seen an apparition of the distant person who mentally desired his presence' to be known. The first successful attempt at this, under conditions that admit of no dispute, was made in 1881 by a personal friend, Mr. S. H. Beard, one of the earliest members of the Society for Psychical Research. On several occasions Mr. Beard, by an effort of his will, was able to cause a phantom

---

[4] A few other striking cases are given in Chapter 10 of my book on Psychical Research in the Home University Library.

of himself to appear, three miles away, to certain acquaintances who were not aware of his intention to make the experiment.

The phantom appeared so real and solid that the percipient thought Mr. Beard himself had suddenly come into the room; and on one occasion the figure was seen by two persons simultaneously. Similar results have been obtained by at least nine other persons, independently of each other, living, in fact, in different parts of the world, more than one carefully conducted and successful experiment being made in each case.[5]

Doubtless these apparitions, though appearing so life-like and substantial, were hallucinations, but by what process is thought able to reproduce itself in a distant mind, and thus cause these phantoms to be projected from it? Either, thought in A. by some unknown means, affects the brain matter in B., and so excites the impression, or thought exists independently of matter. Whichever alternative we take, as Mr. F. W. H. Myers says, —

> "It is the very secret of life that confronts us here; the fundamental antinomy between Mind and Matter.
>
> But such confrontations with metaphysical problems reduced to concrete form are a speciality of our research; and since this problem does already exist — since the brain cells are, in fact, altered either by the thought or along with it — we have no right to take for granted that the problem, when more closely approached, will keep within its ancient limits, or that Mind, whose far-darting energy we are realising, must needs be always powerless upon aught but the grey matter of the brain." ("Proceedings" S.P.R., Vol. X, p. 421.)

Certainly amongst mankind a conscious thought always strives and tends to externalise itself, to pass from a conception to an expression. Creation is the externalised thought of God, and this God-like attribute we, as part of the Universal Mind, share in a partial, limited degree. Our words and actions are a constant, though partial embodiment of our thoughts, effected through the machinery of our nervous and muscular systems. But without this machinery thought can sometimes, as we have shown, transcend its ordinary channels of expression, and act,

---

[5] Full details of these cases will be found in Mr. Myers' *Human Personality,* Vol. I, pp. 293 *et seq.* and pp. 688 *et seq.*

not immediately, but directly, upon another mind, producing not only visual and auditory impressions but also physiological changes.

In fact carefully conducted experiments, some of which I have myself witnessed, have shown that startling physiological changes can be produced in a hypnotised subject merely by conscious or sub-conscious mental suggestion. Thus a red scar or a painful burn can be caused to appear on the body of the subject solely through suggesting the idea.

By some local disturbance of the blood vessels in the skin, the unconscious self has done what it would be impossible for the conscious self to perform. And so in the well-attested cases of stigmata, where a close resemblance to the wounds on the body of the crucified Saviour appear on the body of the ecstatic.

This is a case of unconscious. self-suggestion, arising from the intent and adoring gaze of the ecstatic upon the bleeding figure on the crucifix. With the abeyance of the conscious self the hidden powers emerge, whilst the trance and mimicry of the wounds are strictly parallel to the experimental cases previously referred to.

May not the effects of pre-natal impressions on the offspring (if such cases are proved) also have a similar origin? And if I may make the suggestion, may not the well-known cases of mimicry in animal life originate, like the stigmata, in a reflex action, — as physiologists would say, — below the level of consciousness, created to some extent by a predominant impression? I venture to think that ere long biologists will recognise the importance of the psychical factor in evolution.

Adaptation to environment is usually a slow process spread over countless generations, but here also the same causes, *inter alia*, may be at work. Moreover, even rapid changes sometimes occur. Thus the beautiful experiments of Professor Poulton, F.R.S., have shown that certain caterpillars can more than once in their lifetime change their colour to suit their surroundings. I have seen a brilliant green caterpillar acquire a black skin when taken from its green, environment and placed among black twigs. It is no explanation to say that the nervous stimulus which produced these pigmentary deposits is excited by a particular light acting on the surface of the skin.

Through what wonder-working power is this marvellous change accomplished? Not, of course, through any conscious action of the caterpillar, for even the pupa? of these caterpillars undergo a like change, a light-coloured chrysalis becoming perfectly black when placed on black paper; even patches of metallic lustre, exactly like gold, appear on its integument, as I can testify, when the chrysalis is placed on gilt paper! Does it not seem as if animal Life shared with us, in some degree, certain super-normal powers, and that these colour changes might be due to the influence of causes somewhat analogous to those producing the stigmata, i.e., suggestion, unconsciously derived from the environment? If so, we have here something like the externalising of unconscious thought in ourselves.

To return from this digression. Whether all apparitions are unsubstantial and subjective, due to a telepathic impact from the living or the dead, I am not prepared to say. There are cases which this hypothesis is very difficult to cover, where several people have witnessed the apparition and where it has seemed to have a definite objective existence in successive positions. In any case we need to be on our guard against pressing the telepathic theory to absurd extremes, as some psychical researchers seem disposed to do.

We are in fact, only on the threshold of our knowledge of this obscure and difficult region of enquiry, and humility of mind no less than confidence of hope should be our habit of thought. As Sir Oliver Lodge has remarked, "Knowledge can never grow until it is realised that the question 'Do you believe in these things?' is puerile unless it has been preceded by the enquiry, 'What do you know about them?' " It is invariably those who know nothing of the subject who scornfully say "surely you don't believe in these things!"

There are some remarkable instances where the dying person, before the moment of transition from earth, appears to see and recognise some of his deceased relatives or friends. One cannot always attach much weight to this evidence, as hallucinations of the dying are not infrequent. Here however is a case, one of many recorded in that useful journal Light, which much impressed the physician who narrates it.

Dr. Wilson of New York, who was present at the last moments of Mr. James Moore, a well-known tenor in the United States, gives the following narrative: —

> "It was about 4 a.m., and the dawn for which he had been watching was creeping in through the shutters, when, as I leant over the bed, I noticed that his face was quite calm and his eyes clear. The poor fellow looked me in the face, and, taking my hand in both of his, he said: 'You've been a good friend to me, doctor.' Then something which I shall never forget to my dying day happened, — something which is utterly

indescribable. While he appeared perfectly rational and as sane as any man I have ever seen, the only way that I can express it is that he was transported into another world, and although I cannot satisfactorily explain the matter to myself, I am fully convinced that he had entered the golden city — for he said in a stronger voice than he had used since I had attended him: 'There is mother! Why, mother, have you come here to see me? No, no, I am coming to see you. Just wait, mother, I am almost over. Wait, mother, wait, mother!' "

On his face there was a look of inexpressible happiness, and the way in which he said the words impressed me as I have never been before, and I am as firmly convinced that he saw and talked with his mother as I am that I am sitting here.

"In order to preserve what I believed to be his conversation with his mother, and also to have a record of the strangest happening of my life, I immediately wrote down every word he said. It was one of the most beautiful deaths I have ever seen."

Miss Cobbe in her *Peak in Darien* gives another instance of this kind, but the following narrative is even more striking. It is vouched for by my friend the late Mr. Hensleigh Wedgwood, who contributed it to the *Spectator*. Mr. Wedgwood writes: —

"Between forty and fifty years ago, a young girl, a near connection of mine, was dying of consumption.

She had lain for some days in a prostrate condition, taking no notice of anything, when she opened her eyes, and, looking upwards, said slowly, 'Susan — and Jane — and Ellen!' as if recognising the presence of her three sisters, who had previously died of the same disease. Then, after a short pause, 'and Edward, too!' she continued, — naming a brother then supposed to be alive and well in India, — as if surprised at seeing him in the company. She said no more, and sank shortly afterwards. In course of the post, letters came from India announcing the death of Edward from an accident, a week or two previous to the death of his sister. This was told to me by an elder sister who nursed the dying girl, and was present at the bedside at the time of the apparent vision."

This last instance is difficult to explain away, if correctly narrated. I am also personally acquainted with one or two similar cases, which my informants consider too sacred to be made public. Several remarkable cases of visions of the dying are given in the "Proceedings and Journal of the S.P.R.," which I regret are too long to be quoted here; the reader is specially referred to the following: "Proc," Vol. Ill, p. 93; V, p. 459, 460; VI, p. 294. The evidence seems indisputable that, in some rare cases, just before death the veil is partly drawn aside and a glimpse of the loved ones who have passed over is given to the dying person.

CHAPTER 13

AUTOMATIC WRITING: THE EVIDENCE FOR IDENTITY

"Is there an answering voice from the void,
Or vain and worthless my passionate prayer?
Are all my hopes forever destroyed
In blackness of darkness, depth of despair?"

— F. W. H. Myers.

Let us now enquire what further experimental evidence is afforded by psychical research for survival after death. No candid student of the evidence, so carefully sifted in recent years, can (in my opinion) resist the conclusion that there exists an unseen world of intelligent beings, some of whom, as the succeeding chapters will show, have striven to prove, with more or less success, that they once lived on earth. It would seem as if the mode in which the manifestation of these unseen intelligences takes place varies from time to time. At one period hauntings and poltergeists appear to be most frequent, at another apparitions, at another super-normal physical phenomena, such as were discussed in the earlier chapters; at the present time automatic writing appears to be the most common.

It is interesting to note that automatic writing is also one of the oldest recorded forms of super-normal communication. More than 2,000 years ago it was mentioned by a Hebrew seer as follows: "All this the Lord made me to understand in writing with His hand upon me."[1] Automatic messages may take place either by the automatist passively holding a pencil on a sheet of paper, or by the planchette, or by the "ouija board." In this last method an indicator, — which may be a small board shaped like a planchette, or any other contrivance, — is lightly touched by the automatisms fingers and after a time it moves more or less swiftly to the different letters of the alphabet which are printed on a board below or arranged on a table.

All these modes of communication have the objection that the automatist, even when absolutely above suspicion, may unconsciously guide the pencil or indicator; hence the necessity for a critical examination of the evidence so obtained and of the contents of the messages themselves.[2] In the first place can the communications made through trustworthy automatists or mediums, be reasonably accounted for by thought-transference from those who are sitting with the medium, or telepathy from other living persons who may know some of the facts that are automatically written?

This explanation has indeed been held by some investigators; but even assuming the fact of thought-transference, of which many automatic messages afford an interesting confirmation, that only helps us a little further; clairvoyance may occur, far-seeing as well as far-feeling. Then there is often a curious reflection of the prevailing sentiment of the community, "As if" (Professor James remarks), "the sub-conscious self was peculiarly susceptible to a certain stratum of the Zeitgeist." "It is conceivable," as Mr. Myers remarks,

> "that thought transference and clairvoyance may be pushed to the point of a sort of terrene omniscience; so that to a man's unconscious self some phantasmal picture should be open of all that men are doing or have done. All this might be, but before such a hypothesis as this could come within the range of discussion by men of science there must be a change of mental attitude so fundamental that no argument at present could tell for much in the scale."

But it may be urged that the revival of lapsed memories, and of some of the many unconscious impressions made on our personality,

---

[1] 1. Chronicles xxviii. 19.

[2] The reader will bear in mind that the unseen intelligence may be, and probably is in .mimic cases, only the subliminal of the medium.

may afford an explanation more in harmony with our present state of knowledge and the scientific views of today. This up-rush of past impressions would come as a revelation to the subject, unrecognisable as belonging to his own past experience, and therefore regarded as no part of his own personality, but looked at merely with the curiosity and fainter interest that attaches to the "not me." Moreover, the series of unfamiliar nervous discharges, accompanying the emergence of new sensations and ideas from previously dormant nerve centres, would appear as foreign to the automatist as the reproduction of one's voice in the phonograph, or the reflection of one's face in a mirror, if heard or seen for the first time. The sensation of "otherness" thus produced would give rise to the feeling of another Ego usurping the body, hence the "control" would be designated by some familiar or chance name other than the subject's own, or by a name that appeared to fit the ideas expressed.

But is this explanation sufficient? It may be a *versa causa*, but does it account for *all* the facts that are definitely known about double consciousness and about these automatic and trance communications? Regarding the latter, I know that it certainly does not.

Whilst it disposes of, perhaps, the bulk of the messages usually attributed to disembodied spirits of Satanic agency, it does not cover all the ground. The late Hon. A. Aksakof — a distinguished Russian *savant* — whose opinion, formed after a painstaking and life-long study of the whole subject, is deserving of the highest respect of scientific men as well as of Spiritualists — points out (and the evidence he adduces fully bears out his statement), that the unconscious self of the medium cannot explain all the facts, but that an external and invisible agency is occasionally and unmistakably indicated. The opinion of the Russian savant is corroborated by the experience of other investigators; for instance, I will cite two distinguished and most competent authorities, who have made a careful study of this part of our subject.

In his text-book on "Psychology," the late Professor William James, of Harvard, writes (p. 214) :—

> I am however, persuaded by abundant acquaintance with the trances of one medium that the "control" may be altogether different from any possible waking self of the person. In the case I have in mind it professes to be a certain departed French doctor, and is, I am convinced, acquainted with facts about the circumstances, and the living and dead relatives and acquaintances, of numberless sitters whom the medium

never met before, and of whom she has never heard the names. ... I am persuaded that a serious study of these trance-phenomena is one of the greatest needs of psychology.

Professor W. James not only speaks with authority as an eminent psychologist, but he has had unusual opportunities for a. careful investigation of the case of the well known medium Mrs. Piper, to whom he here refers, and he reiterates, — in a letter to Mr. Myers, published in the "Proceedings of the Society for Psychical Research," Vol. VI, p. 658, — that:—

> I feel as absolutely certain as I am of any personal fact in the world that she knows things in her trances which she cannot possibly have heard in her waking state.

Sir Oliver Lodge, F.R.S., the other witness I will cite, has also made a prolonged study of Mrs. Piper, and he fully endorses Professor James' opinion; he says: —

> Mrs. Piper's trance personality is undoubtedly (I use the word in the strongest sense) aware of much to which she has no kind of ordinarily recognised clue, and of which she, in her ordinary state, knows nothing. But how does she get this knowledge?

That is the question we have to face, and for this purpose what we have to do is to collect truth-telling, *veridical*, messages, and critically examine whether their contents were known to the deceased person and not known to the medium, or automatist, nor to the sitters. This is now being done, and has for many years past been done, by careful and skilled investigators connected with the English and American Societies for Psychical Research. The result has confirmed the opinion I have long held, and expressed in my book *A New World of Thought* (published many years ago), in the following sentences, which remain unchanged: —

There is in my opinion evidence of occasional communications from those who have once lived on earth — not as satisfactory as one would wish, and never a complete revelation of their personality, but in general affording the same trivial and fragmentary presentation that we have in our own dreams. But the messages are more than the incoherent mutterings of a man in his sleep. Behind them there is the same evidence of a combining and reasoning power as we have in our own normal self-consciousness; evidence of an unseen personality, with an intelligence and character of its own entirely distinct from that of the subject's normal self.[3] It has been held by some investigators that this person is only part of the personality of the medium, the transcendental Ego of the unconscious self; but, if so, it is, I am convinced, during trance in touch with those who have once lived on earth, evidence of some extra-terrene communicator certainly exists, unsatisfactory and dream-like though the communication often is. As Professor (now Sir Oliver) Lodge has pointed out concerning Mrs. Piper when her "control" is asked as to the source of its information:—

"She herself, when in the trance state, asserts that she," i.e., her "control," or that part of her which calls itself Dr. Phinuit "gets it by conversing with the deceased friends and relatives of people present .... but even when the voice changes and messages come apparently from these very people themselves, it does not follow that they themselves are necessarily aware of the fact, nor need their conscious mind (if they have any) have anything to do with the process."[4]

This opinion Sir Oliver Lodge expressed in 1894, but the wider experience we have gained in more recent years, especially the evidence of "cross correspondence" (to which I will refer in a moment), has led all serious students of psychical research to the conviction that there is a conscious and designed effort on the part of the unseen communicators to convince us of their survival after death.

In fact the communications appear to fall into two groups, with an indefinite line of demarcation between them. In one group, the cause appears to be the operation of hidden powers that lie wrapped up in our present human personality, and which the peculiar organisation of the medium renders manifest; in the other group the cause appears to be the operation of the same powers, controlled by unseen personalities, who have once lived on earth, or claim to have done so.

That is to say, the unconscious mind of the medium is the instrument from which in the former case and through which in the latter the messages come. We must not, however, conclude that these latter are in every case extra-terrene in their origin, for a telepathic influence from living and distant persons may sometimes be their cause: — as,

---

[3] See the remarkable cases quoted by Ms. Myers in "Proceedings S. P. R.," Vol. VI, p. 341 *et seq.*

[4] "Proceedings S. P. R.," Vol. X, pp. 15 and 17.

for instance, in the well-known case of Rev. P. H. and Mrs. Newnham, where Mrs. Newnham's hand automatically wrote answers to questions previously written down by her husband, and of the purport of which her conscious self was wholly ignorant. This shows how necessary it is to submit all "spiritualistic" communications to the most rigorous scrutiny before deciding on their probable origin.

With full knowledge of all these points before they passed from earth, both Mr. Frederick Myers and Dr. Hodgson were convinced, from their own personal enquiry, that these automatic communications established the fact of survival after death. Since these pioneers in psychical research entered the unseen world, they themselves appear to have specially directed many of the communications, so as to avoid possible telepathy from those on earth, or the emergence of a subconscious memory on the part of the medium.

This they have done by making evident the presence of a combining and reasoning intelligence, apart from and beyond that of the automatist. The significance of the more recent communications — through Mrs. Piper, the late Mrs. Verrall, and several other automatists — which contain what have been called "cross-correspondences" — is precisely this, that they seem inexplicable except on the recognition that some intelligence, which certainly is not the conscious intelligence of any incarnate mind, has planned, coordinated and directed them.

The intricacy and elaboration of these incidents makes them difficult to deal with in a work like this. But it is impossible to pass them by altogether, and an illustration will be given later on. They evince not only the presence of intelligent and selective direction, but also in some cases they contain fresh and impressive evidence indicative of the identity of the intelligence at work. In the last two chapters of my little book on Psychical Research in the Home University series, I have given several instances of these "cross-correspondences," and to these chapters the reader is referred. It is however very difficult to compress into a brief narrative the substance of this evidence, and its cogency can only be felt by a careful perusal of the lengthy papers by Miss Johnson and others published in the *Proceedings of the Society for Psychical Research*.

The enormous difficulty of verifying the identity of the intelligence with that of the deceased person it professes to be, is vastly increased when the claimant is invisible, when "personation" seems to be a common practice, when telepathy is admitted, and when the evidence is of a fitful and fragmentary character. Even in the law-courts we have protracted trials, such as the Tichborne case, when the sole question at issue is the identity of a particular claimant. If the identity of the intelligence which communicates through the medium with a person who has once lived on earth can be established, even in a single instance, all other questions sink into comparative insignificance. Those, however, who will take the trouble critically to examine the ample records of the communications made through the mediumship of Mrs. Piper, which have been published, will find that it needs a great deal of ingenuity and a great many hypotheses to get rid of the inference that we are here, in several instances, actually in touch with the veritable persons who assert they have once lived on earth, and whom we know to have done so. This inference is, of course, a matter of individual judgment, in which no doubt each person's mental bias will come into play, be he as judicial as he will.

Here we find a striking illustration that our knowledge of each other is to a large extent incommunicable to other persons. Those who have had repeated sittings with Mrs. Piper and other genuine mediums for automatic writing or speaking, have been convinced of the survival of friends who have passed from earth. On the other hand, those who have not had such opportunities, but have laboriously read the evidence that has been published, may feel its weight and value, though they may not attain the confident conclusion reached by the investigators themselves. The reason is that we know one another not by any verbal testimony of our identity but by an instant recognition, either from appearance or familiar traits of speech or action. If a long absent friend, whom we may have thought dead, is at the other end of a telephone line, and through loss of voice unable to speak to us except through an intermediary, how difficult it would be for him to prove his identity. To do this he would not talk about current events, but cite trivial incidents in his past life which he hoped we might remember. This experiment with the telephone has actually been made, one person trying to identify himself to another at the other end of the line.

As Dr. Hodgson and others have pointed out, the best proof of identity is to be found in accurate references to incidents of a simple nature, that might be recalled by the sitter but are unknown to the medium or to the public generally. And so we notice that in the messages which purport to come from a deceased friend, trivial incidents are recalled, which are likely to have been unknown to any but the sitter. Such communications may seem silly and worthless to the general reader of the record, but they often carry conviction to the person receiving them. Illustrations of this will be given in the succeeding chapters.

We now come to another interesting point: if in automatic writing the hand of the automatist is controlled and guided by some discarnate spirit we should expect to find, and we do sometimes find, words written in a language unknown to the writer.[5] Still more striking would be the evidence of supernormal guidance if very young children, as yet unable to write in their normal state, could occasionally have intelligible automatic writing coming through them. This, of course, involves the possession of psychic power by such children, and therefore the instances are likely to be rare.

There is however some trustworthy evidence of this kind. Mr. Myers in *Human Personality* (Vol. II, p. 484 *et seq.*) gives a couple of cases which are well attested, wherein children, who had not been taught writing and could not write a word in their normal state, were found to write intelligible words automatically. One was a child nearly five years old who had not learned a single letter of her alphabet, the other a child just four years of age who had no knowledge whatever of writing. This latter case was investigated by Dr. Hodgson, who inspected the writings, and which were made with a pencil held between the middle fingers of the child's left hand. Mr. Myers adds: "I have seen a tracing of the last written phrase 'Your Aunt Emma.'

It is a free scrawl, resembling the planchette writing of an adult rather than the first effort of a child." The child had an Aunt Emma who had died some years before, and the child herself died soon after this unexpected message had come through her hand.

The parents it may be added were not spiritualists, and the mother testifies that their child "had not been taught the alphabet, nor how to hold a pencil."

Further evidence of the super-normal source of these automatic messages will be given in the next chapter; it is obviously of paramount importance to establish the fact of this super-normal source before entering upon the discussion of the contents of the messages themselves.

---

[5] My friend Mr. W. B. Yeats informs me that he has received, not through a professional medium, the most conclusive evidence of this. Words were given in various languages, e.g., Italian, Greek and Latin, known to the control but utterly unknown to the medium. See also "Proceedings S. P. R.," Vol. XI 11, p. 337; XX, p. 30.

CHAPTER 14

PROOF OF SUPER-NORMAL MESSAGES: THE OUIJA BOARD

> "Out of the deep, my child, out of the deep,
> From that true world within the world we see,
> Whereof our world is but the bounding shore."
> — *Tennyson.*

In the previous chapter reference was made to the so-called Ouija board, whereby messages are communicated through the movement of a small triangular table, or indicator, which runs on three legs tipped with felt. The automatists fingers rest lightly on this indicator, which smoothly glides over the board and spells out the messages by pointing to one or other of the letters of the alphabet printed on the board below. Though this method of communication is slow and laborious it has its advantages. Frequently it is successfully used by those who fail to get automatic writing with a pencil; moreover with patience and practice speed and accuracy in indicating the right letters can be obtained.

But the most valuable feature in this method of communication is the suppression of any subconscious guidance of the indicator which can be brought about by careful blindfolding of the sitters.

A small private circle of friends of mine in Dublin have devoted themselves for a few years past to experiments with the ouija board and have obtained some remarkable results. A joint paper by myself and one of the sitters, — the Rev. Savill Hicks, M.A., — was read by the latter before the S.P.R. wherein some of the communications were given.[1] The sitters found when they were carefully blindfolded that the indicator moved with as great ease and precision as when they could see the letters of the alphabet. Questions were promptly answered and the indicator often moved so rapidly that their hands had some difficulty in keeping pace with it: in fact the recorder who took down the communications had frequently to resort to shorthand.

I asked the "control" if I might turn round the board with its alphabet. Instantly the reply was spelt out "Yes, it makes no difference." So the sitters, still blindfolded, raised the indicator and I turned the board so that the alphabet was now upside down to the sitters, and even could they have seen there would have been some difficulty in picking out the right letter. But there was not the least hesitation, the indicator moved as promptly and correctly as before to the right letter. I asked could any friend of mine communicate. A message was spelt out from a deceased friend, whom I will call Sir John Hartley, giving his full Christian and surname correctly, and he sent a message to the Dublin "Grand Lodge of Freemasons": Sir John when on earth had held a very high rank in the Masonic order, though this fact was quite unknown to the sitters.

I then asked one of the sitters to allow me to take his place, and this I did after being securely blindfolded. On putting my fingers on the indicator, along with the two other sitters, the extraordinary vigour, decision and swiftness with which the indicator moved startled me, and it seemed incredible that any coherent message could be in process of delivery. But the recorder had taken down the message which came as follows: "The same combination must always work together in order to obtain the important messages, as it is very tiring unless the same three are present; there is one present who is unsuited for the receiving." The recorder asked who this was and was told that it referred to myself! It was not until we removed the bandages from our eyes that any of the sitters knew the purport of the messages given.[2]

Objection might be made that it is very difficult to blindfold a person effectually by bandaging the eyes. Although the sitters, who were personal friends of mine, declared they could see nothing, it was

---

[1] See also my paper published in the "Proceedings of the American Society for Psychical Research" for September, 1914.

[2] It may be well to state here that I myself am not in the least psychic, and have never had psychical gifts of any kind; perhaps happily so, as one is better able to preserve a detached and critical spirit.

desirable to meet this objection. Accordingly opaque eye screens were made and fastened over the eyes with an elastic cord round the head: a space was cut for the nose so that the screen fitted closely to the cheeks and forehead, and thus resembled the eye screens used by patients after an operation for cataract. I tried one of these screens and found it pleasanter to use than a bandage and absolutely effective in preventing vision. But communications came just as easily when these screens were worn; and a new control unexpectedly came who called himself Peter Rooney.

A new pattern of "board" was now made; this consisted of a sheet of plate glass resting on a table of the same size, beneath the glass an alphabet was placed, and the indicator, which had very short legs tipped with felt, now moved more freely over the smooth glass surface. The letters of the alphabet were on separate bits of thin card, and could be arranged in any way we pleased on the table beneath the plate glass.

A clerical friend, who was an interested but sceptical enquirer, was invited to be present at some of the sittings, and whilst the indicator was rapidly spelling out a communication through the blindfolded sitters, he silently held a large opaque fire screen over the moving indicator and alphabet below; but it made no difference, the message went on, though it could only be read by the recorder bending his head down to see between the screen and the alphabet. I asked my friend, the Rev. W. P. Robertson, M.A., to send me a brief report of this sitting, here it is: —

> "When present with Sir Wm. Barrett at the sitting in question, I observed that the interposition of the opaque screen made no appreciable difference in the speed at which the message was spelt out, and certainly it caused no interruption, much less a cessation of the message. The letters of the alphabet were arranged in three lines and in order beneath the plate glass.
>
> It occurred to me that possibly the sitters knew the position of each letter, as a good typist knows her keyboard, though they might be unconscious of the fact themselves. I ventured to suggest that the letters be jumbled. The sitters agreed and Sir Wm. Barrett and I rearranged the letters at random, the sitters being blindfolded all the time. On resuming with the alphabet thus altered, the movement of the indicator was at first very slow, it travelled three times in and out between the letters and then proceeded to spell out, slowly and deliberately: 'There

is a disturbing person.' Here we laughed and asked the 'control' to indicate which of us was the culprit — the Professor or the clergyman? At this point there occurred what, to my mind, was the most impressive feature of the sitting. We all expected some sort of answer to this question. The shorthand writer said, 'It seems to be writing nonsense now.' The 'nonsense' on examination proved to be — *'ality in the room.'* That is, our question was ignored and the 'control' calmly finished what he intended to say. A second instance of ignoring a question and continuing a sentence that we thought had been completed, occurred at the same sitting.

So far as I could judge the blindfolding of the sitters was *perfect*, and their *bona fides* is to me beyond question. When the opaque screen was held over the board, the letters were visible only to the reporter who bent down to see underneath the screen.

W. P. Robertson.

I have given these details to establish the fact that whatever may have been the source of the intelligence displayed, it was absolutely beyond the range of any normal human faculty. As for the numerous messages that came through the blindfolded sitters, one from the control, Isaac David Solomon, on October 19th, 1912, — just after the first Balkan war had broken out, — was as follows:

"Blood, blood everywhere in the near East. A great nation will fall and a small nation will rise. A great religion will stand in danger. Blood everywhere. News that will astonish the civilised world will come to hand within the next week."

Now, whatever the source of this message it was perfectly true, for within a week afterwards the first victory of the Bulgarians at Kirk Kilisse was announced and later on, as we know, a great nation (Turkey) fell and a small nation (Bulgaria) rose; whilst more recently Europe has been drenched in blood.

This control passed and the American Irishman Peter Rooney, persistently intruded himself and told us the story of his life and recent death. The purport of it was that he had lived a wretched and bad life, mostly in gaol, and, he added, life at last became so unendurable that ten days previously he threw himself under a tramcar in Boston and so committed suicide. It was only afterwards that the blindfolded sitters knew the purport of the message, they were laughing and chatting together during its delivery. To us onlookers it seemed very incongruous, for the message was delivered in the most life-like manner, with evident pain and reluctance leading up to the tragic conclusion.

The next day I wrote to the Governor of the State Prison at Boston, Mass., to the Chief of Police in that city, to the Chief of Police at Boston, Lincolnshire, to the distinguished corresponding member of the S.P.R., Dr. Morton Prince, of Boston, U.S.A., and to Dr. Hyslop, Hon. Sec. of the American S.P.R., asking if any information could be given me concerning this Peter Rooney, and requesting a reply as soon as possible.

In the course of a few weeks I obtained answers to my enquiries. No man of this name was known at Boston in England, no Peter Rooney had been in confinement at Boston Prison, Mass., and no former inmate of that prison had recently committed suicide.

The chief Inspector of Police at Boston, Mass., made a thorough investigation and found that no Peter Rooney had been sent to prison from Boston, or had been committed to the Reformatory, or had committed suicide.

Dr. Morton Prince, of Boston, however, obtained from the Police Records of Boston that a Peter Rooney had fallen from the elevated railway in Boston in August, 1910, had received a scalp wound, was attended by a doctor, laid up for a month, and was still living in his home, York Street, Boston. It was probably only a chance coincidence that a man of the same name had met with an accident in Boston.

The whole elaborate story was therefore fictitious, and characteristic of the dramatic inventions, like externalised dreams, which so often come through these automatic channels, and which are so misleading to the novice and so productive of mischief to the credulous.

Nevertheless other messages subsequently came through another control, giving names and addresses of two persons recently deceased in England, which on investigation proved to be perfectly correct; though the names were entirely unknown to myself or any of the sitters. Such is the curious mixture of truth and fiction which these automatisms so frequently display. I have not space to give details of these two cases, but will cite a later and remarkably veridical communication that came through the ouija board in Dublin.

The sitters in this case were not blind folded, one was the same lady who took part in the former sittings, the wife of a well-known Dublin physician and daughter of the late Professor Dowden, Mrs. Travers Smith. The other was her friend, Miss C, the daughter of a medical man, and evidently possessing great psychic power.

The Pearl Tie-Pin Case.

Miss C, the sitter, had a cousin an officer with our Army in France, who was killed in battle a month previously to the sitting: this she knew. One day after the name of her cousin had unexpectedly been spelt out on the ouija board, and her name given in answer to her query "Do you know who I am?" the following message came: — "Tell mother to give my *pearl tie-pin* to the girl I was going to marry, I think she ought to have it." When asked what was the name and address of the lady both were given, the name spelt out included the full Christian and surname, the latter being a very unusual one and quite unknown to both the sitters.

The address given in London was either fictitious or taken down incorrectly, as a letter sent there was returned, and the whole message was thought to be fictitious.

Six months later, however, it was discovered that the officer had been engaged, shortly before he left for the front, to the very lady, whose name was given; he had however told no one. Neither his cousin nor any of his own family in Ireland were aware of the fact and had never seen the lady nor heard her name, until the War Office sent over the deceased officer's effects. Then they found that he had put this lady's name in his will as his next of kin, both Christian and surname being precisely the same as given through the automatist; and what is equally remarkable, a pearl tie-pin was found in his effects.

Both the ladies have signed a document they sent me, affirming the accuracy of the above statement. The message was recorded at the time, and not written from memory after verification had been obtained. Here there could be no explanation of the facts by subliminal memory, or telepathy or collusion, and the evidence points unmistakably to a telepathic message from the deceased officer.

Other remarkable evidential cases came through the ouija board. One was on the occasion of the sinking of the Lusitania, and Mrs. Travers Smith has kindly furnished me with the following report: —

The Hugh Lane Case.

"On the evening of the day on which news had come that the Lusitania was reported sinking, Mr. Lennox Robinson and I sat at the ouija board; the Rev. Savill Hicks taking the record. We *did not know* that Sir Hugh Lane was on board. We were both personal friends of his, and knew he was in America, but had no idea he was coming back so soon.

"Our usual 'control' came and then the words 'Pray for the soul of Hugh Lane.' I asked 'Who is speaking?' the reply was 'I am Hugh Lane.' He gave us an account of the sinking of the ship and said it was 'a peaceful end to an exciting life.' At this point we heard the stop-press evening paper called in the street and Mr. Robinson ran down and bought a paper. I went out of the room to meet him, and he pointed to the name of Sir Hugh Lane among the passengers.

We were both much disturbed, but continued the sitting. Sir Hugh gave me messages for mutual friends and ended this sitting by saying 'I did not suffer, I was drowned and felt nothing.' "At subsequent sittings he spoke of his will, but never mentioned the codicil now in dispute. He hoped no memorial would be erected to him in the shape of a gallery or otherwise, but was anxious about his pictures. The messages were always coherent and evidential and always came through Mr. Robinson and me.

(Signed) Hester Travers Smith"

This is a very evidential case, for no information of the *death* of Sir Hugh Lane was given until some days later.

Another veridical message, through the same sitters, came to a friend of mine who was in profound distress through the death in battle of his son, an officer with our army in France. This message, together with others, he obtained later on through a lady in London, who knew nothing of my friend beforehand, absolutely convinced him of the identity of his son and of his survival after death. The result was a very happy one; from almost heartbroken grief he is now in serene and perfect confidence of his son's survival.

Besides the foregoing group of sitters, a well-known and esteemed member of the Society of Friends and friend of mine in Dublin, has for several years past had a small private circle of sitters with the ouija board. He has thus obtained some thousands of communications, chiefly from deceased members of his family, which have demonstrated to him the fact of their survival after death, and thus afforded great consolation to himself and other stricken friends. These communications are not evidential to an outsider, but they give some remarkable statements as to the conditions of life and occupation in the unseen world, which are more or less in accordance with similar communications (unknown to these sitters) obtained by others.

A digest of the spirit teachings coming through a medium in America who is much esteemed by Dr. Hyslop, has lately been published by Mr. Prescott Hall in the "Journal of the American Society for Psychical Research" for November and December, 1916. As Mr. Hall points out, if we find on collating a number of communications through different mediums, of different training, in different countries, that they substantially agree upon certain facts as to the nature and conditions of spirit life, the result may be of interest and value.

But this will depend upon the fact whether the descriptions given are not to be found in spiritistic literature and therefore not likely to be the common opinion of mediums generally. Unfortunately it is usual to find such descriptions arc only a reflection of the medium's own opinions and reading, and therefore the product of the memory or subconscious impressions of the medium. This is conspicuous when attempts at scientific or philosophical disquisitions are made by the medium, which rarely exhibit anything more than the grotesque assertions of an ignorant mind.

Mr. Prescott Hall, however, is doing good service in classifying these spirit teachings, examining their source and testing their consistency.

By far the most remarkable and interesting collection of *Spirit Teachings* was published some years ago by the late Rev. Stainton Moses (M.A., Oxon), to whom reference has already been made. These were given through his own mediumship and are well worth careful perusal, together with his book on "Spirit Identity and the higher aspects of Spiritualism."

In the next chapter will be found some glimpses of the spirit world obtained through two ladies, neither of whom were spiritualists; one was a personal friend, and both were of unimpeachable veracity.

CHAPTER 15

FURTHER EVIDENCE OF SURVIVAL AFTER DEATH

"The souls of the righteous are in the hands of God. In the sight of the unwise they seem to die and their departure is taken for misery and their going away from earth to be utter destruction — but they are in peace."[1]

The super-normal character of many of the communications that reach us through the medium or automatist having been established, let us now turn to further evidence of survival and of the identity of the discarnate intelligence, together with occasional glimpses of their condition after death.

Some years ago I was staying at a friend's house in the country, which I will call Hawthorn Manor, and found that my hostess, Mrs. E. — the wife of a lawyer holding a responsible official position, and herself a matronly lady of great acumen and commonsense, the centre of a circle of religious and charitable activity — had accidently discovered that her hand was occasionally impressed by some power she could not control. Long messages, the purport of which were at the time unknown to her, were thus written.

The curious feature of this automatic writing was that it came on her suddenly; when writing up some household accounts she fell into a dreamy or semi-trance-like state, and then felt the fingers of another

---

[1] From the *Wisdom of Solomon*, iii, 1-3.

hand — belonging apparently to an invisible person seated opposite to her — laid on her right hand, and a sudden vigorous scribbling ensued. But the writing was all upside down, each line beginning at her right hand side of the page, and could only be read by turning the page round.

Mrs. E. assured me, and I have no reason to doubt her word, that it was quite impossible for her to write a single word correctly in this way in her normal state. Anyone who will make the attempt will find how difficult such a mode of writing is to execute, especially in the clear and characteristic caligraphy, which here occurred.

Mrs. E. was not a spiritualist and had no knowledge of the subject, in fact rather an aversion to it. Hence no serious attention was given to this abnormal writing until a message came containing certain specific statements, wholly outside the knowledge of herself or husband, which they subsequently discovered to be perfectly true incidents in the life of a deceased relative, who asserted he was present and guiding the lady's hand. Other communications followed, which also were verified. Then on another evening came the instance to which I have referred as affording proof of identity.

The Chatham Case

In this case the communicating intelligence was unknown to Mrs. E. The circumstances, written down at the time, were as follows: — A cousin of my hostess, an officer in the Engineers, named B., was paying a visit to Hawthorn Manor. I was not present, but the facts were sent to me; some, indeed, came under my own knowledge. B. had a friend, a brother officer, Major C, who died after B. left Chatham, and to whose rooms in the barracks he frequently went to play on C.'s piano, both being musical: of this Mrs. E. assured me she knew absolutely nothing. At the sitting in question, much to B.'s amazement, for he was quite ignorant of spiritualism, the Christian name and surname of Major C. were unexpectedly given, followed by the question, addressed to B., "Have you kept up your music?" Then came some private matter of a striking character, when suddenly the unseen visitant interjected the question, "What was done with the books?" "What books?" was asked? "Lent to me," was C.'s reply. "Who lent you the books?" The reply came at once, "A — ," giving the name of another brother officer, of whose existence Mrs. E. was also wholly unaware. "Shall I write to ask A — if he has them?" B. asked. "Yes," was the reply. All present assert on their word of honour they knew of no such loan, nor was the officer named in any of their thoughts, nor had Mrs. E. ever heard A — 's name mentioned before.

A — was written to, and the question about the books incidentally asked, but in reply that came some time after no notice was taken of the question. Two months later, however, B. accidentally met his friend A —, when, in the course of conversation on other matters, A — suddenly exclaimed: "That was a rum thing you asked me about in your letter; I mean about Major C. and the books. I did lend him some books, but I don't know what became of them after his death."

An objector might urge that it is conceivable B. might once have seen some books belonging to A — in Major C.'s room, and afterwards forgotten the fact, and that this latent memory had telepathically (and unconsciously to all concerned) impressed Mrs. E., but obviously this explanation will not cover other cases, some of which I will cite. For these some more elaborate hypothesis must be invented, and our ingenuity becomes severely taxed when we remember that these are only stray illustrations of a growing mass of sifted evidence pointing in the direction of survival after death. Much of this evidence has been published, but other cases are privately known to me, and each case requires new and often absurd assumptions if we attempt to explain it away.

I will now cite some further illustrations of the automatic script that came through my friend Mrs. E.'s hand, and in the earlier stages came in the wonderful manner already mentioned. The remarkable point being that Mrs. E. did not know what her hand had written until the paper was turned completely round and the message read. I know of no other case where messages were written in this inverted script, though there may be such.

"Mirror writing" is not uncommon, that is messages written (as postcards are sometimes written) in a script which can only be read when viewed in a mirror; this art is not so difficult to acquire as inverted writing.

The following communications are also unlike the usual type, inasmuch as they give us a glimpse, — if they are really veridical, — of the state of the soul immediately after death. Mrs. E. assured me that these messages were quite foreign to her thoughts, and entirely beyond her ability to compose. She had lost during the preceding winter a dearly loved brother, who was studying at an engineering college near London. A friend of his, who had been a sufferer, had pre-deceased him, but no thought of this friend was in Mrs. E.'s mind when one evening her hand wrote: —

> "I want you to believe your friends live still and can think of you.... On opening the eyes of my spiritual body I found myself unaltered, no terror, only a strange feeling at first, then peace, a comforted heart, love, companionship, teaching. I am [giving here his full name], and have written this, but your brother [giving the name] is here and wants to speak to you."

After an interval Mrs. E. felt her hand again impelled to write, and the following message came: —

> "I am here [giving her brother's name] and want to tell you about my awakening into spirit life. I was at first dimly conscious of figures moving in the room and round the bed. Then the door was closed and all was still. I then first perceived that I was not lying on the bed, but seemed to be floating in the air a little above it. I saw in the dim light the body stretched out straight and with the face covered. My first idea was that I might re-enter it, but all desire to do this soon left me — the tie was broken. I stood upon the floor, and looked round the room where I had been so ill and been so helpless, and where I could now once more move without restraint. The room was not empty. Close to me was my father's father [giving the name correctly]. He had been with me all through. There were others whom I love now, even if I did not know much of them then. I passed out of the room, through the next, where my mother and were [relatives still in this life], I tried to speak to them. My voice was plain to myself, and even loud, yet they took no notice of all I could say.
>
> I walked through the college rooms; much blackness but some light. Then I went out under the free heavens. I will write more another sitting — power too weak now. Good-night." [His signature follows.]

At another sitting, a night of two later, the same name was written, and the thread of the preceding narrative was abruptly taken up without any preface: —

"I saw the earth lying dark and cold under the stars in the first beginning of the wintry sunrise. It was the landscape I knew so well, and had looked at so often. Suddenly sight was born to me; my eyes became open. I saw the spiritual world dawn upon the actual, like the blossoming of a flower. For this I have no words. Nothing I could say would make any of you comprehend the wonder of that revelation, but it will be yours in time. I was drawn as if by affinity to the world which is now mine. But I am not fettered there. I am much drawn to earth, but by no unhappy chain. I am drawn to those I love; to the places much endeared."

These messages are deeply interesting: some of them were written in my presence and, as I have stated, Mrs. E. in her normal waking consciousness was convinced she could not have composed them. But the subliminal self, the uprush of which Mr. Myers has suggested lies at the root of genius, has gilts far beyond the power of the normal self and it is possible, though not in my opinion probable, that these communications are only the dramatised products of Mrs. E.'s own hidden and unsuspected powers. This explanation, however, fails to account for the veridical messages that came through Mrs. E., giving information beyond the knowledge of any persons present; nor can it explain many of the communications that have come through other automatists, such as the other cases already cited and those which follow.

But why should we think it so extravagant to entertain the simplest explanation — that occasionally a channel opens from the unseen world to ours, and that some who have entered that world are able to make their continued existence known to us? Why *some*, we cannot tell. And why so paltry a manifestation? But is anything paltry that manifests life?

In the dumb agony which seizes the soul when some loved one is taken from us, in the awful sense of separation which paralyses us as we gaze upon the lifeless form, there comes the unutterable yearning for some voice, some sign from beyond; and if, in answer to our imploring cry for an assurance that our faith is not in vain, that our dear one is living still, a smile were to overspread the features of the dead, or its lips to move, or even its finger to be lifted, should we deem any action a paltry thing that assures us death has not yet ended life, and still more that death will not end all? Though it be

"Only a signal shown and a voice from out of the darkness,"

it is not paltry! Only the dead in spirit care not for the faintest, the rudest sign that assures us, who are "slow of heart to believe in all that the prophets have spoken," that the soul lives freed from the flesh, that the individual mind and memory remain, though the clothing of the body and brain be gone.

And it is just this natural human longing that renders a dispassionate consideration of the facts, a calm and critical weighing of the evidence, so difficult and yet so imperative.

This is now being done, as the following case illustrates, with a care that grows by experience, and with an honesty that none can dispute.

Mrs. Holland's Scripts

Some of the most remarkable automatic scripts, — which have been discussed with critical acumen by the Research Officer of the S.P.R., — came to a lady of education and social position resident in India. This lady was not a spiritualist, and at the time had no acquaintance with the members of the Society for Psychical Research. As her family disliked the whole subject she prefers to be known under the pseudonym of "Mrs. Holland." Subsequently, on her return to England, she became personally known to and esteemed by many of the leaders and officials of the S.P.R. Her attention having been once casually drawn to the subject of automatic writing she tried the experiment and to her surprise found her hand wrote both verse and prose without any volition on her part; the first messages were headed by the impromptu lines: —

"Believe in what thou canst not see,
Until the vision come to thee."

Mrs. Holland says she remains fully conscious during the writing, "but my hand moves so rapidly that I seldom know what I am writing." Her interest in the subject increased and she obtained and read Mr. Myers' monumental work *Human Personality*, which was published after Mr. Myers' death. Though she did not know the author, it was natural that much of her automatic script purported to be inspired by him. A careful study of the messages so inspired has compelled the belief that the spirit of Mr. Myers really did control some of these messages. Here for instance is a very characteristic communication purporting to come from Mr. Myers:—

> "To believe that the mere act of death enables a spirit to understand the whole mystery of death is as absurd as to imagine that the act of birth enables an infant to understand the whole mystery of life. I am still groping — surmising — conjecturing.. The experience is different for each one of us. . . . One was here lately who could not believe he was dead; he accepted the new conditions as a certain stage in the treatment of his illness."

Then follows, not quite verbally correct, the first two lines of Mr. Myers' poem St. Paul — a poem which Mrs. Holland declares she had never read and of which she knew nothing whatever. Of course it is possible that she had somewhere seen these lines quoted, though she has no recollection of this. The automatic script is as follows:—

> "Yea, I am Christ's — and let the name suffice ye — E'en as for me He greatly hath sufficed.[22] If it were possible for the soul to die back into earth life again I should die from sheer yearning to reach you — to tell you all that we imagined is not half wonderful enough for the truth — that immortality, instead of being a beautiful dream, is the one, the only reality, the strong golden thread on which all the illusions of all the lives are strung. If I could only reach you — if I could only tell you — I long for power, and all that comes to me is an infinite yearning — an infinite pain. Does any of this reach you, reach anyone, or am I only wailing as the wind wails — wordless and unheeded?" *Proceedings*, S.P.R., Vol. XXI, p. 233.

On another occasion the Myers control wrote: —

> "It may be that those who die suddenly suffer no prolonged obscuration of consciousness, but for my own experience the unconsciousness was exceedingly prolonged."

And again,

---

[2] The actual lines in Mr. Myers' *St. Paul* are: "Christ! I am Christ's! and let the name suffice you, Ay, for me too He greatly hath sufficed."

"The reality is infinitely more wonderful than our most daring conjectures. Indeed, no conjecture is sufficiently daring."

The hypothesis that these messages are due to dramatic creations of Mrs. Holland's subliminal self becomes increasingly difficult to believe when we find other wholly different types of messages purporting to come from Mr. Ed. Gurney and the Hon. Roden Noel, who were also entirely unknown to Mrs. Holland. When they were on earth I knew these distinguished men personally, and was in frequent correspondence with each of them; hence from my own knowledge I can affirm that these communications are singularly characteristic of the respective and diverse temperaments of each.

But there was more than this, for not only was some very striking blank verse written by the Roden Noel control, but mention is made of places and persons associated with Mr. Roden Noel that were unknown to Mrs. Holland. In fact the automatist did not know who was controlling her hand when it wrote: —

"I was always a seeker, — until it seemed at times as if the quest was more to me than the prize, — only the attainments of my search were generally like rainbow gold, always beyond and afar... I am not oppressed with the desire that animates some of us to share our knowledge or optimisms with you all before the time. The solution of the great Problem I could not give you — I am still very far away from it; the abiding knowledge of the inherent truth and beauty into which all the inevitable ugliness of existence finally resolve themselves will be yours in time."

Preceding this had come the following: —

"This is for A.W., ask him what the date, May 26th, 1894, meant to him — to me — and to F.W.H. I do not think they will find it hard to recall, but, if so, let them ask Nora."

Here it is to be noted Mrs. Holland, who was in India, knew nothing of Dr. A. W. Verrall, whose name is suggested by the initials A.W., nor that Mrs. Sidgwick was called Nora (her Christian name being Eleanor) but the whole context eventually suggested to Miss Johnson (the Research Officer of the S.P.R.), to whom the script was sent, a message from Roden Noel, who was known both to Dr. Verrall, Mr.

F. W. H. Myers, and Mrs. Sidgwick. Miss Johnson adds: "It was appropriate we should be told to ask Nora (Mrs. Sidgwick) if we could not find out for ourselves, since he (Roden Noel) was an intimate friend of Dr. Sidgwick." Now the date given was precisely *that of the death of Roden Noel*. Though Mrs. Holland thought she may have once seen some poems of Mr. Noel's, she knew nothing of him personally nor of the date of his death.

The fetish of subliminal or telepathic knowledge is here hard to invoke and becomes absurd when we find one of the earliest of Mrs. Holland's scripts, written in India and purporting to come from Mr. Myers, gives a minute and lengthy description of an elderly gentleman, which ends up as follows: —

> "It is like entrusting a message on which infinite importance depends to a sleeping person. Get a proof, — try for a proof if you feel this is a waste of time without. Send this to Mrs. Verrall, 5, Selwyn Gardens, Cambridge."

When this script was received by Miss Johnson she at once recognised the description as resembling Dr. Verrall, and Mrs. Verrall's address given was perfectly correct. Further, when the script was shown to Mrs. Verrall she said the whole description was remarkably good and characteristic of her husband, who was then living. Mrs. Verrall, who now alas! has also passed into the unseen, states that no portrait or description of her husband had ever been published, nor was her address given in *Human Personality*, which, as stated, Mrs. Holland had read. On being questioned Mrs. Holland declared she had never seen, and had no conception of Mrs. Verrall's address. Of the good faith of Mrs. Holland there is no doubt whatever, and she herself was most anxious to find out whether any of her automatic writing came from her sub-conscious memory.

Other very remarkable cases of supernormal knowledge in Mrs. Holland's script are described in Miss Johnson's long memoir in the Proceedings of the S.P.R., one in particular is worth noting. Mrs. Holland's hand wrote, on January 17th, 1904, — purporting to be under the control of Mr. Myers: —

> "The sealed envelope is not to be opened yet. I am unable to make your hand form Greek characters and so I cannot give the text as I wish — only the reference — 1 COR. XVI., 12 ['Watch ye, stand fast in the faith,

quit you like men, be strong']. Oh I am feeble with eagerness. How can I best be identified! It means so much apart from the mere personal love and longing. Edmund's [Mr. Ed Gurney] help is not here with me just now. I am trying alone amid unspeakable difficulties."

Now Mrs. Sidgwick had asked Mrs. Verrall, who was also a remarkable automatist, as a test to give a favourite text of her husband's and a fairly satisfactory answer was obtained; of this Mrs. Holland knew absolutely nothing, but *on the very same day*, Jan. 17th, 1904, that Mrs. Verrall's script in Cambridge made references to a sealed letter and to a text, Mrs. Holland's hand in India automatically wrote the message just quoted. The text 1 COR. 16, 12, was not the one asked for by Mrs. Sidgwick, but it is the one inscribed in *Greek* over the gateway of Selwyn College, Cambridge, which Mr. Myers constantly passed, and on which, owing to a slight verbal error in the Greek inscription, Mr. Myers had more than once remarked to Mrs. Verrall.

Mrs. Holland had never been in Cambridge, had no connection with the University, and knew absolutely nothing of the Greek inscription on the gateway of Selwyn College.

The text incident may be an example of what has been already referred to as "cross-correspondence," that is two widely separated automatists, giving somewhat similar replies, or giving a sentence the meaning of which is unintelligible until it is supplemented by a further communication through another automatist, who has no knowledge of the other fragmentary message. All this looks as if a single unseen personality controlled the two automatists, in order to avoid any explanation by telepathy or the subliminal self. The interesting point being, as I have pointed out already, that only since the death of Mr. Myers and Dr. Hodgson, — who were familiar with this favourite method of explaining away the significance of these messages, — have numerous cases of cross-correspondence arisen among independent and widely separated automatists.

CHAPTER 16

EVIDENCE OF IDENTITY IN THE DISCARNATE

"The Ghost in man, the Ghost that once was man
But cannot wholly free itself from man,
Are calling to each other thro' a dawn
Stranger than earth has ever seen; the veil
Is rending and the voices of the day
Are heard across the voices of the dark."

— *Tennyson.*

These well-known lines of our great poet are today receiving ampler confirmation than was thought possible a generation ago. In the present chapter I will cite some remarkable evidence of survival obtained through personal friends of my own.

I have previously given illustrations of the wonderful mediumistic power of the Rev. Stainton Moses and of the high regard in which he was held. No one who knew him could for a moment doubt, as Mr. Myers says, "his sanity or his sincerity, his veracity or his honour," and those who knew him personally, as I did, could understand the esteem and affection which his colleagues at University College School and his intimate friends always felt for him. I will here briefly narrate two remarkable cases in favour of the identity of the *soi-disant* spirit which came through Mr. Moses. These cases are well known to those familiar with the literature of spiritualism, but may not be known to many of my readers: —

The Abraham Florentine Case.

In August, 1874, Mr. Moses was staying with a friend, a medical man, in the Isle of Wight, and at one of the "sittings" which they had together a communication was received with singular impetuosity purporting to be from a spirit who gave the name Abraham Florentine, and stated that he had been engaged in the United States war of 1812, but only lately had entered into the spiritual world, having died at Brooklyn, U.S.A., on August 5th, 1874, at the age of eighty-three years, one month, and seventeen days.

None present knew of such a person, but Mr. Moses published the particulars as above stated in a London newspaper, asking at the same time American journals to copy, so that, if possible, the statement made might be verified or disproved.

In course of time an American lawyer, a "claim-agent," who had been auditing the claims of soldiers in New York, saw the paragraph, and wrote to an American newspaper to say that he had come across the name A. Florentine, and that a full record of the person who made the claim could be obtained from the U.S. Adjutant-General's office. Accordingly the headquarters of the U.S. army was applied to, and an official reply was received, stating that a private named Abraham Florentine had served in the American war in the early part of the century. Ultimately the widow of Abraham Florentine was found to be alive.

Dr. Crowell, a Brooklyn physician, by means of a directory, discovered her address in Brooklyn, and saw and questioned the widow. She stated that her husband had fought in the war of 1812, that he was a rather impetuous man, and had died in Brooklyn on August 5th, 1874, and that his eighty-third birthday was on the previous June 8th. He was therefore eighty-three years, one month, twenty-seven days old when he died, the only discrepancy being seventeen for twenty-seven days, a mistake that might easily have arisen in recording the message made through Mr. Moses when entranced in the isle of Wight. Full details of this case were published in Vol. XI of the "Proceedings of the S.P.R."

What are we to say to this evidence? The newspaper files remain to attest the facts, which seem to be absolutely irrefragable.

The only surmise that can be made is that Mr. Moses had seen some notice of the man's death and career in an American newspaper, and either had forgotten the fact or had purposely deceived his friends. But then, this could only have been one of many similar cases of forgetfulness or deception, and before we can assume this we have to prove that Mr. Moses *did* obtain the required information by means of newspapers or other mundane channels of information. This Mrs. Moses is certain he did not, and no one as yet has been able to show that he did, or to find a particle of evidence on behalf of the wearisome and motiveless deception which must, in this event, habitually have characterised a man of spotless integrity and honour. Moreover, it is wholly unlikely an obscure private soldier should have an obituary notice in an American newspaper, or if it were so, that it should have been noted by English readers. In fine, after critically examining this case, Mr. F. W. H. Myers remarks: "I hold that the surviving spirit of Abraham Florentine did really communicate with Mr. Moses."[1] It is, however, necessary to submit every case of "spiritualistic" communication to the most rigorous scrutiny before deciding on its probable origin; what to a novice may seem to have an extra-terrene origin may really be a telepathic influence from some living person or the revival of some forgotten impression.

Long experience in the work of psychical research has shown the danger arising from what has been called *cryptomnesia*, i.e. a hidden memory. This explanation has indeed been suggested by some psychical researchers as possible in the foregoing case (unwarrantably I think), but it cannot apply to the next; which affords another of the remarkable proofs of spirit identity obtained through the automatic writing of Mr. S. Moses.

The Blanchie Abercromby Case.

The following case Mr. Myers considered to be one of extreme interest and value, owing to the fact that only after Mr. Moses' death a series of chances led Mr. Myers to discover additional proofs of its veracity. The spirit purporting to communicate through Mr. Moses was that

---

[1] "Proc. S. P. R.," Vol. XI, p. 407.

of a lady known to Mr. Myers, and who will be called Blanche Abercromby. This lady died on a Sunday afternoon at a country house some 200 miles from London. Of her illness and death Mr. Moses knew absolutely nothing, but the same Sunday evening a communication, purporting to come from her, and stating that "she had just quitted the body," was made to Mr. Moses at his secluded lodgings in London.

A few days later Mr. Moses' hand was again controlled by the same spirit and a few lines were written purporting to come from her and asserted by the spirit to be in her own handwriting, as a proof of her identity. There is no reason to suppose Mr. Moses had ever seen her handwriting, for he had only met her once casually at a séance. The facts communicated to Mr. Moses by the deceased lady were private; accordingly he mentioned the matter to no one, and gummed down the pages of the communication in his notebook and marked it "private matter." When after the death of Mr. Moses his documents were examined by Mr. Myers, he received permission from the executors to open these sealed pages. To his astonishment he found the communication to be from the lady whom he had known, and on comparing the handwriting of the script with letters from this lady when on earth he found the resemblance was incontestable. He submitted the matter to the lady's son and to an expert in handwriting and both affirmed that the spirit writing and that by the lady when living were from the same person. Numerous peculiarities were found common to the two, and the contents of the automatic script were also characteristic of the deceased lady. The ordinary handwriting of Air. Moses is quite different from that which usually comes in his automatic script, and that again was wholly unlike the caligraphy in the present case.

Here no hypothesis of telepathy from the living, or forgotten memory, or the subliminal self of Mr. Moses, affords any explanation, and I regard this case as one of the strongest links in the chain of evidence on behalf of survival after death. As a rule the caligraphy of the automatic script is not the same as that of the person who purports to communicate, nor should we expect it to be so, if the communication be effected by telepathy from the deceased person.

There are however some other cases where the *soi-disant* spirit occasionally seems able to guide the hand of the medium so perfectly as to produce an accurate reproduction of the deceased's handwriting. A notable instance of this occurred in the case of the late Professor Henry Sidgwick, from whom a characteristic communication came through automatic writing to which his signature was affixed. This signature is identical with that in the many letters I received from Prof.

Sidgwick when on earth, and here also there is no reason to believe the medium, a lady I know personally, had ever seen Professor Sidgwick's handwriting.[2] Bearing in mind the hypothesis of cryptomnesia, I will now cite some remarkable messages which were sent to us by my venerable friend the late Mr. Hensleigh Wedgwood, the cousin and brother-in-law of Charles Darwin, and himself a well-known savant. Mr. Wedgwood was deeply interested in psychical research and had many sittings for automatic writing (by planchette) with two valued friends of his, "Mrs. R." and her sister "Mrs. V.," both of whom were psychic.

In the present case Mrs. R. was the automatist, a lady known for some years to Mr.

Fred. Myers, and of whose scrupulous good faith there can be no more question than of that of Mr. Wedgwood himself. Mrs. R. and Mr. Wedgwood sat opposite each other at a small table, the former with her left hand and the latter with his right on the planchette.

Mr. Wedgwood states that the writing came upright to him but upside down to his partner, and so far from guiding the planchette his only difficulty was to avoid interfering with its rapid movement. His partner declared the same, and moreover could not have written rapidly, or at all, in this inverted manner.

Mrs. R.'s notes, confirmed by Mr. Wedgwood, are as follows: —

The David Brainerd Case.

October 10th, Friday, at —, Mr. Wedgwood and I sitting. The board moved after a short pause and one preliminary circling.

"David — David — David — dead 143 years." The butler at this moment announced lunch, and Mr. Wedgwood said to the *soi-disant* spirit, "Will you go on for us afterwards, as we must break off now?"

---

[2] In Human Personality, Vol. II, p. 168, Mr. Myers refers to this element of handwriting as a proof of identity, and gives a remarkable case in point on p. 466. An able, critical paper by Sir H. Babington Smith, C.B., which discusses this and other evidence given by automatic writing, was published in Vol. V of the Proceedings S.P.R.

"I will try."

During lunch Mr. Wedgwood was reckoning up the date indicated as 1747, and conjecturing that the control was perhaps David Hume, whom he thought had died about then. On our beginning again to sit, the following was volunteered: —

"I am not Hume. I have come with Theodora's sister. I was attracted to her during her life in America. My work was in that land, and my earthly toil was cut short early, as hers has been. I died at thirty years old. I toiled five years, carrying forward the lamp of God's truth as I knew it."

Mr. Wedgwood remarked that he must have been a missionary.

"Yes, in Susquehannah and other places."

"Can you give any name besides David?" "

David Bra — David Bra — David Brain — David Braine — David Brain." Mr. W. "Do you mean that your name is Braine?"

"Very nearly right."

Mr. W.: "Try again."

"David Braine. Not quite all the name; right so far as it goes. ... I was born in 1717." Mr. W.: "Are you an American?" "America I hold to be my country as we consider things. I worked at " (sentence ends with a line of D's.) After an interval Mr. Wedgwood said he thought it had come into his head who our control was. He had some recollection that in the 18th century a man named David Brainerd was missionary to the North American Indians. We sat again and the following was written: — "I am glad you know me. I had not power to complete name or give more details. I knew that secret of the district. It was guarded by the Indians, and was made known to two independent circles.

Neither of them succeeded, but the day will come that will uncover the gold." It was suggested that this meant Heavenly truth.

"I spoke of earthly gold." Mr. Wedgwood said the writing was so faint he thought power was failing.

"Yes, nearly gone. I wrote during my five years of work. It kept my heart alive." Mr. Wedgwood writes: —

I could not think at first where I had ever heard of Brainerd, but I learn from my daughter in London that my sister-in-law, who lived with me 40 or 50 years ago, was a great admirer of Brainerd, and seemed to have an account of his life, but I am quite certain that I never opened the book and knew nothing of the dates, which are all correct, as well as his having been a missionary to the Susquehannahs.

My daughter has sent me extracts from his life, stating that he was born in 1718 and not 1717 as planchette wrote. But the *Biographical Dictionary* says that he died in 1747, aged 30.

Mrs. R. writes that she had no knowledge whatever of David Brainerd before this.

The *Biographical Dictionary* gives the following: —

"Brainerd, David. A celebrated American missionary, who signalised himself by his successful endeavours to convert the Indians on the Susquehannah, Delaware, etc. Died, aged 30, 1747." It is perhaps noteworthy in connection with the last sentence of the planchette writing that in the life of Brainerd by Jonathan Edwards extracts given from his journal show that lie wrote a good deal, e.g., "Feb. 3, 1744. Could not but write as well as meditate," etc "Feb. 15, 1745. Was engaged in writing almost all the day." He invariably speaks of comfort in connection with writing.

The other case given by Mr. Wedgwood is too lengthy to quote in detail, but a brief summary is given because, like the preceding, it is one of the few cases where the soi-disani spirit asserts he lived on earth very many years ago.

The Colonel Gurwood Case

In this case the automatist was also Mr, Wedgwood's friend Mrs. R., a lady of unimpeachable integrity as already stated, and the mode of sitting with planchette was the same as described in the previous case. The sitting took place in June, 1889, and is recorded in the Journal of the S.P.R. for that year. Notes of the sitting were written at the time and the planchette writing copied.

As soon as the sitting began planchette wrote that a spirit was present who wanted to draw; forthwith a rough drawing was made of the top of an embattled wall, or mural coronet, from which an arm holding a sword arose. Planchette wrote, "Sorry I can't do better, was meant for a test, J.G." Asked what the drawing represented, the answer came, "Something that was given me." Asked if J.G. was a man or woman, planchette wrote "Man, John G." Mr. Wedgwood said he knew a J. Giffard, was that right? The reply came, "Not Giffard, John Gurwood, no connection of yours." Asked how he died, "I killed myself on Christmas Day, it will be forty-four years ago next Christmas," i.e. in 1845. Asked if he were in the army, the reply came, "Yes, but it was the pen, not the sword that did for me." Asked if pen was right, and if so, was he an author who failed? the reply was "Yes, pen, I did not fail, the pen was too much for me after the wound." Asked where he was wounded the reply was "In the Peninsular in the head, I was wounded in 1810." Asked if the drawing was a crest and had anything to do with the wound planchette wrote "It came from that and was given me, the drawing was a test; remember my name, power fails to explain, stop now." Mr. Wedgwood then recalled that a Colonel Gurwood edited the despatches of the Duke of Wellington, but he had never read any history of the Peninsular war and knew no details of Gurwood's life or of his crest: Mrs. R. was wholly ignorant of the matter.

After the sitting Mr. Wedgwood looked up the matter and found that Colonel Gurwood led the forlorn hope at the storming of Ciudad Rodrigo in 1812,[3] and the Annual Register states that he then "received a wound in the skull which affected him for the remainder of his life." In recognition of his bravery he received a grant of arms in 1812,

---

[3] Planchette wrote 1810, if the figures were correctly read.

which are specified in the Book of Family Crests, — and symbolised in the crest, — as follows, "Out of a mural coronet, a ruined castle in centre, and therefrom an arm, holding a scimitar." The drawing given as a test is practically this crest, though the ruined castle was doubtless too difficult to be drawn by planchette. Furthermore, the Annual Register for 1845 states that Colonel Gurwood committed suicide on Christmas Day that year, in a fit of despondency, and remarks that it was probably owing to the overstrain caused by his laborious work in editing the despatches; this explains the automatic writing, "Pen was too much for me after the wound." None of these facts were known to Mr. Wedgwood or Mrs. R. before the automatic writing came.

In subsequent sittings Colonel Gurwood again controlled planchette and gave some further details of his life, the storming of the fort and names of persons, all of which were found to be correct so far as they could be verified. But the evidential value of these later sittings must be discounted, owing to the fact that Mr. Wedgwood had meanwhile looked up Napier's *Peninsular War* and might have gained some of the information from its pages.

Many other striking illustrations of survival after death might be given, but the reader who is interested must go to the original papers to which I have referred earlier. Sir Oliver Lodge has had some remarkable cases of "spirit identity" through other automatists, and especially through Mrs. Piper, with whom he has had numerous sittings.

These cases he has critically investigated: many of them relate to himself and his family, revealing facts entirely unknown to the medium and at the time unknown to Sir Oliver, which subsequently have been found to be correct. The conviction to which Sir Oliver has been driven, from his own personal and long continued experience, and which he has publicly avowed, is that there is undeniably evidence of survival after death.

One of the most recent cases corroborative of this conclusion relates to messages purporting to come from his gallant and beloved son Lieut. Raymond Lodge, who lost his life in the war. Particulars of this case were read before the Society for Psychical Research, and I made an abstract of that paper, — kindly revised by Sir. O. Lodge, — for insertion in this place. But since then Sir Oliver has published his work "Raymond," where additional evidence is given, and as this book has been so widely read and noticed in the press it seems needless to refer to the matter further.

Moreover, nearly all the evidence I have cited has come through private and unpaid mediums, and this was not the case in all the Raymond messages.

The Right Hon. Gerald Balfour has recently (Dec. 1916) read a paper before the S.P.R., which in the opinion of some competent judges affords the most striking evidence of survival yet obtained. For it apparently demonstrates the continued and vigorous mental activity of the late Professor A. W. Verrall and the late Professor Butcher, both eminent classical scholars. The evidence exhibits a range of knowledge, and constructive ability in framing a classical puzzle, such as could not be accounted for by telepathy, or the subliminal self of the automatist. The automatic script came through a lady who is well known to Mr. Balfour, and to whom reference has already been made under her pseudonym of "Mrs. Willett."

Mr. Balfour affirms with confidence that Mrs. Willett is as little familiar with classical subjects as the average of educated women.

Nevertheless recondite classical allusions like the "Ear of Dionysius" (which forms the title of Mr. Balfour's paper) and other obscure topics were given in the script, the whole forming a literary puzzle which remained insoluble, until later on the script furnished the key. Mr. Balfour says it is difficult to suppose that the materials employed in the construction of this puzzle could have been drawn from the mind of any living person; he believes they must be ascribed to some disembodied intelligence or intelligences, and there are cogent reasons for believing that the real authors were, — as they profess to be, — the late Professors Verrall and Butcher. The paper has been published in the "Proceedings" of the S.P.R. Vol. 1. XXIX.

CHAPTER 17

EVIDENCE FROM ABROAD OF SURVIVAL

"There is no death, what seems so is transition;
This life of mortal breath
Is but a suburb of the life Elysian,
Whose portal we call death."

— *Longfellow.*

It must be borne in mind that competent psychical researchers in other parts of the world besides the United Kingdom have for many years past been at work, and obtained what they deemed to be conclusive evidence of survival. In this chapter I will cite a fragment of the evidence that comes to us from America and Russia.

No investigator of psychical phenomena has given more time to the critical investigation of the evidence on behalf of survival than the late Dr. Hodgson during his residence in the United States. In fact he made this subject practically his sole occupation for many years before his death. He was so far from being credulous that he detected and exposed many spurious phenomena, and in my opinion he carried his scepticism too far as regards other mediums than Mrs. Piper, with whom he had innumerable sittings. At first he attempted to explain away the results he obtained through Mrs. Piper; but ultimately was driven to the spirit hypothesis; his own words are: "Having tried the hypothesis of telepathy from the living for several years ... I have no hesitation in affirming with the most absolute assurance that the 'spirit' hypothesis is justified by its fruits and the other hypothesis is not."

The conclusion at which Dr. Hodgson arrived, after his prolonged and critical experimental study of Mrs. Piper, he summed up in the following words: —

> "At the present time I cannot profess to have any doubt but that the chief 'communicators' to whom I have referred in the foregoing pages [of his report] are veritably the personalities that they claim to be, that they have survived the change we call death, and that they have directly communicated with us whom we call living, through Mrs. Piper's entranced organism."[1]

However improbable sceptics may consider this conclusion, we must remember that Dr. Hodgson began his long and arduous investigation with just the same doubt and even disbelief in the "spiritualistic" hypothesis as any of his critics may entertain. Moreover he was not only a remarkably sane and shrewd investigator, but one specially skilled in exposing fraud and illusion. This was shown, as I have remarked, by his exposure of various alleged spiritualistic phenomena which had mystified and baffled some of the ablest enquirers. Hence those who have not had Dr. Hodgson's experience have no right to place mere notions of what is probable and improbable, or possible and impossible, against his deliberate opinion, arrived at after many years of patient and painstaking enquiry.

If it appeared that any other competent investigator, after an equally exhaustive research, had come to an opposite conclusion, sceptics would be justified in their hesitancy to accept the experimental evidence of survival after death. But this is precisely what cannot be adduced. On the contrary, so far as I know, every trained observer, of any nationality, who has devoted years to a similar experimental research, either has arrived at practically the same conclusion as Dr. Hodgson and other able investigators, or has been forced to admit that the phenomena in question are at present wholly inexplicable.

Since Dr. Hodgson's death his work in America has been chiefly carried on by his friend Dr. J. H. Hyslop, formerly Professor at Columbia University. Dr. Hyslop, who now lives in New York, has devoted his life to this work and is preeminent as an able, courageous and indefatigable

---

[1] "Proc. S.P.R.," Vol. XIII, p. 406.

worker at psychical research. Amid his amazingly voluminous contributions to the "Proceedings" and "Journal of the American Society for Psychical Research" there are numerous papers affording striking evidences of survival after death. This evidence has driven him to abandon the agnostic views he formerly held and become a convinced believer in the spirit hypothesis. As Dr. Hyslop is a trained psychologist his opinion is all the more valuable.

During the last six years Dr. Hyslop has had constant sittings with a lady, Mrs. Chenoweth (pseudonym), who has developed strong mediumistic powers. The following is a brief narrative of one of the evidential cases of survival obtained through Mrs. Chenoweth, whose entire trustworthiness and honesty are not disputed. This case illustrates the trivial nature of the incidents given to afford identification.

The Tausch Case.

Dr. Hyslop states that he received a letter from a lady in Germany, of whom he had never heard before, asking him if he could recommend a psychic, as she had recently lost her husband, and in her great distress wanted to find some evidence that would assure her of her husband's continued existence. Dr. Hyslop answered that he knew of no psychic in Germany, but if she would come to America he would arrange for sittings with a psychic in whom he had confidence. The lady replied that this was impossible, but gave the name (different from her own) and address of a sister in Boston, U.S.A., who might take her place. Accordingly Dr. Hyslop arranged for the sister to meet him, but gave her no information of the psychic's name or address, nor did he give any information to the psychic (Mrs. Chenoweth) of the visitor or the object of the sitting. Before admitting the visitor Dr. Hyslop put Mrs. Chenoweth into a trance state, when the normal faculties are in abeyance; in fact, Dr. Hyslop was satisfied that the medium did not even know whether her visitor was a man or a woman.

Automatic writing by Mrs. Chenoweth's hand began and the unseen communicator indicated that a gentleman was present who was anxious to make his existence known to his wife, that he was a philosopher and a friend of the late Professor William James of Harvard, that his mother was dead, and to indicate his identity pointed to a cavity in his mouth where a tooth had been extracted. Of course none of these facts were known to Dr. Hyslop, but in the hope they might apply to the husband of the lady who wrote to him, he communicated them to the widow in Germany and found they were all correct; her husband had been a lecturer on philosophy, was a friend of Prof. W. James and had lost a tooth, though the cavity was not visible. Then the unseen communicator stated the gentleman just before his decease, had great pain in his head, with confusion of ideas and longed for home, adding that he was not away from home where he died, but it was not like his home. All this turned out to be true, he died in his old home in Germany and not in his home in America.

Then some striking evidence of identity came, the communicator stated the deceased wished to prove that he was not a fool to believe in spirits, and that he was greatly interested in some records which had been lent to him "by his friend James." In response to Dr. Hyslop's enquiries the widow wrote that before her husband's death Prof. James had lent him some records to read which had impressed him. All present at the sitting were of course wholly ignorant of this and of the other incidents. The unseen communicator went on to say that he was fond of fixing things and putting clocks to right; that he used to annotate his books and apparently attempted to sign his name, for the letters T. h. came. In reply to enquiries the widow wrote to Dr. Hyslop that her husband did fuss a great deal about clocks, that he annotated his books and always read with a pencil in his hand. Now the name of the deceased was Tausch, the first and last letters of which were given.

Later on the communicator made great efforts to give his name, by automatic writing through the entranced Mrs. Chenoweth, and without any help from Dr. Hyslop (who of course knew the name but no other particulars) there came "Taussh, Tauch and Taush," phonetically correct. Dr. Hyslop then addressed the communicator in German and got replies in German, among them that the visitor was his "Geschwister," which was correct, though Mrs. Chenoweth (through whom of course the automatic writing came) only knew four words of German, not included in these replies. Other points of interest establishing identity also came, such as that the deceased used to carry a small bag containing his manuscripts and reading glass, and that he had taken a long railway journey shortly before his death. In reply to enquiry Mrs. Tausch wrote that her husband always used to carry a small bag in which he put his manuscripts and eye glasses, and that he had taken a long rail journey shortly before his death.

Dr. Hyslop says, all the incidents described were unknown to him and required confirmation by correspondence with Mrs. Tausch in Germany, the only living person who knew their truth. Nor in all his years of sittings with Mrs. Chenoweth has Dr. Hyslop ever had any communications containing similar incidents to those above described. The name might have been filched by telepathy from Dr. Hyslop's mind, but there is no evidence that Mrs. Chenoweth has the slightest telepathic percipience. Even if Mrs. Chenoweth had known the name and address of Mrs. Tausch in Germany (which, of course, she did not), she could not have communicated with her, as only 36 hours elapsed from the first to the last sitting. There was no one in America who could have given her the information.

I agree with Dr. Hyslop that no adequate explanation of this case by telepathy or subliminal knowledge or collusion on the put of the medium can be given, and that the simplest and most reasonable solution is that the information was derived from the mind of the deceased person.

But I must draw to a close my imperfect selection from the mass of first-hand evidence that is being accumulated in proof of spirit identity.

The following case is chosen because it comes from wholly independent and able investigators in Russia. Here, too, any explanation based on collusion, telepathy, or the knowledge of those present, is out of the question. Unfortunately the evidence is somewhat lengthy, but as it combines the manifestation of physical phenomena with evidence of the identity of the communicating intelligence, it forms an important link between the two classes of phenomena. No paid or professional mediums were present, and the *bona fides* of all taking part appears to be unquestionable.

This case is quoted from Vol. VI of the *Proceedings* of the S.P.R., where the reader will find other similar evidential cases in a valuable paper by Mr. F. W. H. Myers.

The Pereliguine Case.

A sitting was held in the house of M. A. Nartzeff, at Tambof, Russia, on Nov. 18th, 1887. M. Nartzeff belongs to the Russian nobility and is a landed proprietor; his aunt, housekeeper and the official physician to the municipality of Tambof were the only other persons present.

The sitting began at 10 p.m. at a table placed in the middle of the room, by the light of a night-light placed on the mantelpiece. All doors were closed. The left hand of each sitter was placed on the right hand of his neighbour, and each foot touched the neighbour's foot, so that during the whole of the sitting all hands and feet were under control. Sharp raps were heard in the floor, and afterwards in the wall and the ceiling, after which the blows sounded immediately in the middle of the table, as if someone had struck it from above with his fist; and with such violence, and so often, that the table trembled the whole time.

M. Nartzeff asked, "Can you answer rationally, giving three raps for yes, one for no?" "Yes." "Do you wish to answer by using the alphabet?" "Yes." "Spell your name." The alphabet was repeated, and the letters indicated by three raps — "Anastasie Pereliguine." "I beg you to say now why you have come and what you desire." "I am a wretched woman. Pray for me. Yesterday, during the day, I died at the hospital. The day before yesterday I poisoned myself with matches." "Give us some details about yourself. How old were you? Give a rap for each year." Seventeen raps. "Who were you?" "I was a housemaid. I poisoned myself with matches." "Why did you poison yourself?" "I will not say. I will say nothing more." After this a heavy table which was near the wall, outside the chain of hands, came up rapidly three times towards the table round which the chain was made, and each time it was pushed backwards, no one knew by what means. Seven raps (the signal agreed upon for the close of the sitting), were now heard in the wall; and at 11.20 p.m. the séance came to an end.

(Here follow the signatures of all those present, with their attestation.) Those who were present also signed the following attestation: — "The undersigned having been present at the séance of November 18th, 1887, at the house of M. A. N. Nartzeff, hereby certify that they had no previous knowledge of the existence or the death of Anastasie Pereliguine, and that they heard her name for the first time at the above mentioned séance." Enquiries were then made as to the truth of the message purporting to have come from an unknown suicide. Dr. Touloucheff, the official physician who was present at the sitting, and who signed the above documents, states that at first he did not believe there was any truth in the message. For he writes: — "In my capacity as physician of the municipality I am at once informed by the police of all cases of suicide. But as Pereliguine had added that her death had taken place at the hospital, and since at Tambof we have only one hospital, that of the 'Institutions de Bienfaisance,' which is not within my official survey, and whose authorities, in such cases as this, themselves send for the police, or the magistrate; — I sent a letter to my colleague, Dr. Sundblatt, the head physician of this hospital, and without explaining my reason simply asked him to inform me whether there had been any recent case of suicide at the hospital, and, if so, to give me the name and particulars. The following is a copy of his reply, certified by Dr. Sundblatt's own signature.

(Signed) "N. Touloucheff."
"November 19th, 1887.

"My dear Colleague, — On the 16th of this month I was on duty; and on that day two patients were admitted to the Hospital, who had poisoned themselves with phosphorous. The first, Vera Kosovitch, aged 38, wife of a clerk in the public service . . . was taken in at 8 p.m.; the second a servant named Anastasie Pereliguine, aged 17, was taken in at 10 p.m. This second patient had swallowed, besides an infusion of boxes of matches, a glass of kerosene, and at the time of her admission was already very ill.

She died at 1 p.m. on the 17th, and the post-mortem examination has been made today. Kosovitch died yesterday, and the post-mortem is fixed for to-morrow.

Kosovitch said that she had taken the phosphorous in an access of melancholy, but Pereliguine did not state her reason for poisoning herself.

(Signed) "TH. Sundblatt."

When M. Nartzeff was asked if the housekeeper, who was at the sitting, could possibly have heard of the suicide, he replied as follows:—

"In answer to your letter I inform you that my aunt's housekeeper is not a housekeeper strictly speaking, but rather a friend of the family, having been nearly fifteen years with us, and possessing our entire confidence. She could not have already learnt the fact of the suicide, as she had no relations or friends in Tambof, and never leaves the house.

"The hospital in question is situated at the other end of the town, about 5 vcrsts from my house. Dr. Sundblatt informs me, on the authority of the procesverbal of the inquest, that Pereliguine was able to read and write.

(This was in answer to the enquiry whether the deceased could have understood alphabetic communication.)"

There are few cases which in my opinion afford so simple and striking a demonstration of the identity of the discarnate personality as the foregoing. There was no professional medium; all the witnesses concerned give their full names; they are persons of repute, and after the facts were published their testimony was never impugned.

Those who remain in doubt as to the value of the evidence adduced in the foregoing chapters should remember that it is, and probably always will be, impossible to obtain such conclusive logical demonstration of survival after death as will satisfy every agnostic. But "formal logical sequence" as Cardinal Newman said in his *Grammar of Assent*, "is not, in fact, the method by which we are enabled to become certain of what is concrete... The real and necessary method ... is the cumulation of probabilities, independent of each other, arising out of the nature and circumstances of the particular case which is under review," and so the truth of the spirit hypothesis, and of spirit-identity, like the truth of all disputed matters, is to be judged in this way, — that is, by the whole evidence taken together.[2] In concluding this chapter I wish to draw attention to a valuable and brightly written work in two

---

[2] Kant knew nothing of the telepathy or psychical research, but even his critical mind admitted that "in regard to ghost stories, while I doubt any one of them, still have a certain faith in the whole of them taken together."— *Dreams of a Spirit Seer*, p. 88.

volumes, strangely entitled *On the Cosmic Relations*, by Mr. Henry Holt, the widely esteemed American publisher. In this work Mr. Holt gives a mass of evidence obtained by himself, as well as by Dr. Hodgson and others, that has convinced him of the existence of super-normal phenomena, and the impossibility of explaining away by telepathy or otherwise the evidence on behalf of survival after bodily death.

Part 5

CHAPTER 18

CLAIRVOYANCE: PSYCHOLOGY OF TRANCE PHENOMENA

"We all walk in mysteries. We are surrounded by an atmosphere of which we do not know what is stirring in it, or how it is connected with our own spirit. So much is certain, that in particular cases we can put out the feelers of our soul beyond its bodily limits, and that a presentiment, nay, an actual insight into the immediate future, is accorded to it."[1]

Many difficulties and perplexing problems arise in reviewing the brief and imperfect outline of spiritualistic phenomena that I have attempted to give in the preceding pages.

These it is desirable to consider in the present and succeeding chapter.

Some of these difficulties may be removed when we obtain a fuller knowledge of the whole subject. Those of my readers who approach these problems for the first time will, of course, bear in mind that only a fragment of the already accessible evidence could be presented within the compass of a small volume. Moreover, I have been obliged

---
[1] Goethe, "Conversations with Eckermann," Bonn's Library, p. 290.

to omit certain portions of the wide field of psychical research, which have received prolonged and critical investigation, and must be considered in any explanation of spiritualistic phenomena. One of these is telepathy, now largely accepted, and to which I will return in the last chapter; another is alleged clairvoyance. On this latter a few words must now be said.[2]

The term clairvoyance unfortunately is used to denote two distinct aspects of supernormal faculty. In one sense it is employed to express the transcendental perception of distant scenes or of hidden material objects.

That such a faculty exists I have not the least doubt; it may be evoked in the higher stages of hypnotic trance or it may occur in certain sensitives in their normal state.

Mrs. H. Sidgwick has published a searching investigation of what has been called "travelling clairvoyance,"[3] and in my lengthy researches on the so-called Divining — or Dowsing — rod, I have shown that a good dowser unquestionably possesses a somewhat similar faculty, though one unrecognised by science.[4] The term *tele-aesthesia* has been suggested by Mr. F. W. H. Myers for this faculty; implying the perception of terrestrial objects or conditions independently of the recognised channels of sense, and also independently of any possible knowledge derived from telepathy.

The word clairvoyance has also been used to denote the transcendental vision of beings on another plane of existence. It is alleged that many mediums have this faculty in their normal state, or in their entranced condition, and also in their "waking stage" between the two. Here also the evidence on behalf of such a faculty appears to me indisputable; but the difficulty of obtaining conclusive evidence on this point is great, owing to the possible intrusion of telepathy, — that convenient and hard worked hypothesis.

I have little doubt that clairvoyance in both its meanings, as well as telepathy, enter largely into, and afford some explanation of, the communications which purport to come from the spirit world. But we must

---

[2] In a letter published in the *London Times* so long ago as 1876, I said that before we could hope to arrive at any definite Conclusion! upon alleged spirit communications we must know whether clairvoyance and (what is now called) telepathy really exist.

[3] See Proceedings S.P.R., Vol. VII et seq.

[4] See Proceedings S.P.R., Vols. XIII and XV; also for a brief resume of the whole subject see Chap. XII of ray book on Psychical Research in the "Home University Library."

assume telepathy from the dead as well as the living, and we need evidence that the medium actually possesses power as a percipient, or unconscious receiver, of a telepathic impress.

It is quite time experimental psychologists and psychical researchers should admit that super-normal phenomena do occur, and test, as well as propose, various theories, now often advanced without proof.

Students of psychical research will find the most important and critical examination of the psychology of the trance phenomena of spiritualism in the monograph by Mrs. Henry Sidgwick, which fills the bulky volume of the *Proceedings of the S.P.R.* for December, 1915. This laborious research deals with Mrs. Piper's trance phenomena — but applies more or less fully to other genuine mediums — when evidence is also riled of knowledge acquired otherwise than through the senses, whether from the living or from the dead. The object of the paper is to throw light on the question

> "Whether the intelligence that speaks or writes in the trance, and is sometimes in telepathic communication with other minds (whether of the Living or of the dead) is other than a phase, or centre of consciousness, of Mrs. Piper herself."

Mrs. Sidgwick emphatically admits that Mrs. Piper has super-normal means of obtaining knowledge, but comes to the conclusion that Mrs. Piper's trance, and presumably that of other similar mediums —

> "Is probably a state of self-induced hypnosis in which her hypnotic self personates different characters either consciously and deliberately, or unconsciously and believing herself to be the person she represents, and sometimes probably in a state of consciousness intermediate between the two. . . And further . . . she can obtain perfectly, and for the most part fragmentarily, telepathic impressions. . . Such impressions are not only received by her as the result of her own telepathic activity or that of other spirits — spirits of the living or may be of the dead — but rise partially or completely into the consciousness operating in the trance communications, and so are recognized."[5]

---

[5] "Proceedings S.P.R.," Vol. XXVIII, p. 330.

Telepathy from the living, and also sometimes from the discarnate, combined with a real or imaginary dissociation of personality of the medium during the trance state, is therefore Mrs. Sidgwick's view of such phenomena. This was in substance Dr. Hodgson's opinion in the earlier stage of his investigations. But, as Mrs. Sidgwick says, "he had apparently already abandoned this hypothesis when he published his first report." As is well known, and was previously mentioned, Dr. Hodgson and Mr. Myers, like many other critical students, eventually were driven to accept the spirit hypothesis as the most consistent and simplest solution.

Mrs. Sidgwick's conclusions are unquestionably entitled to careful consideration, and doubtless will commend themselves to many psychologists and conservative thinkers. To a large extent, if without presumption I may express an opinion, I believe they are justified, and explain many of the perplexing anomalies, false statements and personation of great names, in these trance communications.

Thus in a sitting with Mrs. Piper, in 1899, the Jewish lawgiver "Moses of old" purported to communicate, and prophesied that in the near future there would be great wars and bloodshed and then the approach of the millennium. But in this great war Russia and France would be on one side against England and America on the other, whilst Germany would not take any serious part in the war. After this "Moses" added a good deal of solemn twaddle.

Then another time Sir Walter Scott purports to communicate and tells Dr. Hodgson that if he wishes to know anything about the planet Mars he was to be sure to call up the novelist, as he had visited all the planets; asked if he had seen a planet further away than Saturn, the *soi-disant* Walter Scott answered "Mercury!" Julius Caesar also purports to control and Madame Guyon; but another and more frequent control was George Eliot (the novelist), who sometimes acts as the communicator, for she says,

> "We speak by thought unless we act upon some machine, so-called medium, when our thoughts are expressed to the controlling spirit who registers them for us."

This may be true enough; but the real George Eliot would never speak so ungrammatically as to say, "I hardly know as there is enough light to communicate," or again, "Do not know as I have ever seen a haunted house," words which are reported to be her own.

Similar grammatical mistakes are made by other educated controls.

But some of the most conclusive evidence of personation is given by the control who purported to be the Rev. Stainton Moses.

The names of three spirit friends (the "Imperator band"), whom the real Stainton Moses could never have forgotten, were given, and "not one of these names is true or has the least semblance of truth," Professor Newbold tells us. Again Dr. Stanley Hall in a sitting with Mrs. Piper, asked if a niece, Bessie Beals, could communicate?

She professed to come and gave various messages at several sittings, but she had never existed, Dr. Hall having given a fictitious name and relationship! Thus it will be seen that we cannot take these communications at their face value, as they are sometimes manifestly false, although presented to the sitter with a dramatic distinctness and corresponding character, which give them a life-like reality.

They probably represent phases of the hypnotic self of Mrs. Piper, created by some verbal or telepathic suggestion from the mind of the sitter. In spite of this unquestionable personation of deceased personalities Mrs. Sidgwick admits that —

> "Veridical communications are received, some of which, there is good reason to believe come from the dead, and therefore imply a genuine communicator in the background" (p. 204).

Here it is well to note the meaning attached to the words "control" and "communicator." By the former is meant the intelligence which is, or professes to be, in direct communication with the sitter through the voice or writing of the medium. By "communicator" is meant the intelligence for which the control acts as amanuensis or interpreter, or whose remarks or telepathic impress the control repeats to the sitter through the medium. This definition, given by Mrs. Sidgwick, is generally accepted.

The difficulties of communicating are necessarily great, as we cannot suppose that a physical process or physical organs of speech and hearing are employed by the communicators. In fact they tell us, as Swedenborg told us long before telepathy was discovered, that spirits converse by thought. Visual perception is sometimes suggested. One unseen communicator says:

> "If you could see me as I stand here, you would see every gesture I make, which is copied by Rector [the control]; he imitates me as I speak to you."

Mental pictures, as Dr. Hyslop has stated, float before the mind of the medium and the difficulty seems to be in selecting the appropriate one. Difficulties of hearing, or telepathic percipience, are also mentioned, especially the difficulty in getting a name. Then there is mind wandering and mental confusion, one communicator, speaking through Mrs. Piper, says: —

> "I am talking as it were through a thick fog and it often suffocates me," and again, "I can't get the right word, my mind is so confused"; "the conditions are suffocating."

The sceptic, of course, will assert this is only the clever way the medium assumes to cloak her ignorance, but there is every reason to believe it represents a genuine difficulty in the transmission of ideas from the unseen to the seen. We know the uncertain conditions of telepathy here, and they may exist on the other side when the control is trying to impress ideas on the sub-conscious self of the medium.

Some light is thus thrown on the scrappy, disjointed, and confused nature of many veridical messages. The primary need of establishing their identity probably explains why the communications are so largely fragmentary reminiscences of the earth life of the deceased.

Whilst the bulk of the communications appear to exhibit a truncated, dream-like intelligence on the part of the deceased, — as if a dream zone intervened between the two worlds, — this is not always the case. Some recent scripts, as in Mr. Gerald Balfour's paper on the Ear of Dionysius, show not only the cooperation of two or more discarnate minds, but also give positive evidence of an ability and wide classical knowledge, quite beyond the power of the automatist. The cryptic allusions, it is true, need considerable ingenuity, learning and skill to make the evidence intelligible to ordinary minds. This recondite mode of communication may be adopted to prevent suspicion that the message is derived from terrene minds by telepathy or other sources of error. Those who have not the necessary time or knowledge to unravel these mosaics of classical scholarship, must rest content with the assurance that competent and unbiassed investigators have been convinced that they afford convincing evidence of the identity of the deceased persons from whom they profess to come.

CHAPTER 19

DIFFICULTIES AND OBJECTIONS CONSIDERED

But trust that those we call the dead
Are breathers of an ampler day
Forever nobler ends."

— *In Memoriam, cxviii.*

In the course of our discussion we have seen a dreary agnosticism, and the materialistic tendency of scientific enquiry and modern commercialism, confronted with the indisputable facts of psychical research. The revolution in thought which those facts imply and necessitate, will in course of time be apparent, and be a great gain both to knowledge and religion.

There remain, however, many unsolved problems. Why are the unseen communicators so seldom conscious of other friends on earth, outside the narrow circle of the sitters? Are earth memories only revived by some association of ideas in the communicator or control with those in the minds of the circle? Why have we no messages that will stand critical enquiry, from the greatest or the saintliest men and women who once lived on earth? Why is there no clear and consistent account of the surroundings, and the occupation, of those who have passed into the spiritual world? These and many other questions naturally arise and we can only hope that in the future more light may be thrown upon these perplexities.

There has certainly been a thinning of the veil which separates us from those who have passed into the unseen, but one is tempted to ask why only a corner of the veil has been lifted here and there, and no full revelation given to us of life in the spiritual world? Moreover, what is given appears so inadequate and so unsatisfying.

But it is probable we shall never be able to see behind the veil with the clearness and assurance that Swedenborg claimed to possess, although he warned others off the ground he trod. There may be, and are I believe, good reasons for this obscure vision.

If everyone were as certain as they are of day following night, that after the momentary darkness of death they would pass into an endless life of brightness and freedom, such as many spiritualists depict, it is possible few would wish to remain on earth. May be multitudes of earth-worn and weary souls would resort to some painless and lethal drug, that would enable them to enter a realm where they hoped their troubles would be forever ended. A vain and foolish hope, for the discipline of life on earth is necessary for us all, and none can hope to attain a higher life without the educative experience of trial and conflict.

Doubtless much of the scepticism that exists in religious minds, as to the genuineness of these automatic communications, arises from the belief that messages which might reach us from beyond this life would authenticate themselves by their elevated wisdom and piety, or by their transcendent knowledge. Such a belief has its root in the popular notion that at death we are suddenly transformed by our passage out of this world into a state of sublime holiness and wisdom, or else of utter and hopeless misery. The good are supposed to enter at once into their final state of endless bliss, and the evil, by their transition from earth, into their final state of an endless Hell. One of the immense benefits which Swedenborg has conferred on theology is the shattering of this crude medieval creed, — not only among his followers, but in a much wider circle; and today the same may be said of spiritualism, which confutes the popular idea of heaven and hell and teaches us the continuity of our existence here and hereafter. Long ago Milton with singular prescience wrote: —

"What if earth
Be but the shadow of Heaven, and things therein
Each to other like, more than on earth is thought?"

DIFFICULTIES AND OBJECTIONS CONSIDERED

Sir Arthur Conan Doyle, who has publicly expressed his belief in Spiritualism, remarks: "We find ourselves in apparent communication with the dead very shortly after they leave us, and they seem to be exactly as they were before we parted"; and he adds that though Spiritualism is in no way antagonistic to Christianity it removes many of the crude conceptions and modifies some of the doctrines which are popularly held.

Turning now to those who, like the Roman Catholics and many others, believe all spiritualistic phenomena to be the work of evil spirits and therefore to be shunned, the best reply is "by their fruits ye shall know them." We are told "to believe not every spirit but prove the spirits whether they are of God." An able Roman Catholic layman, Mr. J. G. Raupert, who has had considerable experience of Spiritualism, has written much on the dangers of this subject, and with much that he says I agree; but like the late Monsignor Benson he naturally regards the whole matter as one banned by his Church, and therefore as he remarks, "it is an eating of the fruit of the forbidden tree of knowledge."[1] Most of the anathemas pronounced against spiritualism by Protestant and Roman ecclesiastics come from the lips of men who know little or nothing of the subject. Some who have taken the trouble to enquire, have come to believe that spiritism reveals the existence of some mysterious power which may be of a more or less malignant character.

Certainly the Apostle Paul in the Epistle to the Ephesians, points to a race of spiritual creatures, not made of flesh and blood, inhabiting the air around us, and able injuriously to affect mankind. Good as well as mischievous agencies doubtless exist in the unseen; this, of course, is equally true if the phenomena are due to those who have once lived on the earth. "There are as great fools in the spirit world as there ever were in this," as Henry More said over 200 years ago. In any case, granting the existence of a spiritual world, it is necessary to be on our guard against the invasion of our will by a lower order of intelligence and morality.

The danger to the medium lies, in my opinion, not only in the loss of spiritual stamina, but in the possible deprivation of that birthright we each are given to cherish, our individuality, our true selfhood;

---

[1] Miss H. A. Dallas has written an admirable little book, dealing with the objections to spiritualism from a religious point of view, and furnishes a cogent reply to many of the points raised by Mr. Raupert.

just as in another way this may be impaired by sensuality, opium, or alcohol.

The great object of our life on earth appears to be, on the one hand, the upbuilding, strengthening, and perpetuation of our separate and distinct personalities; and, on the other, the awakening and development in each of the consciousness of an underlying Unity, which links each person into a larger Personal Life common to all, "in Whom we live and move and have our being"; in a word, the realisation of the fact that we are integral parts and members of one Body. In so far as Spiritualism aids or thwarts these objects its moral effect must be judged; like mysticism, I think it aids the latter object, but is apt to endanger the former.

What I have said, let me once again repeat, has obviously no bearing on prudent scientific enquiry. Indiscriminate condemnation and ignorant credulity are, in truth, the two most dangerous elements with which the public are confronted in connection with Spiritualism.

The explorer speedily discovers that both are out of place, and in the ardour of the search — unless properly equipped and guided by the *lumen siccum* of the scientific spirit — is likely to become engulfed in a Serbonian bog, even if no worse fate befall him.

It is because I feel that in the fearless pursuit of truth it is the paramount duty of science to lead the way, and erect such signposts as may be needed in the vast territory we dimly see before us, that I so strongly deprecate the past and the present scornful attitude of many in the scientific world.

Furthermore, as a famous philosopher has remarked of cognate facts, "The phenomena under discussion are, at least from a philosophical standpoint, of all facts presented to us by the whole of experience, without comparison the most important; it is, therefore, the duty of every learned man to make himself thoroughly acquainted with them."[2]

---

[2] Schopenhauer; who is here speaking of mesmerism and clairvoyance, but his observation applies still more emphatically to the phenomena of Spiritualism. The passage is from the *Versucht uber Geistersehen*, and is quoted in Du Prel's *Philosophy of Mysticism*.

CHAPTER 20

CAUTIONS AND SUGGESTIONS

"How pure of heart and sound in head,
With what divine affections bold
Should be the man whose thought would hold
An hour's communion with the dead."

— *In Memoriam, xciv.*

Before bringing this book to a close, it is desirable we should consider what weight can fairly be claimed for the argument often urged by candid friends, that the dangers of psychical enquiry more than counterbalance its possible usefulness.

I do not deny that there are some risks (in what branch of novel enquiry are there not risks?), but they have been greatly exaggerated, and those who know least of the whole subject are apt to magnify the dangers most.

As a leading weekly Journal has recently said: —

"In any case it is right and reasonable to investigate the phenomena, or alleged phenomena, as long as they are investigated in a scientific spirit. No one proposes to stop chemical enquiry because foolish people may poison themselves or blow themselves up. Similarly, provided the dangers are understood, psychic investigation ought not to be forbidden or hindered merely because certain psychological and moral risks attach thereto."[1]

Public performances of mesmerism by travelling showmen ought to be prohibited by law, in the same way as public performances of the effects of chloroform by a quack doctor should be, and would be, prohibited. But experiments in thought-transference, to say the least, are entirely harmless, so far as my knowledge goes, and I speak with some authority on this matter.[2] All scientific investigations need to be conducted with prudence and common sense, and when these are exercised in psychical research there is no reason to apprehend any dangers, such as may undoubtedly befall those who, with ignorant and unbalanced minds, and from idle curiosity, venture to rush into a region which may prove to them a treacherous psychical quicksand.

Certain precautions in the investigation of spiritualistic phenomena are however necessary and it may be useful to set them forth.

First and foremost as regards those taking part in a séance for physical phenomena, or in the more familiar sittings for automatic writing, trance speaking, or clairvoyance, let me quote the words of that wise and experienced spiritualist Mr. Epes Sargent, who long ago wrote as follows : —

> "The circumstance that scientific persons have, as a general rule, kept aloof from the whole of this subject, partly through a misgiving as to their ability to cope with it, and partly through their own a priori objections and rooted prejudices, has left it largely in the hands of those who, from defective training or from a lack of the critical faculty, have supposed that all which may come from the unseen world must be authoritative and right. Messages that violate all the laws of logic and common-sense have thus been accepted as bona fide communications from the world's great departed thinkers."[3]

This was written some years ago but today it cannot be said that spiritualists are as a body so uncritical as they once were. I have been

---

[1] *Spectator*, Nov. 18, 1916.

[2] It is amusing to hear how often timid and uninstructed friends have said to me that they were sure strange psychical phenomena were "the work of the devil or else electricity"; either or both of these mysterious agencies being, to many persons, the probable cause of all novel and otherwise inexplicable disturbances.

[3] *The Scientific Basis of Spiritualism*, by Epes Sargent, p, 34I.

invited to address their large gatherings and found them as intelligent and anxious to arrive at the truth as any other body of English men and women. What has struck me most forcibly is the spirit of fellowship and freedom of opinion to be found amongst them, and the reverent tone of their devotional meetings. Doubtless the inexperienced are often credulous and too ready to accept the messages given by automatic writing or trance speaking at their face value.

As regards the general and uninstructed public, it is obvious that these phenomena, and the type of alleged clairvoyance described earlier, lend themselves to gross abuse by those charlatans and rogues who prey upon the credulity or the distress of mankind.

This is one of the misfortunes of the whole subject, and has so largely discredited it.

Silly and credulous folk listen and pay for the rubbish that is told them by would-be astrologers, fortune tellers, crystal-gazers, *et hoc genus omne*. There are genuine cases of clairvoyance in the incipent hypnosis induced by crystal-vision, as Mr. Andrew Lang and others have shown; and there are genuine cases of prevision or precognition of events, as Mr. Myers has demonstrated, just as there are veridical dreams and premonitions.[4] But these genuine cases are exceptional and rarely to be found in a certain class of advertising mediums who swindle the public.

Anyone who possesses genuine psychic power has of course a perfect right to be remunerated, when his or her time is occupied by the exercise of that power. There are, I am sure, many honorable and gifted professional mediums, far removed from the charlatans referred to in the last paragraph.

The mischief largely arises when the ignorant public go to such honest psychics and expect an immediate return for their money. The natural tendency of the medium is not to disappoint the sitter, and the temptation therefore arises to supplement genuine by spurious phenomena. It cannot be too often insisted on that super-normal gifts are rare and elusive, and require patience, knowledge and discrimination on the part of the enquirer.

It is for this reason that I should rather dissuade than encourage uninstructed persons to resort to professional mediums. Even those who yearn to pierce the veil for "The touch of a vanished hand and the sound of a voice that is still," would in my opinion, if they have not

---

[4] See on all these subjects the "Proceedings of the S.P.R.," or Myers *Hunan Personality*.

Christian faith, do better to rest content with a perusal of the evidence for survival that is now being accumulated by rigorous and laborious expert enquiry.

It is easier to give than to follow such advice, and some mourners have, after a time, found in quiet, continuous, private sittings with one or two friends, the assurance they longed to obtain. If they are not thereby led to neglect the paramount duties of their life and work and if they preserve a sane and wholesome judgment no harm can result.

In a previous chapter I have referred to one of the most provoking things in these communications, the not infrequent personation of great names in history. The absurdity is so transparent that only the ignorant are misled, but, even with perfectly honest psychics, these freaks of the subliminal self often add to the perplexity of the enquirer and to the contempt of the scoffer. A century before modern Spiritualism arose Swedenborg uttered warnings on the delusive character of many of the communications from "spirits." In the *Arcana Celestia* he says: —

> "When spirits begin to speak with man they conjoin themselves with his thoughts and affections; hence it is manifest none other but similar spirits speak with man and operate upon him.... They put on all things of his memory, thus all things which the man has learned and imbibed from infancy the spirits suppose these things to be their own; thus they act, as it were, a part of man with men." (This we should now call the emergence of the sub-conscious self of the psychic) "Wherefore let those who speak with spirits beware lest they be deceived, when they say that they are those whom they know or pretend to be."

And so Preiswerk, in a German work published in 1856, giving an account of Spiritualism among the Swiss, says it was found "that the communications by table rapping were only an echo and reflection of the mind of the persons engaged." This, as we know, is frequently the case, and indicates that the source of some of the "physical phenomena" may also be the unconscious self of the medium, as I have already suggested.

Very often, I think, we are apt to judge the medium too harshly. We must remember the abnormal condition and loss of normal self-control involved in mediumship, and surely it would be as unjust to charge a deeply entranced medium with conscious fraud as to accuse a somnambulist walking on a housetop with consciously jeopardising his life. It is this weakening of self-control and personal responsibility,[5] on the part of a medium, that constitutes, in my opinion, the chief peril of Spiritualism. Hence the steps of a novice need to be taken with care; even the level-headed should walk warily, and the excitable and emotional should have nothing to do with it; for the fascination of the subject is like a candle to moths, it attracts and burns the silly, the credulous, and the crazy.

Every Spiritualist knows the mischief of promiscuous sittings of ignorant people, and many feel as strongly as I do that paid professional mediums who have been convicted of fraud should be sedulously avoided. Dark séances are also undesirable and should be discouraged. The best sittings I ever had have been in full light; so with Sir W. Crookes' wonderful observations. In fact, Home, I believe, always refused to sit in the dark: and probably with any medium, by patience and perseverance, the light could be gradually increased without serious injury to the results, and with enormous gain to the accuracy and precision of the observations.

Spiritualism has sometimes been accused of creating insanity and fostering immorality. No reliable evidence in support of such sweeping charges has ever been adduced, and unsupported accusations of a similar character are familiar in the history of nearly every new and disturbing phase of thought.

Isolated cases, no doubt, exist; but, as Mrs. Henry Sidgwick points out in an article in the *Encyclopaedia Britannica*, the fact that the delusions of the insane not infrequently take the form of converse with invisible beings" has probably led to this widespread and mistaken inference.

Passing on to other effects produced on the medium, I doubt if any harm has ever resulted from sittings for automatic writing or speaking, in the normal or trance condition.

But there is certainly some evidence indicating that continual sittings for physical phenomena cause an illegitimate and excessive drain on the vitality of a medium, creating a nervous exhaustion which is apt to lead, in extreme cases, to mental derangement, or to an habitual resort to stimulants with a no less deplorable end. If this be the fact we must, of course, be on our guard, as no gain to science would ever justify experiment heedless of a risk so great; but on this point we want more knowledge. Sometimes D. D. Home suffered severely after a

---

[5] *Arcana Celestia*, §§ 6192 and 5850.

long series of séances. Sir W. Crookes states Home was prostrated after some experiments, "pale, speechless and almost fainting he lay upon the floor; showing what a drain on his vital powers was caused by the evolution of the 'psychic force.' " As regards the impression made on the general public by such phenomena, Mr. C. C. Massey, whose intimate acquaintance with the whole subject I have already referred to, wrote to me in 1895 as follows: —

> "Much of the opposition to phenomenal spiritualism (so-called) arises from disgust of the grotesque incongruity between spiritual mysteries and the vulgar manifestations of which the world chiefly hears in connection with this subject."

Everyone outside a lunatic asylum, at least every reverent person, must revolt from the nightmare of a spiritual realm peopled by the quasi ticket-of-leave ghosts so often met with in these manifestations. Compare such buffoonery with our cherished ideals as expressed by Archbishop Trench : —

> "Where thou hast touched,
> O wondrous death,
> Where thou hast come between,
> Lo! there forever perisheth
> The common and the mean."

Well-informed and experienced Spiritualists say that serious risk to the health, both of mind and body, of the medium sitting for physical manifestations, is incurred by any sudden light or violent awakening of the medium from the state of trance. To a scoffing public this plea seems obviously invented to secure immunity from detection of the medium by a sudden seizure in a dark sitting. But the sniffs and scoffs of the ignorant do not advance our knowledge; what we want to know— is there any conclusive evidence one way or the other on this point? We need experienced and unprejudiced physicians to decide this question.

Whatever the conclusion might be, it is really absurd to suppose that the resources of science are so far exhausted that highly-trained investigators cannot determine, with reasonable precision, whether certain physical movements or appearances are due to a known or an unknown cause, without resort to the aid of clumsy and possibly hazardous police expedients.

It certainly appears to be the fact that the best and most conclusive physical manifestations occur when the investigator treats the phenomena as if they were produced by a timid animal, a sensitive living thing that will shrink into obscurity and disappear at a sudden disturbance or surprise of any kind, often by a mental as well as material shock.

Imagine you are watching the unfolding of a rare and highly organised polyp, and observing the capricious movements of its long and sensitive tentacles, and you will be able to realise how a shock or even a sudden ray of light may startle it to instant closure, though it may by training be accustomed to unfold in full and steady light.

In concluding this chapter it may be well to consider briefly what are the best conditions for obtaining evidence in sittings with good psychics. There can be no doubt that suspicion is fatal to success: sympathy, combined with critical faculty, is essential. The relation of faith to psychical research has been well expressed by the late Mr. C. C. Massey and Mr. Stainton Moses. "Faith," Mr. Massey says, "is the condition of evidence, the key to the gate of the invisible world." In reference to this Mr. Moses remarks: —

> "What Mr. Massey calls 'faith' is a predisposition and attention, a sympathetic state of mind which establishes between an observer and a medium a rapport without which no results are to be had that are worth the having. So when the dispassionate critic makes a merit of the absence of prejudice in his mind he does well. It is conceivable that this negative side may render him harmless; it may even enable him to get personal experience under exceptionally favourable circumstances. But, it may be, as Mr. Massey will points out, 'that this negative qualification is not enough, and ... there is need of a positive sympathy' before any real progress can be made."

It is useless for the sceptic to say we do not require "sympathy" when we are testing the evidence for some novel physical or chemical discovery. No, they are dealing with the world of *matter* and must conduct their experiments in such a way that prejudicial effects in their domain do not vitiate the results. But here we are dealing with delicate psychical conditions and must ascertain what are the favourable or unfavourable conditions for success in that region. Mr. Moses goes on to say: —

"If a man goes to a medium with the strongest desire to witness phenomena, but bringing with him the deterrent attitude of mind which is the antipodes of faith, he will most probably fail, unless he is fortunate enough to meet with a fully-developed psychic whom his coldness cannot wholly chill." "I should say," Mr. Massey remarks, "that the most unfavourable disposition to take to a medium is suspicion, and the most favourable is confidence. But this is to deliver oneself over a prey to the deceiver! Yes, such men do get taken in." I agree with Mr. Massey; they do. I also agree with him when he adds, "I believe that their success will be, on the whole, of such an amount and character as more than to compensate for these disadvantages."[6]

Confidence is certainly misplaced when you are sitting with a doubtful or fraudulent medium, and in any case it must not be regarded as synonymous with credulity. It is the most experienced investigator who is the least credulous, and it is also unquestionably true that it is those psychical researchers who bristle with suspicion, that have never been able to obtain conclusive evidence of the physical phenomena of spiritualism. They are not abler or more critical investigators than Sir W. Crookes and other scientific men, who have had overwhelming proofs, but they bring with them a psychical atmosphere that is as unfavourable to success as a damp atmosphere is to the working of a frictional or Holtz electrical machine.

It was said of old "In quietness and confidence shall be your strength," and this attitude of mind, combined with alert observation and unwearied patience, we commend to the psychical researcher who wishes to obtain the best results.

---

[6] *Light*, Oct. 23, 1886.

Part 6

CHAPTER 21

THE LESSON OF PHILISOPHY IN THE INTERPRETATION OF NATURE

"By that I know the learned lord you are!
What you don't touch, is lying leagues afar;
What you don't grasp, is wholly lost to you;
What you don't reckon, think you, can't be true;
What you don't weigh, it has no weight, alas
What you don't coin, you're sure it will not pass!"[1]

In chapter 3, we discussed the objections raised by science and religion to spiritualistic phenomena and briefly referred to the fact that one reason which has prevented the general recognition of these phenomena, is because modern science, or rather the dominant school of scientific thought, is, or perhaps was, essentially materialistic. This school, as Mr. F. W. H. Myers has eloquently said, "insists, in tones louder sometimes and more combative than the passionless air of science is willing to echo or convey, that all enquiries into man's psychical nature, all enquiries which regard him as possibly more than a portion of organised matter, are no longer open, but closed, and closed

---
[1] Bayard Taylor's translation of "Goethe's Faust," Part II, p. 8.

against his aspirations forever." The materialist is imprisoned within the limits of his senses, hence a world which has no continuous relation with his senses has no existence for him. Life without ponderable matter he confidently asserts is impossible, and he prophesies that the atoms of such matter contain within themselves, as Dr. Tyndall asserted in his British Association address, "the promise and potency of every form and quality of life." [2]

Science having done so much for human thought and life, public opinion naturally inclined to the view held by a recent school of scientific thought, which denies the possibility of any life without protoplasm, i.e., a particular grouping of the molecules of matter which forms the basis of all earthly life. Many of our leading physicists have however dissociated themselves from this habit of thought.

So long ago as 1881, that eminent man Professor Balfour Stewart, who has long since passed into the unseen, wrote to me as follows: —

> "It seems quite clear that the scientific recognition of the unseen, is the point wanting in the intellectual teaching of our race, and I do not doubt that this will be provided for."

His confidence seems to have been abundantly justified, for the psychological climate of today is distinctly more favourable to psychical research. Physicists no longer believe in the Lucretian atom "strong in solid singleness," but are pushing the ultimate nature of matter into the realm of the incomprehensible and intangible ether. The mechanistic theory of the universe, which so delights the German mind, is breaking down.

The confident and complacent assumptions of materialism have it is true long been impugned by philosophy. In fact —

> "The common supposition that the material universe and the conscious beings around us are directly and indubitably known, and constitute a world of 'positive' facts, on which reason can certainly pronounce without any exercise of faith ... is an entire mistake, based upon astonishing ignorance of the essential limitations of human knowledge, of which thinkers who lived in the very dawn of philosophy were perfectly aware.

---

[2] "Fragments of Science," Vol. II, p. 210

The fact is, we are equally obliged to transcend phenomena, and to put faith in events and powers and realities which do not appear when we recognise the past, or the distant, or the material universe, or the minds of men, as when we infer the existence of God and of the unseen world."[3]

Matter, the world outside our consciousness, is the mystery to be explained; for we only know matter in terms of consciousness, hence we can never find in matter an intelligible explanation of mind and will. A mechanistic theory of the universe reduces consciousness to a mere by-product of matter, and volition to an illusion of the mind.

And if science replies to this that the premises on which it rests are furnished by immediate experience in the shape of observation and experiment —

"What are we to say about these same experiences when we discover, not only that they may be wholly false, but that they are never wholly true; . . . ninetenths of our immediate experiences of objects are visual, and all visual experiences, without exception, are, according to science, erroneous,"[4]

that is to say, the degrees of brightness, form, or colour whereby we perceive objects are, as optics teaches, not properties of the things seen but sensations produced in us by undulations in the ether. Hence, psychologically regarded, it may be said, as Mr. Balfour goes on to remark, that —

"Our perceptions, regarded as sources of information, are not merely occasionally inaccurate but habitually mendacious."[5]

For instance, every stimulus given to the optic nerve, whether by light, or pressure, or electricity, or a chemical reagent, reveals itself as a flash of light and is so called by us. The same may be said, *mutatis mutandis*, of the other specialised sense organs.

Again, how different would be our concept of the external world if we were deprived of some of our senses, such for example as sight or

---

[3] *The Realistic Assumptions of Modern Science Examined*, by Professor Herbert M.A., p, 455.
[4] *The Foundation of Belief*, by the Rt. Hon. A. J. Balfour.
[5] *The Foundations of Belief*, page 111.

touch; and again how different if we had other gateways of sense, profounder avenues to a knowledge of the world outside ourselves.

If we were restricted to a single sense, such as sight, we should infer all phenomena, all material things, to consist of variations in luminosity or colour. Hence our ideas of the world would expand or contract in proportion to the extent of the means by which that world is perceived.

It is our ignorance, or our forgetfulness, of these facts, our neglect of the vast difference between our perceptions and the realities for which they stand, that gives rise to many of the perplexities we encounter, and some of the conflicts between science and faith.

This is worth a moment's further consideration by those who have not considered the subject.

The first lesson taught by mental philosophy is that all we know of external objects and material phenomena are certain sensations within us, as already remarked; of the things in-themselves we know absolutely nothing.

The things we do know are certain states of consciousness, certain symbols — or *tekmeria*, as the late Dr. Johnstone Stoney, F.R.S., proposed to call them[6] — signs evoked in our mind by events happening in the universe outside our mind. Accordingly we do not perceive the actual material world, nor anything like it, and have not, therefore, the remotest idea of what the thing we call matter is in itself.

We can watch the movements of a telegraphic needle and learn to read the message it brings, but the moving needle does not enable us to perceive the operator at the other end who is causing it to move, nor does it even remotely resemble the operator; its signals give us, it is true, an intelligible message, but it is intelligible only because the intelligence of the operator has been and is related to our intelligence. In like manner the mental signs of our brain and nervous mechanism give us of the material world outside are not the things, nor a resemblance to the things, in themselves; the real world around us, the world of ontology, is absolutely inaccessible to us. But the reason why the material world is intelligible, why we can interpret the signs it gives us, is because there is an intelligence behind the universe which has been and is related to our intelligence.

To the pure materialist the universe is self-sustained and has no deeper meaning than the appearance it presents to our senses; these

---

[6] See a suggestive paper by Dr. Stoney In the "Proceedings of the Royal Dublin Society," Vol. VI, p. 475.

appearances are to him the ultimate reality. If he forms a mechanical theory of nature by endowing atoms with some occult power, or consciousness, he confers on them the very properties which have to be explained. Hence we are driven to believe in a Supreme Intelligence and to regard the universe as the expression of the Divine Thought perpetually sustained by the Divine Will.

This is surely the simplest and truest interpretation of nature.

There are few more honoured names in science than that of Sir John Herschel, and in this connection a passage from one of his essays appears to me so valuable a contribution to our belief in a Supreme Mind that I venture to quote it. The whole essay, like all Sir John wrote, is full of luminous thought.

> "The universe presents us with an assemblage of phenomena — physical, vital, and intellectual — the connecting link between the worlds of intellect and matter being that of organised vitality, occupying the whole domain of animal and vegetable life, throughout which, in some way inscrutable to us, movements among the molecules of matter are originated of such a character as apparently to bring them under the control of an agency other than physical superseding the ordinary laws which regulate the movements of inanimate matter, or, in other words, giving rise to movements which would not result from the action of those laws uninterfered with; and therefore implying, on the very same principle, the origination of force.
>
> "The first and greatest question which Philosophy has to resolve in its attempts to make out a Cosmos — to bring the whole of the phenomena exhibited in these three domains of existence under the contemplation of the mind as a congruous whole — is, whether we can derive any light from our internal consciousness of thought, reason, power, will, motive, design, or not; whether, that is to say, Nature is or is not more inter pit table by supposing these things (be they what they may) to have had, or to have, to do with its arrangements.
>
> "Constituted as the human mind is, it Nature be not interpretable through these conceptions it is not interpretable at all; and the only reason we can have for troubling ourselves about it is either the utilitarian one of bettering our condition by 'subduing Nature' to our use, through a more complete understanding of its 'laws,' so as to throw ourselves into its grooves, and thereby reach our ends more readily

and effectually; or the satisfaction of that sort of aimless curiosity which can find its gratification in scrutinising everything and comprehending nothing. But if these attributes of mind are not consentaneous, they are useless in the way of explanation. Will without motive, power without reason, thought opposed to reason, would be admirable in explaining a chaos, but would render little aid in accounting for anything else."[7]

It was formerly so integral a part of modern scientific thought to regard mind and matter as distinct entities that we forget this common dualistic conception may be an entirely fallacious idea. Just as language is a manifestation of thought and indissolubly connected with it, so matter may be only a manifestation to us of spirit. To human intelligence, spirit is always manifested through matter; so that spirit and matter, like force and matter, or thought and language, seem to us inseverable and even unthinkable apart.

The essential unity which underlies thought and its expression in language affords an interesting analogy to spirit and matter. As a suggestive writer has remarked —

> "Language is the mode in which thought takes shape, its way of becoming known to itself, and therefore dependent on thought for existence, but their relationship is a far more intimate one than that of cause and effect. . . . We cannot 'account for' thought by the laws of language, simply because thought unconsciously makes those laws by way of attaining to a clearer recognition of itself. In the same way we cannot 'account for' mind by the laws of matter, because those laws are, in reality, the principles according to which human intelligence apprehends the material universe. In them, mind recognises itself in the external world. As thought is essentially self-manifesting so the life of the spirit is essentially self-manifesting, hence as language is the utterance of the one so matter is the utterance of the other."[8]

Experimental science is still young and has not wholly emerged from the Cartesian stage of thought where matter and mind, nature

---

[7] "On the Origin of Force," p. 473. "Lectures on Scientific Subjects," by Sir J. F. W. Herschel, Bart., D.C.L., F.R.S., etc.

[8] *Progressive Revelation*, Chap. V, by Miss Caillard, see also my brochure entitled *Creative Thought*, published by Watkins, Cecil Court, London, W.C

and spirit are absolute opposites, their antagonism reconciled only in the Divine incomprehensible Will. As our knowledge progresses and our interpretation of nature becomes more adequate, we begin to recognise that the dualism and antithesis of nature and spirit disappear, and miracles as well as all super-normal phenomena become less incredible, when nature is seen to be, as Novalis said, "an illuminated table of the contents of the spirit."

CHAPTER 22

THE MYSTERY OF HUMAN PERSONALITY

"One Life through all the immense creation runs,
One Spirit is the moon's, the sea's, the sun's.
All forms in the air that fly, on the earth that creep,
And the unknown nameless monsters of the deep —
Each breathing thing obeys one Mind's control,
And in all substance is a single Soul."

— *Virgil.*

A brief consideration of some aspects of human personality was necessary in an earlier portion of this book. It may not be out of place in conclusion to note some of the higher aspects of this subject. We have seen that our personality is a very complex and mysterious thing. Probably in each of us, certainly in many, there are potentialities which far outstrip the capabilities of our conscious voluntary intelligence; nay more, which transcend the limitations of our senses, of space, of time, and even of our thought and consciousness. But if these super-normal faculties exist — and of their existence such acute thinkers as Schopenhauer and E. von Hartmann were convinced — other manifestations of them than those we are acquainted with in spiritualism, somnambulism, hypnotic trance, etc., might be expected.

The dark continent within us, is in fact much more than a hidden record of unheeded or forgotten past impressions; there is an *ultra*-liminal as well as a *sub*-liminal self;[1] something that has higher perceptive powers than our normal consciousness, something in us that is able to respond to directed thought, whether the thinker be "in the body or out of the body," something that links our individual life to the Source of that life, and to the ocean of universal life. This was firmly believed by that great philosopher, Kant, who, anticipating our present knowledge, slight as that is, was led by the mere strength of his penetrating intellect to assert:

> It is therefore, as good as proved . . . that the human soul, even in this life, stands in indissoluble community with all immaterial natures of the spirit world, that it mutually acts upon them and receives from them impressions, of which, however, as man, it is unconscious, as long as all goes well.

And again he says: —

> It is, therefore, truly one and the same subject which belongs at the same time to the visible and to the invisible world, but (since representations of the one world are not associated with ideas of the other) what I think as spirit is not remembered by me as man.[2]

This was also Swedenborg's view. He repeatedly states: —

> Man is so constituted that he is at the same time in the spiritual world and in the natural world: the spiritual world is where the angels are, and the natural world is where men are.

---

[1] Mr. Myers has used the word *supra-liminal* to connote our conscious waking life, but this might perhaps more appropriately be called *cis-liminal* within the threshold of consciousness: I have used the world *ultra-liminal* to signify the higher transcendental self. The great work on *Human Personality* by Mr. Myers (which was published long after this chapter was written in the original edition of this book) should be read by all who wish a fuller knowledge of the subject.

[2] Kant: "Werke" (Rosenkranz), vii, 53, 59, quoted by Dr. Du Prel in his "Philosophy of Mysticism" (Redway, London). This quotation is from Kant's "Dreams of a Spirit-seer," a translation of which is published by Swan Sonnenschein Sc Co. Du Prel's work has been, with loving labour, admirably translated by the late Mr. C. C. Massey, not the least valuable part of the work being the translator's own suggestive preface. Mr. Massey has also rendered great service to English readers by his translation of E. von Hartmann's "Spiritism." Like other candid enquirers, this eminent German philosopher, having with painstaking care made himself acquainted with the facts of Spiritual ism, states that they afford "an urgent challenge to science to enter upon the exact research of this phenomenal province."

Plotinus, who lived in the third century, also held a very similar belief, speaking of men as "amphibia," who live partly in the natural and partly in the spiritual world.

In fact, the teaching of the Neo-platonists and mysticism generally is that the soul has a two-fold life, a lower and a higher.

Iamblichus believed that even in sleep the soul is freed from the constraint of the body and enters on its divine life of intelligence: the night-time of the body being the day-time of the soul.[3] The "ecstasy" of Plotinus, and earlier still of Philo, was, according to them, the temporary liberation of the soul from its finite consciousness and its union with the Infinite.[4] Thus we see the opinion of many of the world's great thinkers in the past is quite in accord with recent evidence, which teaches us that our Ego is more than our self-consciousness reveals. As the roots of a tree are hidden in the earth, so we may regard the root of our Ego as sunk in a world beyond our consciousness, and the Neo-platonic idea — that the soul is only partially known in its normal, or physically-conditioned, consciousness — becomes intelligible.

There is certainly a world beyond our normal consciousness from which neither space nor time divides us, but only the barrier of our sense-perceptions. This barrier constitutes what has been well termed the "threshold of sensibility," and limits the area of our consciousness. In the progress of evolution from lower to higher forms of life this threshold has been successively shifted, with a corresponding exaltation of consciousness. The organism of an oyster, for instance, constitutes a threshold which shuts it out from the greater part of our sensible world; in like manner the physical organism of man forms a threshold which separates him from the larger and transcendental world of which he forms a part.

But this threshold is not immovable. Occasionally in rapture, in dream, and in hypnotic trance it is shifted, and the human spirit temporarily moves in "worlds not realised" by sense. In the clairvoyance of deep hypnotic sleep, and in somnambulism, the threshold is still

---

[3] See that delightful and well-known work, Vaughan's "Hours with the Mystics." Professor Harnack's article on "Neo-platonism," in the *Encyclopedia Briiannica*, should be read by all who are interested in this subject.

[4] Indeed, a belief in the soul's power to have commerce with the spirit-world has a place in Greek philosophy as early as the 6th century B.C., for Aeschylus was echoing a Pythagorean doctrine when he wrote, "The mind in sleep is bright with eyes" (to receive spiritual impressions). I am indebted to my friend the Rev. M. A. Bayfield for this and many other valued suggestions in this book.

further shifted and a higher intelligence emerges, with a clearness and power proportional to the more complete cessation of the functions and consciousness of our ordinary waking life.

This intelligence, as has been shown above, has powers and perceptions wider and deeper than those of the normal waking consciousness. Accordingly, since the exercise of these faculties in our daily life is apparently hindered by our bodily organism, we may infer that when we are freed from "this muddy vesture of decay," and the soul enters on its larger life, these faculties will no longer be trammelled as they are now. As, one by one, the avenues of sense close forever, the threshold of sensibility is not suddenly removed; and so, as our loved ones pass from us, it is probable that in most cases the "dawn behind all dawns" creeps gently upward, slowly awakening them to the wider and profounder consciousness that, for good or ill, awaits us all.

> "Peace, peace! he is not dead, he doth not sleep,
> He hath awaken'd from the dream of life." [5]

---

[5] Shelley: "Adonais."

CHAPTER 23

THE DIVINE GROUND OF THE SOUL REINCARNATION

"All outward vision yields to that within,
Whereof nor creed nor canon holds the key;
We only feel that we have been
And evermore shall be."

— *Bayard Taylor.*

The transcendental phenomena we have been discussing so far from excluding, of necessity presuppose the "Divine ground of the soul," to use a phrase of the mystics. Encompassing the super-normal within us, lies the supernatural, in the true meaning of that word. For "Behind consciousness itself must certainly be placed the ultimate Reality of which consciousness offers only a reflection or faint representation."[1] The intimacy and immediacy of the union between the soul and God, the Infinite manifesting itself in and through the finite, is the fundamental idea, not only of the mystics, but of the New Testament, and of all great Christian thinkers.

The attainment of this profounder consciousness, and therefore of our full personality, is, however, the province of religion, the "true

---

[1] See upon this subject the striking work on "Personality" In the Rev. J. R. Illingworth, especially Lecture 2 and the note on p. 240, where the views of von Hartmann and Lotze are contrasted.

theme of which is not the future life but the higher life." This knowledge of God, not of the methods of his working, but the consciousness of His presence, is what is meant by religion. From this point of view it is obvious Spiritualism is not and cannot be a religion, which rests essentially upon those higher instincts of the soul we call faith. For, as Canon Scott Holland says in "Lux Mundi" (p. 15) —

> "Faith is the power by which conscious life attaches itself to God. . . . Faith, then, opens an entirely new career to creaturely existence; and the novelty of this career is expressed in the word 'Supernatural.' The supernatural world opens upon us as soon as faith is in being."

In this sense also spiritualism cannot even afford to us knowledge of the supernatural, as it is often claimed to do.[2] In its true meaning supernatural knowledge is incommunicable from without; it is the voice of the Spirit to the spirit, or, as Plotinus said, "The flight of the Alone to the alone," for "the soul must be very still to hear God speak." Of this Divine unveiling the humblest human souls have knowledge, no less than the greatest prophets and poets.

> "For more than once when I
> Sat all alone, revolving in myself
> The word that is the symbol of myself,
> The mortal limit of the Self was loosed,
> And past into the Nameless, as a cloud
> Melts into Heaven. I touch'd my limbs, the limbs
> Were strange, not mine — and yet no shade of doubt
> But utter clearness, and thro' loss of Self
> The gain of such large life as match'd with ours
> Were Sun to spark — unshadowable in words,
> Themselves but shadows of a shadow-world."[3]

It is this "loss of self," this self-surrender, which enables the consciousness of God to enter into our life. Our own will dies and God's will lives in us, and in so far as this is the case we attain the

---

[2] In Appendix "A" I have discussed more fully the conflicting popular notions that Spiritualism is on the one hand a "recrudescence of superstition" and on the other, "evidence of the supernatural."

[3] Tennyson: "The Ancient Sage."

object of our earthly existence, that is, the realisation of a higher and wider consciousness, the discovery of our true personality, which is immortal. This cannot persist until it has been attained, and its attainment is the Way of Life; as Lotze says, "Perfect personality is in God alone."

In other words, when we are conscious of the Divine life and love dwelling within us, our human life becomes a conscious partaker of the endless life of God; without this consciousness human life is not only unsatisfying but unenduring.[4]

Here let me remark that the inference commonly drawn that spirit communications teach us the necessary and inherent immortality of the soul is, in my opinion, a mischievous error. It is true they show us that life can exist in the unseen, and — if we accept the evidence for "identity" — that some we have known on earth are still living and near us, but entrance on a life after death does not necessarily mean immortality, i.e., eternal persistence of our personality; nor does it prove that survival after death extends to all.

Obviously no experimental evidence can ever demonstrate either of these beliefs, though it may and does remove the objections raised as to the possibility of survival.

There are many who believe with the devout and learned Henry More, and other Platonists, together with several eminent thinkers of the present day, such as Professor McTaggart, that the survival of the soul after death involves the assumption of its pre-natal existence. If so, as Mr. C. C. Massey has said, "The whole conception of immortality undergoes an important change if we regard the personal consciousness with its Ego as a mere partial and temporary limitation of a larger self, the growth of many seasons, as it were, of earthly life." The lack of any memory of our past existences, if such there were, has been urged against the idea of reincarnation, but this may be only a temporary eclipse. It is possible that recollection of our past lives may gradually return, as in the course of our spiritual progress we gain a larger life and deeper consciousness: the underlying subliminal life, may be the golden thread that binds into one all our past and future lives.

---

[4] This view of potential immortality was and is held not only by some learned theologians, both ancient and modern (see Rev. Ed. White's "Life in Christ"), but also by not a few devout and eminent scientific men such as the late Sir G. G. Stokes, a past President of the Royal Society of London.

As this question of reincarnation is at present attracting much attention it may be of interest to quote another sentence or two from the devout and suggestive writer named above : —

> "We may find," remarks Mr. C. C. Massey, "the ground of reincarnation in an attraction to this world or principle of life...Whatever has brought us here once will presumably bring us here again and again till the motive power changes....
>
> Regeneration (a new-nature) alone exempts from reincarnation; the bonds of desire to the external nature being thus severed, all the tendrils of attachment to it are thus eradicated.... The idea of Christianity it seems to me—is that this attachment is broken (for all who desire it broken) by attachment to the Personal Power that has, in principle, accomplished the rapture. The Buddhist says 'conquer desire,' but that is only negative: Christ supplies the positive; desire Him and you are already free from the grip of earthly desire: for the two desires cannot co-exist."[5]

Doubtless some readers will consider the foregoing remarks out of place in this book, but the subject of Spiritualism is so intimately connected with, and throws so much light on, the whole question of eschatology, that I have ventured to enter upon an inexhaustible subject, one of age-long interest and discussion. Immortality, Matthew Arnold defined as 'living in the eternal order which never dies'; but the soul craves for more than an impersonal existence of love and goodness, truth and beauty, which are in the eternal order, timeless and boundless.

Let us however recognise our ignorance, we cannot see far ahead, "We have but faith: we cannot know." It may be as Indian philosophy teaches, and the learned Dominican martyr, Bruno, believed, that human personality, the individualisation of the soul, is but a fleeting event, which in the infinite bosom of time has only an ephemeral stability and duration, though as a portion of the Divine life it is immortal. The whole universe was to Bruno, as to many later thinkers, a living Cosmos, an eternal transmutation of the World-soul, of the ever present Divine Word.

Certainly all religions must admit that God is the centre, and the manifestation of God the circumference, of all existence. Within this

---

[5] *Thoughts of a Modern Mystic*, edited by Sir W. F. Barrett, Kegan Paul, Trench & Co.

vast circle lies the whole creation, like the myriad cell life in the human body. Each of these cells in our body has a life of its own, yet all are related to a unitary consciousness, a personality which far transcends the life of each cell. Some mysterious mode of intercommunication possibly exists, even would-appear to exist, between the individual cells and the sub-conscious self.

Thus also we may conceive the human race as the constituent cells, the many members, of the one Body to which all are related and yet all transcended in the one supreme ineffable Being. Nor can we doubt that some mode of communication and influence passes between the Creator and all creaturely existence. For —

> "All are but parts of one stupendous whole,
> Whose body Nature is, and God the soul."

"Inevitably," Frederick Myers remarks, "as our link with other spirits strengthens, as the life of the organism pours more fully through the individual cell, we shall feel love more ardent, wider wisdom, higher joy; perceiving that this organic unity of Soul, which forms the inward aspect of the telepathic law, is in itself the Order of the Cosmos, the Summation of Things."

On the possibility of this Divine influx some light is thrown by the discovery of Telepathy, the implications of which we will briefly consider in the concluding chapter.

CHAPTER 24

TELEPATHY AND ITS IMPLICATIONS

"Each creature holds an insular point in space;
Yet what man stirs a finger, breathes a sound,
But all the multitudinous beings round
In all the countless worlds, with time and place
For their conditions, down to the central base,
Thrill, happy, in vibration and rebound,
Life answering life across the vast profound,
In full antiphony, by a common grace?" [1]

I have dealt in this book mainly with Spiritualistic phenomena; it was not my intention here to treat of other subjects of psychical research, most of which are of a less startling character and some, like hypnotism and telepathy, are, in my opinion, almost as fully established as many of the accepted truths of science. We have added considerably to the weight of evidence since Schopenhauer wrote: "Who at this day doubts the facts of mesmerism and its clairvoyance is not to be called sceptical but *ignorant*. And this remark would now apply to other branches of our enquiry. Deeply interesting scientific problems lie before us in the immediate future. I can only hint at some of these.

In Thought-transference is it the idea or the word that is transmitted; is it the emotion or the expression of the emotion? I believe it is the

---
[1] Mrs. Browning: Sonnet on "Life."

former in both cases. But if so, may not this afford a hint towards the possibility of an interchange of thought amongst men in spite of differences in language? Language is but a clumsy instrument of thought, "consisting as it does of arbitrary signs, it is a rudiment of a material system,"[2] and we may expect it to disappear under the action of evolutionary forces. For how much more perfectly should we be able to transmit complex ideas and subtle emotions by the naked intercourse of minds than by the mechanism of speech.

Or again, may not the *animals* share with man this power? Evidence exists that domestic animals often perceive apparitions, and are frequently keener in their perception than man. It would be worthwhile to try whether animals are open to telepathy; will a favourite dog, for example, respond to the unuttered call of his name, no sense perception reaching him? The habits of ants and bees seem to indicate the possession of a mode of communication unknown to us. If our domestic animals are in any degree open to thought-transference, may we not thus get into somewhat closer communion with them? But leaving aside such speculations, the wider recognition of the fact of thought transference will inevitably lead to its culture and development. Does it not already play some part in the growing sense of sympathy and humanity we find in the world around? But if it were as common here among men, as it is doubtless common in the intercourse of the spiritual world, what a change would be wrought! If we were involuntarily sharers in one another's pleasures and pains, the brotherhood of the race would not be a pious aspiration or a strenuous effort, but the reality of all others most vividly before us; the factor in our lives which would dominate all our conduct. "What would be the use of a luxurious mansion at the West End and Parisian cooks if all the time the misery and starvation of our fellow creatures at

---

[2] Isaac Taylor: *Physical Theory of Another Life*, p. 102. This book, written nearly fifty years before telepathy was heard of contains some suggestions very like the above, though I was unaware of this till quite lately. Owing to the use of the phrase *thought-reading*, the absurd idea is prevalent that thought-transference means reading all the thoughts in another's mind. Only a dominant idea in the agent's. mind is passed on to the percipient, and that apparently requires an effort of will, so that filching one another's thoughts is not possible, and the sanctity and privacy of our minds must always be within our power and possessions, so long as we retain our true selfhood. Professor H. Drummond, in his "Ascent of Man," has also the same idea as I. Taylor: "Telepathy," he remarks, "is theoretically the next stage in the evolution of language," p. 233.

the East End were telepathically part and parcel of our daily lives? On the other hand what bright visions and joyous emotions would enter into many dreary and loveless lives if this state of human responsiveness were granted to the race! For, as Shakespeare says, in one of his Sonnets (XLIV.) : —

> "If the dull substance of my flesh were thought, Injurious distance would not stop my way."

It may be that telepathy is the survival of an old and once common possession of the human race that has fallen into disuse and almost died out with the growth of language.

More probably, I think, it is a rudimentary faculty, or possibly an early and special case of the great human *rapport* which is slowly awakening the race to the sense of a larger self.

> ... A heart that beats in all its pulses with the common heart
> Of human-kind, which the same things make glad,
> The same make sorry."

In relation to psychical enquiry, however, one often hears the question still raised "Of what use is it?" When all is said and done, and the facts we are slowly accumulating are generally recognised and accredited, what will be the gain? None at all to such as Peter Bell, to whom a primrose by the river's brim will only excite regret that he cannot eat or drink it; none to the simple, contented heart; none to those saints whose supreme faith has enabled them to transcend all earthly doubt, and who daily "live as seeing Him who is invisible"; but very much to the rest of mankind, in whom most of us are included.

For, as the learned Dr. Glanville says in the dedication of his famous *Saducismus Triumphatus*, "these things relate to our biggest interests; if established, they secure some of the outworks of religion, and regain a parcel of ground which bold infidelity hath invaded." But our scope is wider than Glanville had before him, and our philosophical need is greater. A false and paralysing materialistic philosophy must either disappear or be reconstructed, when the phenomena we attest can no longer be denied; and so, too, the popular assaults on the Christian religion, based on its incredibility, will be deprived of much of the force they now possess in certain minds.

The most profound change in human thought that has occurred since the Christian era will, in all probability, follow the general recognition by science of the immanence of a spiritual world. Faith will no longer be staggered by trying to conceive of life in the unseen; death will no longer be felt to have so icy a grip over even Christian hearts; miracles will no longer seem to be the superstitious relics of a barbarous age; the "prayer of faith" will no longer find an adequate explanation in the subjective response it evokes, nor the "Word of the Lord" in mere human aspiration. On the contrary, if, as I hold, telepathy be indisputable, if our creaturely minds can, without voice or language, impress each other, the Infinite and Overshadowing Mind is likely thus to have revealed itself in all ages to responsive human hearts. To some gifted souls were given the inner ear, the open vision, the inspired utterance, but to all these comes at times the still small voice, the faint echo within us of that larger Life which is slowly but surely expressing itself in humanity as the ages gradually unfold. Wordsworth felt this when he wrote,

"Not less I deem that there are Powers
Which of themselves our minds impress."

But even to those who prefer to regard these phenomena from a purely scientific aspect there will be great gain. I have already alluded to the possible solution which they afford of many perplexing, and at present inscrutable, scientific problems, the opening up of new regions of fruitful experimental enquiry, the impulse they will give to a truer psychology and a healthier philosophy. But in addition to this, they will tend to bring more forcibly before our minds the solidarity of the race, the immanence of the unseen, the dominance of thought and spirit — in a word, the transcendent unity and continuity of life.

Our scientific as well as our political memories are short-lived. We only see vividly that in the midst of which we live. What has gone before us is as if it had not been and never could be. So the science of today forgets, as has been well said,

"That the tendency of all the earlier systems of physical philosophy was to supernaturalise natural actions, whereas the tendency of modern science is to force into the phenomenal world ultimate causes that must ever be ultra-phenomenal. The older writers on physical science delighted in symbolical designs in which the forces of nature were represented each at his appointed work, and over all they placed a cloud from which issued the hand of God, directing the several agents of the Universe."[3]

The symbol is not unjust, for,

"Tis the sublime of man,
Our noontide majesty, to know ourselves
Parts and proportions of one wondrous whole!
... But 'tis God
Diffused through all, that doth make all one whole."[4]

We are not isolated in or from the great Cosmos, the light of suns and stars reaches us, the mysterious force of gravitation binds the whole material universe into an organic whole, the minutest molecule and the most distant orb are bathed in one and the self-same medium. But surely beyond and above all these material links is the solidarity of mind.

As the essential significance and unity of a honeycomb is not in the cells of wax, but in the common life and purpose of the builders of those cells, so the true significance of nature is not in the material world but in the Mind that gives to it a meaning, and that underlies and unites, that transcends and creates, the phenomenal world through which for a moment each of us is passing.

THE END

---

[3] Rodwell: Preface to *Dictionary of Science*.
[4] Coleridge: *Religious Musings*.

APPENDIX A

SUPERSTITION AND THE SUPERNATURAL MIRACLES

1.

The spiritualistic phenomena we have described in this book are usually characterised by sceptics as a "recrudescence of superstition,"[1] and by believers as "evidence of the supernatural." If either of these statements are true they have serious and far-reaching consequences, and as they are both supported by some authority, it is eminently desirable we should examine these assertions carefully. And, first, what is the meaning to be attached to "superstition" on the one hand,[2] and "supernatural" on the other? Supersition (Lat., *superstitio*) is etymologically the standing over a thing in amazement or awe. By so doing we shut out the light of enquiry and reason; where this light enters superstition fades away, so that we no longer enshroud a mystery by standing over it, but begin to understand it. Superstition is, therefore, the antithesis of understanding, and of that faith in the intelligibility of the universe which is the sheet anchor of science and the lode-star of all intellectual progress.

The definition given by a learned writer, Sir G. W. Cox, seems to me near the truth, if supplemented by the clause I have added in brackets,

---

[1] Leading review in *Nature*, Vol. LI, 1894, p. 22.

[2] Johnson gives several definitions; the best is "unnecessary fear." Cicero says it is "a certain empty dread of the gods." Plutarch's definition, in his interesting essay on Superstition, resembles this.

viz. Superstition is a belief not in accordance with facts [wherein a false cause is assumed for a fact or occurrence], and issues in superstitious practices when such a belief is regarded as capable of affording help or injury. Hence, when a primary hypothesis is not only erroneous, but unrelated to the facts in question, we have the basis of superstition and its attendant evils, though the deductive reasonings from that hypothesis may be irrefragable. The witch mania was thus a horrible superstition. False ideas of the Cosmos are fruitful sources of absurd and sometimes revolting superstitions.

We are now in a position to test the first assertion: Is spiritualism — using the word in the sense earlier defined — a superstition? Certainly it is, if not in accordance with facts; but those who assert this are the very persons who, on a *priori* grounds, deem the facts impossible or unverifiable, and have therefore never given to the subject any painstaking Study whatever.

Those who have been eye witnesses and made it a subject of laborious investigation, at first hand, assert that certain phenomena entirely new to science do exist, that the facts are there; in fine, although differences of opinion may exist as to the interpretation of those facts, no one has yet proved that a belief in these phenomena is utterly groundless, On the contrary, every painstaking and honest investigator who has endeavoured to prove this, so far as I know, has failed, and many as such have eventually changed sides.

Superstition

But if this be so, it is obvious that, with regard to these phenomena, the primary hypothesis of many scientific and educated men today — which leads them to reject the evidence adduced — is not in accordance with fact; and such a belief issues in a conduct opposed to the attainment of truth. Is it not, therefore, the average man of science, the average public opinion of today, that is on this subject foolishly superstitious? Nor must we forget the consequences of this erroneous belief upon the holders themselves. As the able and thoughtful writer, whose definition of superstition I have adopted, has said: — "It follows that every belief and every practice not based on, or not in accordance with, actual fact, must have an injurious effect on the mental and moral state of the thinker or actor. How great may be the mischief so produced, and how far it may check the growth of all literature, art, and science, the reader may gather from the 9th chapter of Hallam's 'Middle Ages."[3] We are all familiar with one mischievous effect of this erroneous habit of thought on the part of the materialistic school of scientific thought. Starting from the fundamental principle of the denial of an unseen or spiritual world, everything is made to give way to that; albeit the ludicrous arrogance of this denial is obvious when we consider the narrow limits both of our knowledge and of our senses. According to this school, "any solution of a he difficulty is more probable than one which would concede that a miracle had really occurred. This explains their seeming want of candour, and why they meet with evasions, proofs that seem to be demonstrative."[4] These are the words a former learned Provost of Trinity College, Dublin, Dr. Salmon, applies to the Biblical critics of that school, and they are equally true of many ferocious sceptics in connection with Psychical Research.

2.

Nature and the Supernatural

Let us now examine the second and opposite assertion, that Spiritualism is "evidence of the supernatural." Putting aside that school of thought which denies the supernatural *in toto*, numerous attempts have been made to define the word supernatural. Strictly speaking, as God is the Creator and Source of all things, He only can be over or above Nature. Archbishop Whately remarks: —

"As Nature is another word to signify the state of things and course of events God has appointed, nothing that occurs can be strictly called supernatural. Jesus Himself describes His works, not as violations of the laws of Nature, but as 'works which none other man did.' *Superhuman* would, perhaps, be a better word than supernatural." But this was not the idea of the writers either in the Old or New Testaments. Their idea was one common to the age in which they lived, viz., that

---

[3] *Dictionary of Science*, by Dr. Brande, F.R.S., and Sir G. W. Cox, M.A.; Art., "Superstition."

[4] Of such it has been truly remarked, "There is a bigotry of unbelief quite as blind and irrational, involving quite as thorough an abnegation of the highest faculties of the human mind, as can possibly be the case with the bigotry of superstition. — Rev. J. J. Has: *Are Miracles Credible?*

of the arbitrary action of a Supreme Being breaking in upon the ordinary course of events for a special purpose; a miracle was thus a sign or wonder wrought in order to attest His existence and power. Obviously, until science had given us conclusive evidence of an undeviating order in Nature, there could be no clear idea of a miracle as involving a violation of that order, no correct view of the "supernatural." An interesting discussion on the meaning of the word supernatural is to be found in Dr. Horace Bushnell's suggestive and well-known work, *Nature and the Supernatural*. Bishop Butler gives a sound view of the matter.

He says in his "Analogy," Part I, chap. I: "The only distinct meaning of that word [natural] is — stated, fixed, or settled; since what is natural, as much requires and presupposes an intelligent agent to render it so, i.e., to effect it continually or at stated times; as what is supernatural or miraculous does to effect it for once. And from hence it must follow that persons' notion of what is natural will be enlarged in proportion to their greater knowledge of the works of God, and the dispensations of His providence. Nor is there any absurdity in supposing that there may be beings in the universe whose capacities and knowledge and views may be so extensive, as that the whole Christian dispensation may to them appear natural, i.e., analogous or conformable to God's dealings with other parts of His creation; as natural as the visible known course of things appears to us." Similarly St. Augustine remarked: "Miracles do not happen in contradiction to nature, but only in contradiction to that which is known to us of nature." This is the view held by most modern theologians.

In fine, as a former Savilian Professor of Geometry in the University of Oxford, the Rev. Baden Powell, F.R.S., said in his admirable series of essays on the "Order of Nature," p. 232, *et seq.*: — "The limits of the study of nature do not bring us to the *supernatural* ... if at any particular point science finds a present limit, what is beyond science is not therefore beyond nature; it is only unknown nature; when we cease to trace law we are sure law remains to be traced. Whatever amount of the marvellous we encounter in the investigation of facts, such extraordinary phenomena will be sure at some future time to receive their explanation. As Spinoza argued, we cannot pretend to determine the boundary between the natural and the supernatural until the whole of Nature is open to our knowledge.... From the very conditions of the case it is evident that the supernatural can never be a matter of science or knowledge, for the moment it is brought within the cognisance of reason it ceases to be supernatural." From this point of view it will be seen that Spiritualism is not and cannot be "evidence of the supernatural." The popular meaning attached to the word supernatural is, however, "Some occurrence which affords evidence of an unseen or spiritual world outside ourselves, and therefore not belonging to the present or visible order of nature." In this sense only but still improperly we might speak of certain well-attested spiritualistic phenomena as supernatural.

Definition of Miracles

Those who deny all miracles assume they know all the laws of the universe. On such men argument is wasted and they must be left alone if they refuse to listen to good evidence. As Archbishop Whately in an Essay on Superstition, wisely says, "If either Roman Catholics, or any others, will give sufficient proofs of the occurrence of a miracle, they ought to be listened to; but to pretend to, or to believe in, any miracle without sufficient proof is clearly superstition." In view of the phenomena of Spiritualism, I would venture to suggest the definition that miracles are supernormal and therefore rare manifestations of mind, and as such they may be evidence either (*i.*) of the Infinite Mind, or (*ii.*) of a finite mind in the unseen, or (*iii.*) of a higher transcendental part of the human mind.

Another and vital distinction must be drawn between miracles which are voluntary exhibitions of super-normal power for a Divine purpose; and miracles, such as some of the phenomena we have been considering, which are manifestations of an intelligence and a power wholly beyond the control of the psychic, and with which his volition is concerned only so far as the withdrawal of any opposing mental condition. Of these latter (relative miracles) it is probable that the progress of research may render the miracle of today the accepted scientific fact of to-morrow. But the former being self-determined are not in the same category, and therefore will remain, as Kant says, among "events in the world the operative laws of whose causes are, and must remain, utterly unknown to us." It will thus be seen that the common Protestant belief that miracles, using this term in its widest sense, are credible in Scripture, but incredible out of it, is inaccurate. As Dr. Bushnell has well shown, so far from the age of miracles being past, there is unbroken testimony, from the apostolic times to the present, of the existence of miracles, i.e., evidence of a super-normal character on behalf of the existence and operation of unseen Intelligence.

APPENDIX B

NOTE BY PROF. BALFOUR STEWART LL.D. F. R. S.

I have read with much interest the paper by Professor Barrett, on some Physical Phenomena commonly called Spiritualistic witnessed by him. He expresses his conclusions in the following words: "Assuming the evidence to be trustworthy, I, for one, believe it points to the conclusion that, under conditions which are so restricted that we are not put to intellectual confusion by frequent interruptions of the ordinary course of material laws, mind occasionally and unconsciously can exert a direct influence upon lifeless matter." As this is a subject to which I have given a good deal of thought, I trust the Psychical Society will allow me to make one or two remarks upon it, and I am very sure my friend, Professor Barrett, will not object to this course.

Viewing the "Conservation of Energy" as the representative of physical laws, I nevertheless do not regard it in its birth, at least, as anything else than a scientific assertion — a very sagacious one, no doubt, but yet an assertion. We are in profound ignorance not only of the ultimate constitution of matter, but of the nature of those forces which animate the atom and the molecule. Under these circumstances, chiefly to advance physical knowledge by means of a working hypothesis, but partly, it may be, as a weapon against visionaries, we have formulated an assertion known as the "Conservation of Energy." It is unquestionable that this so-called law has greatly extended our knowledge of physics; nor have we met with any strictly physical experiment capable of repetition under fixed conditions that is inconsistent with this law. Now, what should be our course of action when a visionary comes before us with some variety of "Perpetual Motion?" The moral certainty that we are invaded by presumptuous ignorance is, no doubt, a sufficiently good excuse for not discussing the project. But we have a less objectionable method of dealing with such a man by asking him to put his project in execution, and to produce his machine, which we will then carefully examine. The fact that no such machine has been produced, and, as I said before, that no physical experiment contradicts the great laws of Energy, goes surely very far to justify us in regarding these laws as true — as laws which hold in what I may call the physical market of the world, ruling the physical transactions between man and man.

But there are many who are not content with such a limited application of physical laws. In the first place, they repudiate the doctrine of freewill because they regard it as being inconsistent with such laws; secondly, they repudiate the possibility of what are called miracles; and, lastly, they repudiate (with contempt) the evidence for telepathy, and more especially that for Spiritualistic phenomena which has come before the Society for Psychical Research.

One consequence of this mental posture is that interminable discussions have arisen between a certain class of men of science and the supporters of Christianity, the latter of whom have been far from judicious in their method of defence. These have until recently considered miracles as Divine interferences with ordinary laws, and hence as abnormal and intellectually incomprehensible occurrences, while the Protestant theologians have imagined that the power to work miracles ceased with the Apostles.

This latter doctrine was probably assumed as a polemical weapon at the time of the great controversy with the Church of Rome. It goes without saying that this method of looking at things will not recommend itself to men of science, and thus an embittered and useless discussion has continued between two classes of men, neither of whom has seemed to be either able or willing to enter into the position assumed by the other.

Of late years, however, miracles have come to be regarded not as breaks of law, but as phenomena embracing a higher law — a doctrine which is a great advance upon its predecessor. Now the question naturally arises, if there be this higher law, may there not be occasional traces of it to be met with in the world, even at this present age? It is, I think, exceedingly unfortunate that a large class of theologians have attempted to decide this question in the negative.

It is not a question for them to decide, but for those who investigate matters of fact.

This is in reality the question upon which the Psychical Society are engaged, and the circumstances which I have mentioned appear to me to lend an unusual importance to their investigations. Let us begin by allowing that the laws of Energy dominate the scientific marketplace, and the scientific dealings between man and man. We are, I conceive, extending this scientific assertion so far.

But are we justified in extending it further? Are we, for instance, justified in asserting that under the very different conditions of things contemplated by the Psychical Society there may not be at least an apparent and prima facie breakdown of these laws; and more especially, are we justified in absolutely shutting our eyes to all evidence that may be brought before us in favour of such apparent interruptions? I cannot think so. We must examine everything. Because a scientific statement applies to one set of conditions, must it necessarily apply to everything else? I have always thought that this had to be ascertained by investigation, and not by dogmatic assertion, and I therefore conceive that our Society is abundantly justified in applying the Baconian method of research to all occurrences.

APPENDIX C
EUSAPIA PALADINO

After the favourable reports by Professor Charles Richet and Sir Oliver Lodge upon their experiments with Eusapia, further séances were held with her at Cambridge in 1895.[1] I was not present, and, indeed, have never had the opportunity nor the desire to experiment with Eusapia, but those present at Cambridge came to the conclusion, on what appeared to them to be an adequate trial, that there was clear evidence of trickery on the part of Eusapia,[2] although Sir Oliver Lodge adhered to his opinion that the phenomena he witnessed in the Ile Roubaud were genuine.[3] This opinion was corroborated by that of the eminent physiologist, Professor Charles Richet. After the séances at Cambridge he for a time suspended his judgment, but subsequently, both in conversation with myself and on other occasions, has stated that he was absolutely convinced of the super-normal character of some of the manifestations which occur with Eusapia. This also was the opinion of the well-known astronomical writer, Camille Flammarion, who in his work, *Les Forces Naturelles Inconnues*, deals at length with the phenomena occurring with Eusapia, and is convinced of their super-normal character.

But the most remarkable testimony in favour of Eusapia came from some of the leading scientific men of Italy, men specially trained in the

---

[1] See "Journal of the S.P.R.," Vol. VI, p. 306.
[2] *ibid.*, Vol. VII, p. 148.
[3] *ibid.*, p. 135.

investigation of psychological and physiological phenomena. Perhaps the most notable witness was the late Professor Lombroso, who conducted the investigation of Eusapia's powers in his laboratory in the University of Turin, every precaution being taken against fraud. The result was that Lombroso publicly bore witness to the genuineness of these extraordinary physical manifestations. The opinion of so experienced and able a criminologist as Lombroso — whose high scientific status is recognised throughout Europe — necessarily carried great weight. In an article published in 1908 in the "Annals of Psychical Science," Lombroso refers to various phases of these phenomena, including phantasms and apparitions of deceased persons. He points out that sometimes several phenomena occurred simultaneously, and hence were beyond the power of one person to perform, and also that there is evidence of the intrusion of another will, which could not be attributed to the medium or to any person present, but which was in opposition to all, and even to the control, "John." He lays stress upon the importance of these facts in relation to the hypothesis that the occurrences are explicable by the "psychic forces" of the medium and circle alone: an hypothesis which at an earlier stage of the enquiry he himself adopted, but which he now regards as inadequate.

Independent testimony came from Dr. Enrico Morselli, Professor of Neurology and Psychiatry (mental therapeutics), In the University of Genoa, who presided over a set of séances with Eusapia in that city.[4] The control of the medium was very strict. Her hands and feet were held by Dr. Morselli and Sig. Barzini, editor of the *Corriere della Sera*, who states that he was present "with the object of unmasking fraud and trickery," but was in the end convinced of the reality of some of the phenomena. The person of the medium was thoroughly searched before the séance, and the room was also searched; the light was never entirely extinguished.

Under these conditions Dr. Morselli testifies to the occurrence of the following phenomena: movements of the table, raps on the table and sounds on musical instruments without contact; complete levitations of the table; movements of objects at a distance from the medium seen in the light, and, also, the operation of self-registering instruments by the unseen agency; *apports*, i.e., objects brought into the room from outside; the sound of human voices not proceeding from any visible

---

[4] A very full report of these is given in the Annals of Psychical Science for February, March, May, and June, 1907.

person; impressions on plastic substances of hands, feet and faces; the appearance of dark prolongations of the medium's body, of well delineated forms of faces, heads and busts. Although entirely sceptical at the outset of his experiments he declares himself convinced that most of the phenomena alleged to occur with Eusapia are "real, authentic, and genuine."

Dr. Morselli was disposed to interpret these phenomena by what he terms the hypothesis of special *psychic or bio-dynamic* forces; that is to say, he attributes them to some peculiar power emanating from the person of the medium. This is practically the psychic force theory of many earlier English investigators.

Shortly after the séances held under the direction of Dr. Morselli in the University of Genoa, another series of experiments, in Turin, was conducted by Doctors Herlitzka, C. Foa, and Aggazzotti; Dr. Pio Foa, Professor of Pathological Anatomy, being present at the most remarkable of this set of experiments. The séances yielded similar positive results to those held by Professors Lombroso and Morselli.

Another competent witness is Dr. Giuseppe Venzano, stated by Dr. Morselli to be an "excellent observer." He contributed an important article to the "Annals of Psychical Science" (August and September, 1907), containing a detailed record and critical analysis of his experiences with Eusapia, under conditions of strict control, and sometimes in the full light given by an electric lamp of sixteen-candle power. Dr. Venzano, in the course of his experiments with Eusapia, the light in the room being sufficient to enable both the medium and his fellow-sitters to be clearly seen, perceived a woman's form beside him, felt her touch and heard her speak: the form spoke with fulness of detail of certain family affairs not known to anyone present except himself. The whole incident is a most amazing one, and Dr. Venzano states that, in his opinion, any explanation of this experience based on the possibility of fraud or of hallucination is impossible.

Professor Philippe Bottazzi, Director of the Physiological Institute at the University of Naples, having read the report of Dr. Morselli's experiments at Genoa, made an attempt to verify the phenomena by means of an elaborate and carefully arranged set of self-registering instruments, in the hope of obtaining an automatic graphic record of the psychic force exercised by the medium. Such a record would negative the hypothesis of hallucination or misdescription on the part of the observer. These important experiments, carried out with the collaboration of several able professors of the same University, were remarkably successful, and Professor Bottazzi's article concludes by stating that these experiments have "eliminated the slightest trace of suspicion or uncertainty relative to the genuineness of the phenomena. We obtained the same kind of assurance as that which we have concerning physical, chemical, or physiological phenomena. From henceforth sceptics can only deny the facts by accusing us of fraud and charlatanism."[5] In 1909 three members of the S.P.R., the Hon. Everard Feilding, Mr. W. W. Baggally and Mr. Hereward Carrington were commissioned by the Society to carry out another serious investigation with this medium.

The selection was specially made with a view to the qualifications of the investigators. Mr. Carrington was a clever amateur conjuror, and for ten years had carried on investigations on these physical phenomena in the United States. His book on this subject shows his familiarity with the methods adopted by fraudulent mediums and his cautious attitude towards all such experiences. Mr. Baggally was also an amateur conjuror with much experience, and had come to a negative conclusion as to the possibility of any genuine physical phenomena. Mr. Feilding's attitude was the same, and, moreover, he had had extensive experience in investigating physical phenomena.

The result of this investigation was that all three of these well-qualified men were convinced of the absolute genuineness of the remarkable super-normal phenomena they witnessed at their hotel in Naples. Since then they have had another series of séances which yielded quite different results and in which they obtained nothing convincingly supernormal and much that was obviously normal and probably spurious. The same thing was also found in sittings with Eusapia in America.

How can we reconcile these conflicting results? I am not concerned to defend Eusapia, on the contrary I am more disposed to loathe her, but we must be fair, and give even the devil his due. Like other psychics, especially those who exhibit similar amazing super-normal phenomena, she is most sensitive to "suggestion," even when unexpressed; and in the trance, when her consciousness and self-control are largely inhibited, she is the easy prey of external influences. In the absence of the steadying though subconscious, influence of a high moral nature, she unblushingly cheats whenever the conditions are unfavourable for the production of supernormal phenomena. We have no right

---

[5] See Annals of Psychical Science, September, 1907, p. 149; October, 1907, p. 260; December, 1907, p. 377; where a full account of these experiments will be found, with illustrations showing the tracings made by the self-registering instruments.

to assume that she is wholly conscious of so doing, for Professor Hyslop has shown that mediumship is often accompanied with abnormal bodily as well as mental conditions. We know little or nothing of what constitutes the peculiar faculty or environment for the necessary production of these physical phenomena.

If they are due, as some have thought, to an externalization of the nerve force of the psychic, it is not improbable that the degree of this externalization will vary with the favourable or unfavourable mental state of those present. We may even conceive that when this psychic force is restricted or not externalized, it may create movements of the limbs of the psychic which will cause her to perform by normal actions (in perhaps a semi-conscious state) what under good psychical conditions would be done super-normally. This would produce the impression of intentional fraud. Every one who has had much experience in these perplexing investigations knows that what seems purposeless and stupid fraud often intrudes itself, after the most conclusive evidence of genuine phenomena has been obtained. It is this which renders the whole enquiry wholly unfitted for the hasty and unskilled investigator.

APPENDIX D

SUGGESTIONS FOR INVESTIGATORS IN CONDUCTING PSYCHICAL EXPERIMENTS

There are many earnest enquirers who wish to know how to conduct experiments for the investigation of psychical phenomena, and a few suggestions to this end may therefore be useful.

1. *Thought-transference.*

Although the evidence for telepathy is both abundant and weighty, additional evidence is always welcome especially with a view to a better knowledge of the conditions of success. A recent paper by Professor Gilbert Murray, Litt. D., giving a record of his own successful experiments, in guessing incidents thought of by others, should be read in this connection; it will be found in the "Proceedings of the S.P.R." for Nov., 1916. Professor Murray points out how important it is to avoid tedium and lack of interest in all concerned in the experiment. Hence experiments in guessing a card or a number, though useful and necessary for statistical purposes, soon bore and weary the percipient, defeating the end in view. In my original experiments with the children of the Rev. A. M. Creery, 35 years ago, I found the same thing; and in the report of these experiments which Myers, Gurney, and myself published in the first volume of the *Proceedings* S. P. R. (1882) we stated that the more varied the experiments were made the better were the results obtained. Always remember that the essential thing is to keep alive the interest of the percipient.

Further, it is necessary to avoid distraction of the mind, or any disturbances, and also emphatically to avoid any special anxiety for success. Make the conditions as stringent as possible, but at the same time endeavour to conduct the experiments as if they were an amusing game. Nor should the agents, — that is the persons who have selected the subject to be guessed, — mentally exert themselves as if they were studying a difficult proposition. It is not the conscious part of our personality that is effective, but the sub-conscious; possibly thought transference occurs universally. If this is so it would appear that only in a limited number of persons does the telepathic impact emerge into the consciousness of the percipient. In this emergence delay often occurs, hence all the "guesses" should be noted down, as occasionally it will be found that an earlier impression emerges in place of, or with, a later one.

Again Professor Murray confirms what I noticed long ago, that when the "agent" holds the hand of the percipient very often better results are obtained. This is worth further investigation, care being taken to avoid anything like "muscle reading" or hyperaesthesia.

A series of experiments should not be continued too long at one time, as sometimes it is found the trials tire or exhaust the percipient. Some correspondents have told me the experiments produce giddiness, etc. (see note on p. 57, "Proc S.P.R.," Vol. I). But I myself have never noticed this, nor seen any ill effects from these experiments, nor from experiments on "dowsing" (see Chap. 8 of my little book on Psychical Research, Home University Library).

2. *The Dowsing Rod and the Pendule Explorateur.*

Various autoscopes, as I have called them, can be used to reveal involuntary muscular action on the part of the automatist. The forked dowsing rod is the simplest and most widely successful, but the twisting of the rod is no evidence of any super-normal faculty, nor does it imply success in the discovery of underground water or metallic ores. Its movement is due to involuntary and unconscious muscular action, and may be caused by any sub-conscious suggestion arising in the mind of the dowser.

The same explanation covers the motion of the so-called *pendule explorateur*, a ring or other small object suspended by a thread held between the fingers of one hand; or passed over the ball of the thumb, the elbow resting on the table. An alphabet arranged in a circle round the *pendule*, will enable words to be spelt out as the *pendule* swings to each letter.[1] It is tedious, but very amusing and curious results sometimes are found; unexpected messages and answers to questions may be given. If the holder of the *pendule* be blindfolded and the alphabet re-arranged, it will be seen how much is due to his unconscious muscular action and involuntary mental guidance.

In both these cases, however, as in the use of all other *autoscopes*, certain persons will be found who possess super-normal power, and the results so obtained cannot be explained away by any human faculty hitherto recognized by official science. In the case of the good dowser, — who may be a child or wholly unlettered person of either sex, or a distinguished man like the late Mr. A. Lang or others of note, — the faculty of clairvoyance reveals itself, not by a conscious perception but by an automatic action such as the twisting of the rod, whenever the object of search is found; whether it be a hidden coin, or underground spring, or metallic lode. On the continent the pendule is often used for the same purpose, but when messages are spelt out by its means the explanation falls under the next heading.

3. *Automatic Writing, the Ouija Board, etc.*

Here we come to a branch of psychical research which probably excites the most interest, and in which caution is necessary. Those who are new to the subject should read the suggestions given in Chapter 20 and refer to p. xviii of the Preface. Young persons, and those who have little to interest or employ their time and thought—should be strongly discouraged from making any experiments in this perplexing region.

Moreover, it not infrequently happens, as some friends of mine found, that after some interesting and veridical messages and answers to questions had been given, mischievous and deceptive communications took place, interspersed with profane and occasionally obscene language. How far the sitters' subliminal self is responsible for this, it is difficult to say; they were naturally disquieted and alarmed, as the ideas and words were wholly foreign to their thoughts, and they threw up the whole matter in disgust.

With this preliminary caution, and urging all investigators to preserve a sane and critical spirit, the best results can be obtained when

---

[1] Two centuries ago the forked dowsing-rod was used for the same purpose and messages purporting to come from different planets were recorded!

two or more friends agree to sit regularly at some convenient and quiet hour.

A pencil may be held on a sheet of paper or a planchette used or the ouija board, as described earlier. This last autoscope usually furnishes the easiest, though the most tedious, mode of automatic action. It has also the advantage that the person, or two persons, who touch the travelling indicator, can be carefully blindfolded and the alphabet rearranged without their knowledge. If messages can thus be obtained, the conscious, or unconscious and unintentional, movement of the indicator by the sitters, can thus be eliminated more or less perfectly.

If after a few trials no results are obtained the circle should be changed and others allowed to try. When any messages are received, it is well to question the unseen intelligence and ascertain what are the best conditions and who is the most promising medium. Unwearied patience and regular sittings will be found necessary to obtain the best results. Whether the game is worth the candle, the enquirers must decide for themselves; personally I don't think it is, except for those engaged in purely psychological investigation.

4. Physical Phenomena.

These are less easy to obtain; though table-tilting and the movements of other objects touched by the sitters often occur, and may usually be traced to the unconscious and involuntary muscular action of the sitters. Raps and the movement of objects without contact, cannot be so explained; nor can all of the remarkable motions of bodies which occur with contact.

This will be clear from a perusal of Chapters 4 and 5 dealing with physical phenomena. When raps first occur in a private circle, they are usually very faint ticks, and grow in loudness and frequency with continued sittings.

Perhaps the best rules for the conduct of circles sitting for spiritistic phenomena are those long ago published by "M.A. (Oxon)" — the Rev. Stainton Moses.

After instructing sitters to place their hands flat on the upper surface of the table round which they sit, he goes on to say: —

> "Do not concentrate attention too fixedly on the expected manifestation. Engage in cheerful but not frivolous conversation. Avoid dispute or argument. Scepticism has no deterrent effect, but a bitter spirit of

opposition in a person of determined will may totally stop or decidedly impede manifestations. If conversation flags, music is a great help, if it is agreeable to all, and not of a kind to irritate the sensitive ear. Patience is essential, and it may be necessary to meet ten or twelve times at short intervals, before anything occurs. If after such a trial you still fail, form a fresh circle.

An hour should be the limit of an unsuccessful séance.

"If the table moves, let your pressure be so gentle on its surface that you are sure you are not aiding its motions.

After some time you will probably find that the movement will continue if your hands are held over, but not in contact with, it. Do not, however, try this until the movement is assured, and be in no hurry to git metal "When you think that the time has come, let someone take command of the circle and at t a> spokesman. Explain to the unseen Intelligence that an agreed code of signals is desirable, and ask that a tilt may be given as the alphabet is slowly repeated, at the several letters which form the word that the Intelligence wishes to spell. It is convenient to use a single tilt for No, three for Yes, and two to express doubt or uncertainty.

"When a satisfactory communication has been established, ask if you are rightly placed, and if not, what order you should take. After this ask who the Intelligence purports to be, which of the company is the medium, and such relevant questions. If you only satisfy yourself at first that it is possible to speak with an Intelligence separate from that of any person present, you will have gained much.

"The signals may take the form of raps. If so, use the same code of signals, and ask as the raps become clear that they may be made on the table, or in a part of the room where they are demonstrably not produced by any natural means, but avoid any vexatious imposition of restrictions on free communication. Let the Intelligence use its own means.

It rests greatly with the sitters to make the manifestations elevating or frivolous and even tricky.

"Should an attempt be made to entrance the medium, or to manifest by any violent methods, ask that the attempt may be deferred till you can secure the presence of some experienced Spiritualist. If this request is not heeded, discontinue the sitting. The process of developing a trance-medium is one that might disconcert an inexperienced enquirer.

"Lastly, try the results you get by the light of Reason.

Maintain a level head and a clear judgment. Do not believe everything you are told, for though the great unseen world contains many a wise and discerning spirit, it also has in it the accumulation of human folly, vanity, and error; and this lies nearer to the surface than that which is wise and good.

Distrust the free use of great names. Never for a moment abandon the use of your reason. Do not enter into a serious investigation in a spirit of idle curiosity or frivolity. Cultivate a reverent desire for what is pure, good, and true. You will be repaid if you gain only a well-grounded conviction that there is a life after death, for which a pure and good life before death is the best and wisest preparation."

APPENDIX E

The concluding sentence above must be read in connection with the various theories of these physical phenomena which I have given in Chapter 9. For my own part I consider all these manifestations are so closely associated with the subliminal self of the medium, that it would be rash to infer they proceed from a discarnate human personality; though the Russian case cited earlier in this book, as well as Rev. S. Moses' own experience, supports the view that in some cases they may do so.

As a rule the higher and more spiritual the content of the messages, the less palpable and material is their manifestation. The silent "communion of saints" is very far removed from a spiritistic séance. Telepathic such communion may be, and probably is, but, as the mystics in all ages have taught, calmness of body and mind is essential,

> "Some have striven
> Achieving calm, to whom was given
> The joy that mixes man with Heaven."

And "Into that silent heaven the Great Soul floweth in,"
as Plotinus tells us.

Paperbacks also available from White Crow Books

Elsa Barker—*Letters from a Living Dead Man*
ISBN 978-1-907355-83-7

Elsa Barker—*War Letters from the Living Dead Man*
ISBN 978-1-907355-85-1

Elsa Barker—*Last Letters from the Living Dead Man*
ISBN 978-1-907355-87-5

Richard Maurice Bucke—*Cosmic Consciousness*
ISBN 978-1-907355-10-3

Arthur Conan Doyle—*The Edge of the Unknown*
ISBN 978-1-907355-14-1

Arthur Conan Doyle—*The New Revelation*
ISBN 978-1-907355-12-7

Arthur Conan Doyle—*The Vital Message*
ISBN 978-1-907355-13-4

Arthur Conan Doyle with Simon Parke—*Conversations with Arthur Conan Doyle*
ISBN 978-1-907355-80-6

Meister Eckhart with Simon Parke—*Conversations with Meister Eckhart*
ISBN 978-1-907355-18-9

D. D. Home—*Incidents in my Life Part 1*
ISBN 978-1-907355-15-8

Mme. Dunglas Home; edited, with an Introduction, by Sir Arthur Conan Doyle—*D. D. Home: His Life and Mission*
ISBN 978-1-907355-16-5

Edward C. Randall—*Frontiers of the Afterlife*
ISBN 978-1-907355-30-1

Rebecca Ruter Springer—*Intra Muros: My Dream of Heaven*
ISBN 978-1-907355-11-0

Leo Tolstoy, edited by Simon Parke—*Forbidden Words*
ISBN 978-1-907355-00-4

Leo Tolstoy—*A Confession*
ISBN 978-1-907355-24-0

Leo Tolstoy—*The Gospel in Brief*
ISBN 978-1-907355-22-6

Leo Tolstoy—*The Kingdom of God is Within You*
ISBN 978-1-907355-27-1

Leo Tolstoy—*My Religion: What I Believe*
ISBN 978-1-907355-23-3

Leo Tolstoy—*On Life*
ISBN 978-1-907355-91-2

Leo Tolstoy—*Twenty-three Tales*
ISBN 978-1-907355-29-5

Leo Tolstoy—*What is Religion and other writings*
ISBN 978-1-907355-28-8

Leo Tolstoy—*Work While Ye Have the Light*
ISBN 978-1-907355-26-4

Leo Tolstoy—*The Death of Ivan Ilyich*
ISBN 978-1-907661-10-5

Leo Tolstoy—*Resurrection*
ISBN 978-1-907661-09-9

Leo Tolstoy with Simon Parke—*Conversations with Tolstoy*
ISBN 978-1-907355-25-7

Howard Williams with an Introduction by Leo Tolstoy—*The Ethics of Diet: An Anthology of Vegetarian Thought*
ISBN 978-1-907355-21-9

Vincent Van Gogh with Simon Parke—*Conversations with Van Gogh*
ISBN 978-1-907355-95-0

Wolfgang Amadeus Mozart with Simon Parke—*Conversations with Mozart*
ISBN 978-1-907661-38-9

Jesus of Nazareth with Simon Parke—
Conversations with Jesus of Nazareth
ISBN 978-1-907661-41-9

Thomas à Kempis with Simon Parke—*The Imitation of Christ*
ISBN 978-1-907661-58-7

Julian of Norwich with Simon Parke—*Revelations of Divine Love*
ISBN 978-1-907661-88-4

Allan Kardec—*The Spirits Book*
ISBN 978-1-907355-98-1

Allan Kardec—*The Book on Mediums*
ISBN 978-1-907661-75-4

Emanuel Swedenborg—*Heaven and Hell*
ISBN 978-1-907661-55-6

P.D. Ouspensky—*Tertium Organum: The Third Canon of Thought*
ISBN 978-1-907661-47-1

Dwight Goddard—*A Buddhist Bible*
ISBN 978-1-907661-44-0

Michael Tymn—*The Afterlife Revealed*
ISBN 978-1-970661-90-7

Michael Tymn—*Transcending the Titanic: Beyond Death's Door*
ISBN 978-1-908733-02-3

Guy L. Playfair—*If This Be Magic*
ISBN 978-1-907661-84-6

Guy L. Playfair—*The Flying Cow*
ISBN 978-1-907661-94-5

Guy L. Playfair —*This House is Haunted*
ISBN 978-1-907661-78-5

Carl Wickland, M.D.—
Thirty Years Among the Dead
ISBN 978-1-907661-72-3

John E. Mack—*Passport to the Cosmos*
ISBN 978-1-907661-81-5

Peter & Elizabeth Fenwick—
The Truth in the Light
ISBN 978-1-908733-08-5

Erlendur Haraldsson—
Modern Miracles
ISBN 978-1-908733-25-2

Erlendur Haraldsson—
At the Hour of Death
ISBN 978-1-908733-27-6

Erlendur Haraldsson—
The Departed Among the Living
ISBN 978-1-908733-29-0

Brian Inglis—*Science and Parascience*
ISBN 978-1-908733-18-4

Brian Inglis—*Natural and Supernatural: A History of the Paranormal*
ISBN 978-1-908733-20-7

Ernest Holmes—*The Science of Mind*
ISBN 978-1-908733-10-8

Victor Zammit—*Afterlife: A Lawyer Presents the Evidence.*
ISBN 978-1-908733-22-1

Casper S. Yost—*Patience Worth: A Psychic Mystery*
ISBN 978-1-908733-06-1

William Usborne Moore—
Glimpses of the Next State
ISBN 978-1-907661-01-3

William Usborne Moore—
The Voices
ISBN 978-1-908733-04-7

John W. White—
The Highest State of Consciousness
ISBN 978-1-908733-31-3

Stafford Betty—
The Imprisoned Splendor
ISBN 978-1-907661-98-3

Paul Pearsall, Ph.D. —
Super Joy
ISBN 978-1-908733-16-0

All titles available as eBooks, and selected titles available in Hardback and Audiobook formats from www.whitecrowbooks.com

www.ingramcontent.com/pod-product-compliance
Lightning Source LLC
LaVergne TN
LVHW041541070426
835507LV00011B/860